SPIRITUAL PROGRESSION
PROGRESSION
—IN THE—
LAST DAYS

SPIRITUAL PROGRESSION
—— IN THE ——
LAST DAYS

—— BLAINE M. ——
YORGASON

Deseret Book Company
Salt Lake City, Utah

Library of Congress Catalog Card Number: 94-26155

ISBN 0-87579-913-2

Printed in the United States of America

10   9   8   7   6   5   4   3   2   1

To my friend Gregg C.,
who first introduced the modern
wilderness to my thinking

Contents

Acknowledgments

I express appreciation to Paul Allen, CEO; Dan Taggart, President; and their company, Infobases International, for the wonderful gospel research tools they provide. With either the LDS Historical Library or the Gospel Library running in my CD ROM drive, it rarely takes more than a few seconds to go from thinking of a topic to reading what has been said about it either scripturally or by one or another of the Brethren. These are wonderful tools, for which I am very grateful.

I also express gratitude to Sheri Dew for her unfailing friendship and confidence; to Jack Lyon for his kind and patient editing; to Ron Millett for his tremendous support and friendship; and to all the staff at Deseret Book. They are a great publishing house, and it is a privilege working with them.

Introduction

Several years ago, under assignment from my stake president, I wrote a series of seven lessons for the stake missionaries over whom I had been called to preside. These lessons were designed to explain the principles of the gospel and to show how living these principles correlated with effective missionary work. Within the next year I expanded these lessons considerably and sent them in letter format to my three eldest children, who were serving missions at the time in Arizona, England, and Norway.

Shortly thereafter my brother Brenton and I were encouraged to work together and "fictionalize" these letters, add more topics, and publish them as a series of twelve booklets entitled *The Gospel Power Series*. And within another year, condensed, altered, and added to, much of this material was brought under one cover and published as *Spiritual Survival in the Last Days*.

In the four years since the writing of our book, as I have studied the scriptures and the works of the Brethren, I have become convinced that the material described in *Spiritual Survival* is only the first segment in a dramatic journey of the spirit. What follows, then, is a sequel, which no doubt contains mistakes and omits many things that ought to be covered, but which is my best effort to explain the next portion of the journey I believe the Lord is encouraging us to make.

As President Howard W. Hunter has said: "Developing spirituality and attuning ourselves to the highest influences of godliness is not an easy matter. It takes time and frequently involves a struggle. It will not happen by chance, but is accomplished only through deliberate effort and by calling upon God and keeping his commandments. . . . None of us has attained perfection or the zenith of spiritual growth that is possible in mortality. Every person can and must make spiritual progress. The gospel of Jesus Christ is the divine plan for that spiritual growth eternally. ("Developing Spirituality," *Ensign*, May 1979, pp. 25–26.)

For those who may feel so drawn upward, I hope you will read, ponder, and, enjoy.

The Need
for Spiritual
Progression

CHAPTER

1

The Last Days

Troops, Rebels Fight Furiously in Rwanda

An estimated twenty thousand people have been slain in a week of savage ethnic violence.

Study Shows Vitamin A May Cause Cancer

After ten years of study, scientists find that beta carotene may cause cancer.

Serbs Block Movement of U.N. Observers

In some instances observers are being held hostage.

2 Utah Families Held Hostage by Intruders

The families were blindfolded and gagged but not bound.

2 Men Arrested So Far in String of 35 Burglaries

Investigators look at additional suspects and new cases.

Pharmacist Accused of Violating FDA Rules

Man who cuts costs for his customers is charged.

Couple Recounts Days of Terror in Rwanda

Fighting is the result of a decades-old struggle between the Hutu and Tutsi ethnic groups.

Scam Bilks Navy of $3 Million

Thief caught almost by accident.

U.S. Mistakenly Downs Own Copters

More than twenty killed in deadly mistake over Iraq.

Parents Seek Protection from Kids

Nearly one-third of Boston restraining orders are for parents afraid of their children.

Police Chief Requests Probe into Shooting

Allegations of racism, excessive force, and police bias surface when cop attacker is slain.

3 More Suspects Arrested in Hostage Taking

Man, wife, and three teenagers linked to robberies. One man remains at large.

UDOT Wiretapper Says He Had Misgivings

Says he suspected the tap was illegal but did as he was told.

West Jordan Man Stabbed to Death in Family Fight

Woman claims self-defense; investigators agree.

Addict Robs Pizzeria, Uses Threat of AIDS

Wielding can-opener, robber threatens to use own blood as weapon.

The above headline articles, taken from two consecutive weekday editions of my local paper, indicate that we live in an incredibly unstable world, something that should surprise no one. Natural disasters are becoming pandemic, wars rage around the globe, crime is everywhere, and even in our homes there seems to be no safety.

Two Studies

In 1984 Dr. George Gallup issued a report titled "Religion in America." He summarized that the people in America, at least, didn't know how to strengthen their families; their self-respect was terribly fragile; and they had no real idea of where to turn in order to find God. "America . . . ," he wrote, "appears to be confronted with a giant paradox: Religion is growing in importance among Americans but morality is losing ground. On the one hand, levels of religious involvement remain high: Nine in 10 state a religious preference, seven in 10 are church members and six in 10 attend religious services in a given month. A majority, furthermore, say they are more interested in religious and spiritual matters today than they were five years ago.

"On the other hand, widespread cheating is found in all levels of society and two-thirds of Americans hold the view that the level of ethics in the U.S. has declined during the last decade. . . . Some light is shed on the paradox of religion gaining ground but morality slipping by the results of a recent Wall Street Journal/Gallup survey. The survey shows very little difference in the behavior of the churched and unchurched on a wide range of items including lying, cheating and pilferage."

This portion of the report concluded that people were looking for a missing element, a divine connection that really worked in their lives: "While it may be true that the population is less spiritually committed than in the past, the vast majority say they wish their personal religious faith were stronger and that they want religion to play a greater role in society" (*The Gallup Report,* no. 222, March 1984, pp. 1, 6).

If good people were looking for that missing element of spirituality ten years ago, then today they must surely be desperate for it. In all problem categories itemized by Dr. Gallup, conditions have only worsened, sometimes dramatically. Pete Du Pont, writing for Scripps Howard News Service, recently editorialized: " 'Of all the dispositions and habits which lead to political prosperity, religion and morality are indispensable supports' (George Washington, in his farewell address, 1796).

"Two hundred years later, the father of our country would be stunned by the state of his republic. Crime has reached heights he could never have imagined, and religion, a fundamental force behind settling the New World, faces constant challenge from government.

"These two occurrences are not merely coincidental. Washington of 1796 has a lesson for Washington in 1994; the subversion of religion in America can only lead to lower community morality and higher crime.

"The numbers tell a grim tale. Since 1965, almost every cultural measure shows decay. The crime rate has more than tripled. The Department of Justice estimates that eight out of 10 Americans will be the victims of violent crime at some point in their lives. Illegitimate births are up 400 percent. The percentage of single parent families has increased 2 1/2 times.

"During the same period, the practice of religion in America has declined as well. Church attendance has lagged across the nation. Sunday School attendance has declined from 47 million to 28 million young people."

Du Pont then refers "to the work of British sociology

professor Christie Davies, who correlated the decline in religious participation with the rise in societal violence in England across a full century of experience.

"During the last half of the 19th century," he continues, "there was a decrease in England's crime rate, illegitimacy rate and drug and alcohol abuse. But those indices flattened, reversed and then increased markedly in the next 50 years. This 'U-curve in deviant behavior,' as Davies calls it, resulted from a 'change in the entire culture and morality of the society, and particularly in the way children are brought up . . . a change in the very character of the people.'

"Using Sunday School attendance as an indicator of spiritual activity, Davies notes that while it was falling by two-thirds from 1900 to the 1970s, police reports of serious crimes rose from three per 1,000 people to four per 100 people. By 1980 it was five per 100 people, an 80-year increase in violence of 17 times."

Du Pont summarizes that until the majority of the people start reaffirming their basic values, the most important of which is religion, there is little hope for our future. (Pete Du Pont, "Assault on Religion Parallels Alarming U.S. Increase in Crime," *Deseret News*, April 10, 1994, p. A16).

In the October 1993 General Conference, President Gordon B. Hinckley fervently addressed this theme. Quoting from a *Wall Street Journal* article, he said: " 'Since 1960, the U.S. population has increased 41%; the gross domestic product has nearly tripled; and total social spending by all levels of government [has experienced] more than a fivefold increase. . . .

" 'But during the same . . . period there has been a 560% increase in violent crime; a 419% increase in illegitimate births; a quadrupling in divorce rates; a tripling of the percentage of children living in single-parent homes; more than a 200%

increase in the teenage suicide rate' (William J. Bennett, "Quantifying America's Decline," *Wall Street Journal*, 15 Mar. 1993)." In his talk President Hinckley then quoted Alexander Solzhenitsyn as saying, "The West . . . has been undergoing an erosion and [an] obscuring of high moral and ethical ideals. The spiritual axis of life has grown dim" (Gordon B. Hinckley, "Bring Up a Child in the Way He Should Go," *Ensign*, November 1993, pp. 54, 59).

Many in America, because they know not where to turn for comfort and direction, are simply giving up. "If you can't beat 'em, join 'em" has become far more than a catch-phrase, especially for young people, as criminal and gang activity has proliferated, sexual improprieties escalated, illiteracy and poverty grown by leaps and bounds, and fear filled the hearts and minds of men and women everywhere. No wonder the elements are in commotion and the Lord has been forced to declare, "Darkness covereth the earth, and gross darkness the minds of the people, and all flesh has become corrupt before my face" (D&C 112:23).

What of the Mormons?

And what of members of the Church of Jesus Christ of Latter-day Saints? How do we stack up? While exact statistics are not readily available, we rarely have more than a 50 percent activity level in our U.S. stakes ("active" meaning that an individual attends one meeting in three months), the percentage of full tithe payers is far below 50, and those who attend the temple is obviously as low. In fact, in a recent local meeting attended by the author, it was reported that more adult male members in the Salt Lake Valley hold the Aaronic Priesthood than hold the Melchizedek Priesthood.

In other words, while a large majority of Mormons say our

religion is important to us, and while we resist all efforts to convert us to other faiths, sometimes even arrogantly disdaining them, yet our own doctrines and beliefs remain obscure to us and are therefore of little consequence or benefit as we muddle our way through mortality.

Disdaining Spirituality

Even more serious is the fact that in our ignorance of spiritual things we frequently criticize our brothers and sisters in Christ who are striving to draw nearer to Him and who are enjoying the gifts of the Spirit. Truly the sophisticates of this Church, vainglorious individuals who are learned enough in the ways of men to believe they are wise, so loudly proclaim their temporal gospel that many are convinced their only salvation lies in the arm of flesh. Thus is the Savior crucified again and again, His message of salvation left to peal in blocked-up ears, and the people allowed to stumble onward toward their own well-earned destruction. Is it any wonder that the Prophet Joseph felt forced to exclaim: "That which was looked upon by the ancient saints as among the greatest favors and blessings, viz., revelation from God and communion with Him by dreams and by visions, is now looked upon by the religious world as the height of presumption and folly. The ancient saints considered their condition most deplorable when Jehovah would not speak to them; but the most orthodox religionists of this age deem it quite heterodox to even admit the probability that He ever will speak again. O my soul! language fails to paint the absurdity and abomination of such heaven-opposing and truth-excluding dogmas; and were it possible for those bright seraphs that surround the throne above, and bask in the sunbeams of immortality, to weep over the inconsistency and irrationality of mortals, the earth must be bedewed with celestial tears. My humble advice to all such is, that they repent and cast far from them these wicked traditions . . . lest the Lord speak to them in His wrath, and vex them in His sore displeasure" (Joseph Smith, *History of the Church of Jesus Christ of Latter-day Saints*, 7 vols., 2nd ed. rev., edited by B. H. Roberts [Salt Lake City: The Church of Jesus Christ of Latter-day Saints, 1932–51], 4:497).

A Personal Experience

A close friend of mine is striving to bring his life more in line with the doctrines of Christ so he will be better able to deal with these calamitous times. Recently he had a sad confrontation with some members of his family. These were "active" Latter-day Saints, by the way, good people whom he loved. Yet when he tried to explain to them what had become important to him, what really mattered, he discovered that they had grown complacent or outright scornful of spiritual issues. They scoffed when he spoke to them of receiving a little personal revelation through the power of the Holy Ghost, and they laughingly referred to him as an extremist, a fanatic, one who couldn't keep both feet in the real world. "As if I really wanted to," my friend added in his letter describing these events to me.

He then pointed out to them that when the angel showed Nephi the great and spacious building (the pride and wisdom of the world), it was peopled to a great extent by the house of Israel (modern Church members), who had "gathered together to fight against the twelve apostles of the Lamb" (1 Nephi 11:35). "Are these people you?" he asked his loved ones. "Are you the scoffers and the scorners and the simply complacent?"

While they only laughed harder, as if in answer to his own question he found himself reading that same evening in the scriptures of a day in the immediate future when "the arm of the Lord [shall] fall upon the nations. And then shall the Lord set his foot upon this mount, and it shall cleave in twain, and the earth shall tremble, and reel to and fro, and the heavens also shall shake. And the Lord shall utter his voice, and all the ends of the earth shall hear it; and the nations of the earth shall mourn, and *they that have laughed shall see their folly. And calamity shall cover the mocker, and the scorner shall be consumed; and they that have watched for iniquity shall be hewn down and cast into the fire*" (D&C 45:47–50; emphasis mine).

Reading on, he discovered that Christ was referring to the house of Israel (see D&C 45:51–52) in this dire prophecy, those Church members who have gathered into the great and spacious building of Nephi's vision. And then he wrote me that he knew what would befall his loved ones if they didn't wake up.

"Why," he asked as his letter continued, "is it so hard? Like Nephi I have labored diligently to write, to persuade my children, and also my family, to believe in Christ, and to be reconciled to God; for I know that it is by the grace of Christ that we are saved, after all we can do. That is why I talk of Christ, I rejoice in Christ, I preach of Christ, and I write of all the different things we can do to come to Christ, that my children and perhaps a few others may know to what source they may look for a remission of their sins [see 2 Nephi 25:23, 26].

"That," he went on, "has become my obsession, my hope, my joy, my life; to bring myself and those I love to Christ, where we may all be redeemed from hell and encircled about eternally in the arms of His love [see 2 Nephi 1:15]. Thus, having not wasted the days of our probation through the pursuit of worldly trivia, but instead obtaining and then retaining a remission of our sins through His precious blood which was spilled in our behalf, we will all experience eternal joy together.

"How simple it all seems!" he concluded. "How profound it really is! And how extremely difficult it turns out to be. It is no wonder that Jacob warned us against wasting the days of our mortal probation in pursuit of the world [see 2 Nephi 9:27], for coming unto Christ and obtaining and then retaining a remission of our sins requires a lifetime of diligent effort—an endurance race that must be run until the end of our mortal lives or it simply cannot be won."

The whole issue my friend raised puts me in mind of a prophecy I read recently that is attributed to Joseph Smith. Mosiah Hancock recorded that as the Prophet visited one day with him and his father, Levi Hancock, Joseph foretold the travels of the Saints as they crossed the plains and settled in the valley of the Great Salt Lake. Joseph said, "You will build cities to the North and to the South, and to the East and to the West; and you will become a great and wealthy people in that land. But, the United States will not receive you with the laws which God desires you to live, and you will have to go to where the Nephites lost their power. They worked in the United Order for 166 years, and the Saints have got to become proficient in the laws of God before they can meet the Lord Jesus Christ, or even the city of Enoch. . . .

"*You will live to see men arise in power in the Church who will seek to put down your friends and the friends of our Lord and Savior, Jesus Christ. Many will be hoisted because of their money and the worldly learning which they seem to be in possession of; and many who are the true followers of our Lord and Savior will be cast down because of their poverty*" (Mosiah Lyman Hancock, *Autobiography of Mosiah Hancock* [1834–1865], compiled by Amy E. Baird, Victoria H. Jackson, and Laura L. Wassell; typescript, BYU, p. 19; grammar has been standardized; emphasis mine).

How sad it is that some of us, as divinely sired brothers and sisters, have come to such a point that we are willing to put down others. How sad that we have followed so thoroughly the very path of wickedness and worldliness we have so frequently been warned against. How sad that we have come to the very time when "plagues, pestilence, famine, and disease such as the world has never before seen; . . . scourges, tribulation, calamities, and disasters without parallel; . . . strife, wars, rumors of wars, blood, carnage, and desolation which overshadow anything of past ages; . . . the elements being in commotion with resultant floods, storms, fires, whirlwinds, earthquakes—all of a proportion and intensity unknown to men of former days; . . . evil, iniquity, wickedness, turmoil, rapine, murder, crime, and commotion among men almost beyond comprehension" (Bruce R. McConkie, *Mormon Doctrine*, 2nd ed. [Salt Lake City: Bookcraft, 1966], p. 691) are all about us. How sad that some of us choose to become part of the problem rather than part of the solution.

The Fulness of the Gospel to Be Taken from Unrighteous Members

One of the more interesting prophecies concerning such members of the latter-day Church, which has already begun its fulfillment, was given by the resurrected Christ to the Nephites: "Thus commandeth the Father that I should say unto you: At that day when the Gentiles shall sin against my gospel, and shall reject the fulness of my gospel, and shall be lifted up in the pride of their hearts above all nations, and above all the people of the whole earth, and shall be filled with all manner of lyings, and of deceits, and of mischiefs, and all manner of hypocrisy, and murders, and priestcrafts, and whoredoms, and of secret abominations; and if they shall do all those things, and shall reject the fulness of my gospel, behold, saith the Father, *I will bring the fulness of my gospel from among them.*

"And then will I remember my covenant which I have

13

made unto my people, O house of Israel, and I will bring my gospel unto them. And I will show unto thee, O house of Israel, that the Gentiles shall not have power over you; but I will remember my covenant unto you, O house of Israel, and ye shall come unto the knowledge of the fulness of my gospel" (3 Nephi 16:10–12; emphasis mine).

According to the Lord, the term *Gentiles* refers not only to us as a nation but also to us as a Church and a people (see D&C 109:60). Therefore, this is a warning to us. The fulfillment of this prophecy of the last days began in the early 1830s with general persecution of the Saints, continued in the 1880s when the U.S. government passed laws preventing Latter-day Saints from entering into the fulness of the new and everlasting covenant of marriage, and continues today as, among other things, the Spirit of the Lord withdraws from unrighteous members who refuse to repent.

But because God loves us and doesn't want to see this happen, He declared in 1829: "Behold, the world is ripening in iniquity; and *it must needs be that the children of men are stirred up unto repentance,* both the Gentiles and also the house of Israel" (D&C 18:6; emphasis mine).

So we on this earth and in this land, even as members of the Church, are in the midst of it, this stirring up unto repentance that the Lord has promised us. And that is what the last days are all about—a time when the commotion of all things will stir up unto repentance all those who will repent, enabling them to avoid the destruction and even spiritual annihilation that others will suffer.

Spiritual Preparation Necessary

Several years ago my wife and I went to great lengths to set aside what we considered an adequate full year's storage for our family. In fact, it was so complete that we began feeling pretty secure. Then came a warm, pleasant Saturday morning in June that found me in my hammock teaching my eldest son how to mow the lawn. Actually, it would make me ready to learn about true preparation.

Suddenly our morning was interrupted by loudspeakers and wailing police sirens. We were ordered to evacuate our home immediately, and the next time we saw our home and food storage, both had been utterly destroyed (along with everything else we owned) by the filthy, contaminated waters emanating from the ruptured Teton Dam in Southeastern Idaho. So much for that sort of security and preparation.

But the surprising lesson, which took some time to sprout in my benumbed mind, was that it didn't really matter that our food supply and all else had been destroyed. As a wise stake president finally explained to me, because we had been endeavoring to be obedient to the counsel of inspired Church leaders, with our food storage program and numerous other things, we were blessed by Heavenly Father beyond belief, with all sorts of protection that was far more significant than not going hungry. In other words, we had been spiritually prepared.

Though many years have passed since that flood, nothing really has changed. If we are going to survive these days of turmoil and evil and be prepared for the coming of the Lord, then it needs to be by preparation that is significantly more than physical. We must be stirred up unto repentance and renewed spiritual growth or progression.

Brigham Young's Dream

At noon on February 17, 1847, as Brigham Young lay ill at Winter Quarters, he dreamed that he went to see Joseph Smith.

After pleading to be reunited with the Prophet and being told that the time was not right, President Young asked if Joseph at least had a word of counsel for the Saints.

Brigham Young related: "Joseph stepped toward me and looking very earnestly, yet pleasantly, said, 'Tell the people to be humble and faithful, and be sure to keep the spirit of the Lord and it will lead them right. Be careful and do not turn away the still small voice; it will teach them what to do and where to go; it will yield the fruits of the kingdom. Tell the brethren to keep their hearts open to conviction, so that when the Holy Ghost comes to them, their hearts will be ready to receive it. They can tell the Spirit of the Lord from all other spirits; it will whisper peace and joy to their souls; it will take malice, strife, and all evil from their hearts, and their whole desire will be to do good, bring forth righteousness and build up the Kingdom of God. Tell the brethren if they will follow the Spirit of the Lord they will go right. Be sure and tell the people to keep the Spirit of the Lord, and if they will, they will find themselves just as they were organized by our Father in Heaven, before they came into the world. Our Father in Heaven organized the human family, but they are all disorganized and in great confusion.'

"Joseph then showed me the pattern, how they were in the beginning. This I cannot describe, but I saw it, and saw where the priesthood had been taken from the earth (and then restored) and how it must be joined together, so that there would be a perfect chain, from Father Adam to his latest posterity. Joseph again said, 'Tell the people to be sure and keep the Spirit of the Lord and follow it, and it will lead them just right'" (In Preston Nibley, *Exodus to Greatness* [Salt Lake City: Deseret News Press, 1947], p. 329).

We Must Come unto Christ

Six times in Brigham Young's dream, Joseph Smith counseled Church members to get and keep the Spirit of the Lord. And that counsel, I believe, is the key to anyone's spiritual progression in these last days. To obtain Christ's Spirit, however, we must come to Him. Over and over we hear the commandment "Come unto Christ." Lest we be confused by the meaning of this commandment, Moroni explains: "I would exhort you that ye would come unto Christ, and lay hold upon every good gift, and touch not the evil gift, nor the unclean thing. . . .

"Yea, come unto Christ, and be perfected in him, and deny yourselves of all ungodliness; and if ye shall deny yourselves of all ungodliness and love God with all your might, mind and strength, then is his grace sufficient for you, that by his grace ye may be perfect in Christ; and if by the grace of God ye are perfect in Christ, ye can in nowise deny the power of God.

"And again, if ye by the grace of God are perfect in Christ, and deny not his power, then are ye sanctified in Christ by the grace of God, through the shedding of the blood of Christ, which is in the covenant of the Father unto the remission of your sins, that ye become holy, without spot" (Moroni 10:30, 32–33).

Jesus adds: "He that believeth these things which I have spoken, him will I visit with the manifestations of my Spirit, and he shall know and bear record. For because of my Spirit he shall know that these things are true. . . .

"Come unto me, O ye Gentiles, and I will show unto you the greater things, the knowledge which is hid up because of unbelief. Come unto me, O ye house of Israel, and it shall be made manifest unto you how great things the Father hath laid up for you, from the foundation of the world; and it hath not come unto you, because of unbelief. Behold, when ye shall rend that veil of unbelief which doth cause you to remain in your awful state of wickedness, and hardness of heart, and blindness of mind, then shall the great and marvelous things which have been hid up from the foundation of the world from you—yea, when ye shall call upon the Father in my name, with a broken heart and a contrite spirit, then shall ye know that the Father hath remembered the covenant which he made unto your fathers, O house of Israel" (Ether 4:11, 13–15).

"Therefore, sanctify yourselves that your minds become single to God, and the days will come that you shall see him; for he will unveil his face unto you, and it shall be in his own time, and in his own way, and according to his own will" (D&C 88:68).

Coming unto Christ, then, is true spiritual progression. And each of us must do this in the exact manner prescribed by the Lord and His prophets if we are going to spiritually survive this great time period known as the last days.

2

Power from on High

In early-day Kirtland, the newly converted Latter-day Saints came to Christ under the inspired direction of Joseph Smith, and their classic experiences are worthy of note. But first, a little background.

In December of 1830 Joseph wrote in his journal: "To the joy of the little flock, which in all, from Colesville to Canandaigua, New York, numbered about seventy members, did the Lord reveal the following doings of olden times, from the prophecy of Enoch" (*History of the Church*, 1:132–33). Then followed part of the segment of the book of Enoch that is presently in chapters 6 and 7 of Moses in the Pearl of Great Price.

The Book of Enoch

Two aspects of Enoch's prophecy are germane to our discussion. The first is that Enoch declared that he had been in the presence of the Lord. Enoch wrote, "I turned and went up on the mount; and as I stood upon the mount, I beheld the heavens open, and I was clothed upon with glory; and I saw the Lord; and he stood before my face, and he talked with me, even as a man talketh one with another, face to face" (Moses 7:3–4).

At least as significant was the following: "Enoch continued to call upon all the people . . . to repent; and so great was the faith of Enoch, that he led the people of God, and their enemies came to battle against them; and *he spake the word of the Lord,* and the earth trembled, and the mountains fled, even according to his command; and the rivers of water were turned out of their course . . . *so great was the power of the language which God had given him"* (Moses 7:12–13; emphasis mine).

God's Language of Power

Of course, the language God had given Enoch, and the power by which such marvelous deeds were accomplished, was the language of the Holy Priesthood. However, though Joseph now held the Melchizedek Priesthood, he did not yet know the language of power to which the scripture referred. He needed additional powers, or keys, as the Lord was soon to call them, to accomplish specific tasks. Granted to mortals through sacred ordinances, it was undoubtedly such keys of access to God that comprised Enoch's language of power and that enabled the ancient prophet to ultimately bring all his people into God's presence.

While we ordinarily use the word *keys* to refer to the right to preside in the Church, the word is sometimes used in other ways. Thus, a decade after receiving the priesthood, Joseph Smith said: "We behold the Keys of this priesthood consisted in [a person's] obtaining the voice of Jehovah [so that He will talk with him] in a familiar and friendly manner, that he continued to him the Keys, the Covenants, the power and the glory with which he blessed Adam at the beginning . . . for all the ordinances and duties that ever have been required by the priesthood under the direction and commandments of the Almighty in any of the dispensations, shall all be had in the last dispensation" (*The Words of Joseph Smith*, Andrew F. Ehat and Lyndon W. Cook, comps. [Provo, Utah: Brigham Young University Religious Studies Center, 1980], p. 42; hereafter cited as *Words*).

The Prophet also wrote: "Now the great and grand secret of the whole matter, and the *summum bonum* of the whole subject that is lying before us, consists in obtaining the powers of the Holy Priesthood. For him to whom these keys are given there is no difficulty in obtaining [revelation]" (D&C 128:11).

Of course, this clear understanding of power or keys to the access of God was Joseph's in the 1840s, not in 1830, because the Lord had not yet made it all known to him. His task, therefore, was to continue seeking, for clearly he needed more information in order to bring his people into the presence of the Lord.

Power from on High

On January 2, 1831, while still residing in New York, the Prophet received from the Lord a tantalizing commandment: "Ye should go to the Ohio; and there I will give unto you my law; and *there you shall be endowed with power from on high*" (D&C 38:32; emphasis mine).

Joseph Smith knew of his own experiences with God and Christ, he knew of the ministering of angels that he had enjoyed, and he longed for others to experience them as he had. He had learned that when all conditions are met, mortals can truly stand in the presence of the eternal Gods, behold and converse with them face to face, and not be upbraided (James 1:2–6).

Nor was Joseph alone. Not only did he have numerous scriptural examples from both the Bible and the Book of Mormon of men and women who had beheld angels and Christ in ancient times, but already in his own day a select few had enjoyed such privileges. For instance, the Three Witnesses had beheld the angel Moroni as well as the plates from which the Book of Mormon had been translated, and Oliver Cowdery had also seen John the Baptist and Peter, James, and John.

Additionally, during a conference in June of 1830, only two months after the Church had been organized, Newel Knight "saw heaven opened, and beheld the Lord Jesus Christ, seated at the right hand of the majesty on high" (*History of the Church*, 1:85). Joseph Smith, who recorded this supernal event in his journal, stated that Newel's experience inspired his heart "with joy unspeakable" and was calculated to "fill us with awe and reverence for that Almighty Being, by whose grace we had been called to be instrumental in bringing about, for the children of men, the enjoyment of such glorious blessings as were now at this time poured out upon us" (ibid.).

Commanded to Seek the Face of the Lord

Before we go further, it might be wise to discuss the fact that members of Christ's church are commanded to seek His face, to seek during their mortal lives to be brought into His actual presence. This doctrine was formalized years later by Joseph Smith when he said: "God hath not revealed anything to Joseph, but what He will make known unto the Twelve, and even the least Saint may know all things as fast as he is able to bear them. For the day must come when no man need say to his neighbor, Know ye the Lord; for all shall know Him (*who remain*) from the least to the greatest" (ibid., 3:380).

In 2 Chronicles 7:14 we read: "If my people, which are

called by my name, shall humble themselves, and pray, and seek my face, and turn from their wicked ways; then will I hear from heaven, and will forgive their sin, and will heal their land." And the Psalmist sang: "When thou saidst, Seek ye my face; my heart said unto thee, Thy face, Lord, will I seek" (Psalm 27:8). And in two separate revelations that are now part of the Doctrine and Covenants, the Lord said through Joseph: "Every soul who forsaketh his sins and cometh unto me, and calleth on my name, and obeyeth my voice, and keepeth my commandments, *shall see my face and know that I am*" (D&C 93:1; emphasis mine). "And *seek the face of the Lord always,* that in patience ye may possess your souls, and ye shall have eternal life" (D&C 101:38; emphasis mine).

Hence, Newel Knight's experience in beholding the face of Jesus, while the first that we know of (other than Joseph's) in this dispensation, was certainly not supposed to be the last.

For mortals to know the Lord as Joseph knew Him, however, and to bring themselves into His presence, required power of some sort from on high—priesthood power that had not yet been fully granted to the young church. But now Joseph had the promise of the Lord that he would be endowed with it in Ohio. Therefore, by January of 1832 he and Emma were on their way to the wilderness outpost of Kirtland, and the excited families of the Saints followed as quickly as they were able.

The Prophet/Teacher

As the Saints gathered to Kirtland in what seemed almost a human flood, the Prophet labored diligently to teach them as he was being taught by the Lord. And he was being taught at an amazing rate; nearly a third of the revelations in the Doctrine and Covenants were received between August 1831 and April 1834.

As rapidly as he could, Joseph disseminated this information, though he was quickly learning that the task was formidable. Still, meetings were held several times a week, and the doctrines of the kingdom were expounded to the usually eager people by himself and numerous others. Later Joseph said: "It is my meditation all the day and more than my meat and drink to know how I shall make the Saints of God to comprehend the visions that roll like an overflowing surge, before my mind. O how I would delight to bring before you things which you never thought of, but poverty and the cares of the world prevent. . . . I have labored hard and sought every way to try to prepare this people to comprehend the things that God is unfolding to me" (*Words*, pp. 196, 198; spelling standardized).

The thought that some of his beloved Saints might fail must have been troubling to Joseph, for he warned: "The mystery, power and glory of the priesthood is so great and glorious that the angels desired to understand it and cannot: why, because of the tradition of them and their fathers in setting up stakes and not coming up to the mark in their probationary state" (ibid., p. 247; spelling standardized).

Joseph wasn't alone in wondering why so many people had a difficult time listening to and accepting what he knew was divine truth. Dr. Isaac Watts, a recent convert and citizen of Kirtland, wrote a hymn about Joseph Smith, part of which states:

> Why was I made to hear thy voice,
> And enter while there's room,
> While thousands make a wretched choice,
> And rather starve than come[?]
> (In Kenneth W. and Audrey M. Godfrey, Jill Mulvay Derr, *Women's Voices* [Salt Lake City: Deseret Book Company, 1982], p. 50.)

Others See Christ

Yet by and large Joseph's counsel seemed to be working, for gradually others reached the spiritual level where they could see and know as he had seen and known. On February 16, 1832, at the Johnson Farm in Hiram, Ohio, where Joseph and others were working on the new translation of the Bible, he and Sidney Rigdon beheld in vision not only the Father and the Son but also all the holy angels and those who are sanctified before His throne (see D&C 76:19–24). And three months later, during conference in June of 1832, Lyman Wight, Harvey Whitlock, and the Prophet Joseph saw both the Father and the Son in heavenly vision (see Levi Hancock Journal, LDS Historical Department, Salt Lake City, pp. 91–92).

According to D&C 121:33, this was only the beginning of the visions and revelations that the Lord had promised would be poured out upon the heads of the Latter-day Saints.

Further Instructions from on High

In September of 1832, in response to a prayer of inquiry from Joseph and six other elders, the Lord declared: "This greater Priesthood administereth the gospel and holdeth the key of the mysteries of the kingdom, even *the key of the knowledge of God. Therefore, in the ordinances [of the priesthood], the power of godliness is manifest.* And without the ordinances thereof, and the authority of the Priesthood, the power of godliness is not manifest unto men in the flesh; *For without this no man can see the face of God, even the Father, and live. Now this Moses plainly taught to the children of Israel in the wilderness, and sought diligently to sanctify his people that they might behold the face of God; But they hardened their hearts and could not endure his presence;* therefore, the Lord in his wrath, for his anger was kindled against them, swore that they should not enter into his rest while in the wilderness, which rest is the fulness of his glory. Therefore, he took Moses out of their midst, and the Holy Priesthood also" (D&C 84:19–25; emphasis mine).

For Joseph this must have been both exhilarating and sobering. From his study of the Old Testament he knew that before the wrath of the Lord had been kindled against the Israelites, Moses had been able to prepare Aaron, Nadab, Abihu, and seventy of the elders of Israel so that they were able to behold the face of Jehovah (see Exodus 24). More, he had done so through the use of certain keys, which had been specifically designed by God to give the righteous access to Him— even *"the key of the knowledge of God."*

At least as significantly, Joseph now understood that bringing the Latter-day Saints into the presence of God, so that they could behold His face, was far more than just a nice thing to do. Rather, at some point it was essential for a person's exaltation. Furthermore, seeing the face of Christ was something to be initiated rather than being simply waited for. However, if the people hardened their hearts against Joseph and the information he would yet reveal to them from the Lord, then as He had done with the children of Israel, the Lord in his wrath would almost certainly kindle his anger against them and take away their privilege of beholding His face.

Of course, Joseph did not want that. No matter what it took, he obviously wanted the Latter-day Saints to be an Enoch people rather than a Moses people. And so he continued to seek further information about how that could be brought to pass.

The School of the Prophets

Just after Christmas in 1832, Joseph Smith received a revelation commanding him to organize a "school of the prophets" (see D&C 88:118–141). According to the revelation, the brethren needed to attend such a school to prepare to better serve one another through increased knowledge and understanding.

The school began meeting in Kirtland the end of January 1833 in a room that was upstairs above the Gilbert/Whitney store. Those meetings, attended by twenty-one individuals who were there by special invitation or calling, provided the setting for many remarkable spiritual experiences and in-depth discussions of the principles of the gospel.

To these brethren Joseph stated: "To receive revelation and the blessings of heaven it [is] necessary to have our minds on God and exercise faith and become of one heart and mind" (Kirtland Council Minute Book, LDS Church Archives, pp. 3–4).

Regularly the school met and received instructions. Zebedee Coltrin, one of those who had been called to attend, said that every time they were called together to attend to any business, they gathered in the morning about sunrise, fasting, and partook of the sacrament, and before going to school they washed themselves and put on clean linen. Then they gathered to prayer (Salt Lake School of the Prophets Minutes, October 3, 1883, p. 56).

Zebedee Coltrin's Experiences

Brother Zebedee Coltrin further stated: "About the time the school was first organized some wished to see an angel, and a number joined in the circle, and prayed. When the vision came, two of the brethren shrank and called for the vision to close or they would perish, these were Brothers Hancock and Humphries. When the Prophet came in they told him what they had done and he said the angel was no further off than the roof of the house, and a moment more he would have been in [our] midst" (ibid.).

One of the more unusual experiences pertaining to obtaining the visions of heaven happened to Joseph Smith, Oliver Cowdery, and Zebedee Coltrin. Apparently Brother Coltrin had just returned from a mission and was invited to accompany Joseph, Oliver, and Sidney Rigdon to a conference in New Portage. He records: "Next morning at New Portage [I] noticed that Joseph seemed to have a far off look in his eyes, or was looking at a distance, and presently he, Joseph, stepped between Brothers Cowdery and [me] and taking [us] by the arm, said, 'Lets take a walk.' [We] went to a place where there was some beautiful grass, and grapevines and swampbeech interlaced. President Joseph Smith then said, 'Let us pray.' [We] all three prayed in turn—Joseph, Oliver and [I]. Bro. Joseph then said, 'Now, Brethren, we will see some visions.'

"Joseph lay down on the ground on his back and stretched out his arms. . . . He told me to lie by his side with my head resting upon his arm, and Oliver in like manner upon the other side. We did so, all three looking heavenwards. As I looked I saw the blue sky open . . . and [we] saw a golden throne, on a circular foundation, something like a lighthouse, and on the throne were two aged personages . . . [whose] faces shown with youth . . . having white hair and clothed in white garments. They were the two most beautiful and perfect specimens of mankind [I] ever saw. . . . Joseph asked us if we knew who they were. We answered 'No.' Joseph said, 'That is father Adam and mother Eve.' . . . Adam was a large broadshouldered man, and Eve, as a woman, was as large in proportion" (Salt Lake School of the Prophets Minutes, 1883, pp. 68–70; Papers of Zebedee Coltrin, LDS Church Archives; spelling and punctuation standardized; the preceding account is a combination of information from both sources).

A Major Heavenly Vision

On March 18, 1833, the Prophet Joseph promised the school that those among them who were pure in heart should see another vision. The record states: "I exhorted the brethren to faithfulness and diligence in keeping the commandments of God, and gave much instruction for the benefit of the Saints, with a promise that the pure in heart should see a heavenly vision; and after remaining a short time in secret prayer, the promise was verified; for many present had the eyes of their understanding opened by the Spirit of God, so as to behold many things. . . . Many of the brethren saw a heavenly vision of the Savior, and concourses of angels, and many other things, of which each one has a record of what he saw" (*History of the Church*, 1:334–35).

John Murdock, one of those present, wrote of the experience: "About midday the visions of my mind were opened, and the eyes of my understanding were enlightened, and I saw the form of a man, most lovely; the visage of His face was round and fair as the sun; His hair a bright silver grey, curled in most majestic form; His eyes a keen penetrating blue; and the skin of His neck a most beautiful white. He was covered from the neck to the feet with a loose garment of pure white—whiter than any garment I had ever before seen. His countenance was most penetrating, and yet most lovely. . . . The vision was closed up. But it left on my mind the impression of love, for months, that I never before felt to that degree" (Autobiographical sketch, *Utah Genealogical and Historical Magazine*, April 1937, p. 61).

And Zebedee Coltrin said: "I saw a personage walk through the room, from East to West, and Joseph asked if we saw him. I saw him and suppose the others did, and Joseph answered 'That is Jesus the Son of God our elder brother.' Afterward Joseph told us to resume our former positions in prayer, which we did. Another person came through. The Prophet Joseph said this was the Father of our Lord Jesus Christ. I saw him. . . . I experienced a sensation like a consuming fire of great brightness, for He was surrounded as with a flame of fire, which was so brilliant that I could not discover anything else but His person. I saw his hands, his legs, his feet, his eyes, nose, mouth, head and body in the shape and form of a perfect man. His appearance was so grand and overwhelming that it seemed I should melt down in His presence, and the sensation was so powerful that it thrilled through my whole system and I felt it in the marrow of my bones. The Prophet Joseph said: Brethren, now you are prepared to be the apostles of Jesus Christ, for you have seen both the Father and the Son, and know that they exist and that They are two separate personages" (Salt Lake School of the Prophets Minutes, October 3, 1883, pp. 58–60).

Truly were the Saints making progress in bringing themselves into the presence of the Savior.

3

Wondrous Heavenly Manifestations

Once the members of the School of the Prophets had been brought into the Lord's rest, "which rest is the fulness of his glory" (D&C 84:24), Joseph began to focus on bringing the same blessings to all the members of the Church. To do that, of course, he needed to help them obtain the endowment of power the Lord had promised. This endowment was to be a gift of knowledge derived from revelation, a gift of power emitting from God, a gift of the very language of God that Enoch had understood and used. It consisted of instructions relating to the laws of God, including the principle of obedience, and was designed to give the Saints keys by which they could ask for and receive blessings (see D&C 124:95, 97).

Joseph declared that while many would not initially comprehend this endowment, bearers of the priesthood should prepare for it by purifying themselves, cleansing their hearts and their physical bodies in order that they might be prepared and able to overcome all things (see *History of the Church*, 2:309).

And of course, understandable or not, such a wondrous gift of power was usually reserved for presentation to the people of God within a temple. As Joseph said: "The keys are certain signs and words . . . which cannot be revealed . . . till the Temple is completed—The rich can only get them in the Temple—the poor may get them on the Mountain top as did Moses" (*Words*, pp. 119–20).

Apparently the Lord considered the Latter-day Saints in Kirtland sufficiently rich to build a temple, for so he had commanded in December of 1832 (see D&C 88:118–41). However, five months later, in June of 1833, the Lord chastised the Church for their delay in building the temple and admonished them to move forward quickly (see D&C 95). Repenting, the Saints began construction on June 6, 1833, following a plan that had been revealed in open vision to Joseph and his two counselors, Sidney Rigdon and Frederick G. Williams (Kate B. Carter, comp., *Our Pioneer Heritage* [Salt Lake City: Daughters of Utah Pioneers, 1967–76], 10:198).

Building the Temple

For three years, while they endured abject poverty, the several hundred Saints scattered throughout the United States and Canada pooled their resources and labored to construct the temple. Frequently Joseph served as foreman in the stone quarry. All the brethren who were not on missions labored every spare minute; the sisters under Emma Smith's direction made stockings, pantaloons, and jackets for the workmen; and Saints away from Kirtland sent money—ultimately between forty thousand and sixty thousand dollars cash was spent on the building. It was a terrible sacrifice for them all. Yet Joseph said, "A religion that does not require the sacrifice of all things never has power sufficient to produce the faith necessary unto life and salvation" (*Lectures on Faith*, compiled by N. B. Lundwall [Salt Lake City: N. B. Lundwall, n.d.], p. 58). And developing within his people a "faith necessary unto life and salvation" had become Joseph's greatest goal.

Of course this cost him, too. As the time for bringing all the Saints into the presence of the Lord approached, Joseph said, "[I am] weary with continual anxiety and labor, from [setting the quorums] in order, and in striving to purify them for the solemn assembly, according to the commandment of the Lord" (*History of the Church*, 2:388).

Power to Open the Heavens

Though the temple had not yet been completed and dedicated, work had progressed sufficiently by January of 1836 that Joseph decided it was time to begin presenting sacred ordinances to the people, thus empowering them to part the veil and come into the presence of the Lord. And as he had no doubt expected, from January 21 to May 1, 1836, as meetings were regularly held, "probably more Latter-day Saints beheld visions and witnessed other unusual spiritual manifestations than during any other era in the history of the Church" (Milton V. Backman, Jr., *The Heavens Resound* [Salt Lake City: Deseret Book Company, 1983], p. 285).

The first meeting, on January 21, was particularly significant. Oliver Cowdery said of it: "On the night of January 21, 1836, Joseph began to present the Lord's endowment to the Saints. At that time he introduced a number of ordinances designed to purify those who received them. It was during many of the meetings when these ordinances were introduced, that the heavens were opened for so many of the participants"

(Oliver Cowdery, "1836 Diary," *BYU Studies,* vol. 12, 1972, p. 419).

At that meeting the First Presidency and about three dozen others gathered together about candle-light. After spiritual anointings and blessings, the heavens were opened to Joseph and others, and Joseph beheld the celestial kingdom of God and the glory thereof. He saw the transcendent beauty of the gate through which the heirs of that kingdom will enter, which was like unto circling flames of fire; also the blazing throne of God, whereon was seated the Father and the Son. He saw the beautiful streets of that kingdom, which had the appearance of being paved with gold. Many of the brethren who received the ordinances that evening also saw glorious visions. Angels ministered unto them, the power of the Highest rested upon them, the house was filled with the glory of God, and they all shouted hosanna to God and the Lamb. Some then saw the face of the Savior, and others were ministered unto by holy angels, and the spirit of prophecy and revelation was poured out in mighty power; and loud hosannas, and glory to God in the highest saluted the heavens, for they all communed with the heavenly host (see *History of the Church,* 2:379–82).

On the day following, the apostles and presidents of the Seventy received their anointings, after which many saw heavenly beings, members were blessed with the gift of tongues, and, as Joseph said, "angels mingled their voices with ours" (ibid., p. 383).

The spiritual manifestations continued. On Thursday, January 28, during a meeting in which the Prophet attended to the sealing of what had been administered, Zebedee Coltrin again saw the Savior, this time nailed to the wood of the cross, "high and lifted up" (Salt Lake School of the Prophets Minutes, October 11, 1883, pp. 68–70; Papers of Zebedee Coltrin, LDS

Church Archives). Others beheld heavenly beings, and Joseph saw a glorious vision (see *History of the Church*, 2:387).

Harrison Burgess wrote of this same meeting: "I will here relate a vision which was shown to me. It was near the close of the endowments—I was in a meeting for instruction in the upper part of the Temple, with about a hundred of the High Priests, Seventies and Elders. The Saints felt to shout 'Hosannah' and the Spirit of God rested upon me in mighty Power and I beheld the room lighted up with a peculiar light such as I had never seen before. Soft and clear and the room looked to me as though it had neither roof nor floor . . . and I beheld Joseph and Hyrum Smith and Roger Orton enveloped in the light. Joseph exclaimed aloud, 'I behold the Savior the Son of God.' Hyrum, 'I behold the angels of Heaven.' Br. Orton exclaimed, 'I behold the chariots of Israel.' All who were in the room felt the power of God to that degree that many Prophesied and the power of God was made manifest, the remembrance of which I shall never forget while I live upon the earth" (Harrison Burgess File, LDS Church Historical Department, meeting of January 28, 1836).

On Saturday, February 6, the Prophet called together all who had been anointed so they could receive the sealing of all their blessings. Many who were obedient to his instructions received unusual blessings. Some saw visions. Others were filled with the Spirit and spoke in tongues, and some prophesied. Joseph declared it a time of rejoicing long to be remembered (*History of the Church*, pp. 391–92).

Brigham Young Sees Angels

One other incident is worthy of note. In a journal entry dated November 8, 1857, Wilford Woodruff wrote: "President Brigham Young related the circumstances of their seeing a circle of about 40 persons dressed in white robes . . . in the upper story of the Temple in Kirtland during the spring of [1836] after the Endowments. There was no person in that room at the time that was mortal, yet the room was filled with light and many personages did appear clothed in white and frequently went to the windows and looked out so that the Brethren in the street could see them plainly. Brother Young and Truman Angell stood together in the street and looked at them a long time. W. W. Phelps says he saw them for three hours. They were visible by all the Brethren present. Brother Angell said they must have stood some two feet from the floor. If they were only the size of common men they could not have been seen from the place where they stood except it should be the head, and those personages appeared nearly down to the waist as they looked out of the window with a front view" (*Wilford Woodruff's Journal, 1833–1898*, edited by Scott G. Kenney [Midvale, Utah: Signature, 1984], 5:53; spelling and punctuation standardized).

The Dedication

By the time the temple was ready for dedication on Sunday, March 27, 1836, literally hundreds of people had experienced divine manifestations. Erastus Snow wrote: "The number of all that were anointed and blessed in the house of the Lord in Kirtland was about three hundred and sixty. When all were anointed, the blessings were sealed by the presidency. Then we all, like as did Israel when they surrounded Jericho, with one united voice gave a loud shout of Hosanna, Hosanna, Hosanna, to God and the Lamb; Amen, Amen, and Amen. When this was done the Holy Ghost shed forth upon us; some spoke in tongues, some interpreted, others prophesied, some received visions of the judgments that were to be poured out upon this generation, others saw Zion in her glory, and the angels came and worshipped with us, and some saw them, yea, even 12 legions of them, the Chariots of Israel and the horsemen thereof" (as quoted in Joseph William Olsen, Thesis, "Biography of Erastus Snow," Brigham Young University, 1935, p. 19; spelling and punctuation standardized).

On March 27, following Joseph Smith's dedicatory prayer, which had been given him by revelation (see D&C 110), the sacred "Hosanna Shout" rang forth once again. And once again heavenly messengers made themselves manifest to many in attendance.

According to George A. Smith: "On the first day of the dedication, President Frederick G. Williams . . . who occupied the upper pulpit, bore testimony that the Savior, dressed in his vesture without seam, came into the stand and accepted of the dedication of the house, that he saw him, and gave a description of his clothing and all things pertaining to it" (*Journal of Discourses*, 26 vols. [London: Latter-day Saints' Book Depot, 1854–86], 11:10).

That evening in a special meeting of 416 (or 316) holders of the priesthood, many of those present saw the glory of God come down upon the temple like a cloud of fire and heard the sound of a rushing wind, and beheld cloven tongues of fire above the heads of many of the brethren (ibid., p. 426). George A. Smith said: "Many individuals bore testimony that they saw angels, and David Whitmer bore testimony that he saw three angels passing up the south aisle, and there came a shock on the house like the sound of a mighty rushing wind, and almost every man in the house arose, and hundreds of them were speaking in tongues, prophesying or declaring visions, almost with one voice" (ibid.).

Zebedee Coltrin added: "In the Kirtland Temple I have seen the power of God as it was in the day of Pentecost and cloven

tongues of fire have rested on the brethren and they have spoken with other tongues as the Spirit gave them utterance. . . .
The angels of God rested upon the temple and we heard their
voices singing heavenly music" (Papers of Zebedee Coltrin).

Angels on the Temple

On Thursday following the dedication, as many of the
Saints had gathered for a day of fasting, Prescinda Huntington
reported that a small girl came running in her door exclaiming
that the meeting was being held on top of the meeting house.
At first Prescinda dismissed her, but the child was so insistent
that at length she stepped forth to look. She says: "There I saw
on the temple angels clothed in white covering the roof from
end to end. They seemed to be walking to and fro; they
appeared and disappeared . . . [and had done so for the second
or third time] before I realized that they were not mortal men.
Each time in a moment they vanished, and their reappearance
was the same. This was in broad daylight, in the afternoon. A
number of the children in Kirtland saw the same" (Edward W.
Tullidge, *The Women of Mormondom* [New York: Tullidge &
Crandall, 1877], pp. 207–8).

The Visit of Christ, Moses, Elias, and Elijah

The most transcendent spiritual manifestation of all
occurred a week after the dedication. Following the afternoon
worship service, Joseph Smith and Oliver Cowdery retired to
the Melchizedek Priesthood pulpits in the west end of the
lower room of the temple. The canvas partition, called the veil,
was lowered so that they could pray in private. They wrote of
the occasion, "The veil was taken from our minds, and the eyes
of our understanding were opened" (D&C 110:1). They saw a
series of remarkable visions. The Lord Jesus Christ appeared,

accepted the temple, and promised to manifest himself therein if, he said, "my people will keep my commandments, and do not pollute this holy house" (D&C 110:8; see also vv. 2–9).

Moses next appeared and restored "the keys of the gathering of Israel from the four parts of the earth, and the leading of the ten tribes from the land of the north" (v. 11). Elias then conferred "the dispensation of the gospel of Abraham" (v. 12). Finally, in fulfillment of Malachi's prophecy (see Malachi 4:5–6) and Moroni's promise (see D&C 2) to "turn the hearts of the fathers to the children, and the children to the fathers" (D&C 110:15), Elijah appeared to the Prophet and Oliver testifying that "the keys of this dispensation are committed into your hands" in preparation for "the great and dreadful day of the Lord" (v. 16). Through the sealing keys that were restored by Elijah, Latter-day Saints could now perform saving priesthood ordinances in behalf of their kindred dead as well as for the living. However, these sacred ordinances for the dead were not introduced to the members of the Church until the Nauvoo era.

"This great day of visions and revelation occurred on Easter Sunday, 3 April 1836. What better day in the dispensation of the fulness of times to reconfirm the reality of the Resurrection? That weekend was also the Jewish Passover. For centuries Jewish families have left an empty chair at their Passover feasts, anticipating Elijah's return. Elijah has returned—not to a Passover feast, but to the Lord's temple in Kirtland" (*Church History in the Fulness of Times* [Salt Lake City: The Church of Jesus Christ of Latter-day Saints, 1989], p. 167).

An Interesting Note

Concerning the ordinances as performed in the Kirtland Temple, LDS scholars Lyndon W. Cook and Andrew F. Ehat write: "In the Kirtland Temple in 1836, after attending to the ordinance of the washing of the feet, Joseph Smith said he had 'completed the organization of the church, and . . . [had given] all the necessary ceremonies' (*History of the Church*, 2:432 or *Teachings*, p. 110). However, four days later, he was given greater keys of authority and knowledge which he did not confer on the leaders of the Church until the Nauvoo period (see D&C 110). So while the Prophet's statement made in Kirtland refers to the finalization of all offices within the Church priesthood structure and sets the basic structure of temple ordinances, the Prophet's statement to the Relief Society . . . ('He spoke of delivering the keys of the Priesthood to the Church and said that the faithful members of the Relief Society should receive them in connection with their husbands, that the Saints whose integrity has been tried and proved faithful, might know how to ask the Lord and receive an answer' [*History of the Church*, 4:604]) portends that the same priesthood organization as finalized in Kirtland would be endowed with the greater keys and knowledge as revealed later to Joseph Smith by Elias and Elijah. This greater knowledge eventually effected a considerable enlarging of the scope and meaning of temple ordinances, transforming the Kirtland Temple ordinances to their Nauvoo counterparts *without* changing the order of these ordinances (see *History of the Church*, 2:309 or *Teachings*, p. 91)." (*Words*, p. 140, footnotes).

As the spiritual manifestations experienced by most of the several hundred Saints in Kirtland are contemplated, it is an easy matter to understand why historians refer to the period as a latter-day Pentecost—a time of rich outpourings of the Spirit as the members gave their all for their beloved Savior. For this they were rewarded with the supernal blessing of being brought into His presence and enjoying the eternal love and felicity He manifests for all so blessed.

CHAPTER

4

Joseph's Triumph
and Defeat

With the dedication of the Kirtland Temple, Joseph's lofty desire of establishing a Zion for this priesthood generation of the last days had begun its fulfillment. Truly had the Lord blessed His people as they struggled and sacrificed to expand their city, construct a temple to the Most High God, and become a holy people like the ancient Saints of Enoch. Like Enoch's people, these Latter-day Saints were led by a mighty prophet to whom the Lord revealed His will and who had also been given keys of priesthood powerful enough to open the heavens. These keys Joseph freely passed on to the Lord's people through what the Lord termed the "endowment," thus giving all so blessed power to bring themselves back into His presence. And like Enoch's people, a remarkable number in this generation did so, seeing and hearing glorious heavenly manifestations during that season of rejoicing.

Surely they must have felt as did the Nephites following

the appearance of the Lord: "They were in one, the children of Christ, and heirs to the kingdom of God. And how blessed were they! For the Lord did bless them in all their doings" (4 Nephi 1:17–18).

A Tragic Apostasy

Sadly, a period of great apostasy followed immediately thereafter, and many of the Saints succumbed to the entice-ments of Satan and the cares of the world. In August some of the apostates made an armed attempt to take over the temple. Though this was foiled after a few terrifying moments, and the men were ultimately disfellowshipped, it was only the begin-ning. Warren Parish, Apostle John F. Boynton, and others orga-nized a group dedicated to overthrowing Joseph Smith, whom they considered to be a fallen prophet. As a result of this apos-tasy, fifty leading brethren were excommunicated, and they joined in the general persecution of the Saints being perpetrated by the non-Mormons.

Hepzibah Richards, sister of Willard Richards, wrote: "For the last three months we as a people have been tempest tossed, and at times the waves have well nigh overwhelmed us. . . . A dreadful spirit reigns in the breasts of those who are opposed to this Church. They are above law and beneath whatever is laudable. Their leading object seems to be to get all the prop-erty of the Church for little or nothing, and drive [the Saints] out of the place" (Letter, March 23, 1838, *Women's Voices*, edited by Kenneth W. Godfrey, Audrey M. Godfrey, and Jill Mulvay Derr [Salt Lake City: Deseret Book Co., 1982], pp. 76–77).

Between November 1837 and June 1838, possibly two or three hundred Saints withdrew from the Church in Kirtland, and a significant number also left the Church in Missouri. In that nine-month period, the Three Witnesses, a member of the

First Presidency (Frederick G. Williams), four members of the Twelve Apostles, and several members of the First Quorum of Seventy left the Church. Because Brigham Young continually defended Joseph Smith no matter what was said, his life was threatened, and he was forced to flee to Missouri on horseback.

Thus began a mass exodus of the Latter-day Saints from Geauga County, as more than sixteen hundred people abandoned their homes and property and entered into a new colonizing adventure in the wilderness of western America.

At the beginning of 1838 Joseph Smith wrote: "A new year dawned upon the Church in Kirtland in all the bitterness of the spirit of apostate mobocracy; which continued to rage and grow hotter and hotter, until Elder Rigdon and myself were obliged to flee from its deadly influence, as did the Apostles and Prophets of old . . . to escape mob violence, which was about to burst upon us under the color of legal process to cover the hellish designs of our enemies, and to save themselves from the just judgment of the law" (*History of the Church*, 3:1).

A Spirit of Worldliness Was behind the Apostasy

On both continents Jesus taught: "No man can serve two masters: for either he will hate the one, and love the other; or else he will hold to the one, and despise the other. Ye cannot serve God and mammon" (Matthew 6:24; 3 Nephi 13:24). And Hugh Nibley adds: "The first commandment given to the Saints in this last dispensation, delivered at Harmony, Pennsylvania, in April of 1829, before the formal incorporation of the Church, was an ominous warning: 'Seek not for riches but for wisdom' (D&C 6:7)—all in one brief mandate that does not allow compromise. Why start out on such a negative note? The Lord knew well that the great obstacle to the work would be what it always had been in the past. The warning is repeated throughout the Doctrine and Covenants and the Book of Mormon again and again. The positive and negative are here side by side and back to back, making it clear, as the scriptures often do, that the two quests are mutually exclusive—you cannot go after both, you cannot serve both God and Mammon, even if you should be foolish enough to try" (Hugh Nibley, *Approaching Zion* [Provo and Salt Lake City: Foundation for Ancient Research and Mormon Studies and Deseret Book Company, 1989], p. 343).

After examining all the information available, it appears obvious that a great many of the Kirtland Saints somehow lost track of the wisdom of God and shifted their allegiance from God to mammon, or the things of the world. Eliza R. Snow apparently understood the cause of the spiritual decline of the Saints perfectly, for she said that many members felt that "prosperity was dawning upon them . . . and many who had been humble and faithful . . . were getting haughty in their spirits, and lifted up in the pride of their hearts. As the Saints drank in the love and spirit of the world, the Spirit of the Lord withdrew from their hearts, and they were filled with pride and hatred toward those who maintained their integrity" (*History of the Church*, 2:487–88, footnotes).

A growing spirit of speculation in Kirtland was further evidence of this. Many people had borrowed money at inflated prices in order to purchase land for resale at a substantial profit. Warren Cowdery said that these members were "guilty of wild speculation and visionary dreams of wealth and worldly grandeur, as if gold and silver were their gods, and houses, farms and merchandise their only bliss or their passport to it" (*Messenger and Advocate*, May 1837, p. 509).

"Then came the crash of 1837, brought on by those same shrewd, hardheaded businessmen," Hugh Nibley writes.

" 'During this time,' [Heber C.] Kimball recalled, 'I had many days of sorrow and mourning, for my heart sickened to see the awful extent that things were getting to.' Many apostatized and 'also entered into combinations to obtain wealth by fraud and every means that was evil.' Later, Kimball returned to Kirtland again after a mission to England: 'The Church had suffered terribly from the ravages of apostasy.' Looking back over many years, he recalled that 'the Ohio mobbings, the Missouri persecutions, the martyrdom, the exodus, nor all that Zion's cause has suffered since, have imperiled it half so much as when mammon and the love of God strove for supremacy in the hearts of His people.' Note that they were torn between God and Mammon, and 'no man can serve both!' " (*Approaching Zion*, p. 347).

Brother Nibley says: "Every step in the direction of increasing one's personal holdings is a step away from Zion, which is another way of saying, as the Lord has proclaimed in various ways, that one cannot serve two masters: to the degree in which he loves the one he will hate the other, and so it is with God and business, for *mammon* is simply the standard Hebrew word for any kind of financial dealing" (ibid., p. 37).

"From the very first there were Latter-day Saints who thought to promote the cause of Zion by using the methods of Babylon. Indeed, once the Saints were told to make friends with the Mammon of unrighteousness (D&C 82:22), but that was only to save their lives in an emergency. We have the word of the Prophet Joseph that Zion is not to be built up by using the methods of Babylon. He says, 'Here are those who begin to spread out buying up all the land they are able to do, to the exclusion of the poorer ones who are not so much blessed with this world's goods, thinking to lay foundations for themselves only, looking to their own individual families and those who are to follow them. . . . Now I want to tell you that Zion cannot be built up in any such way'" (ibid., p. 20–21; spelling standardized).

Of course, any time such worldliness takes precedence over the things of the Spirit, then the Spirit of God departs and apostasy occurs. President Spencer W. Kimball said: "Today we worship the gods of wood and stone and metal. Not always are they in the form of a golden calf, but equally real as objects of protection and worship. They are houses, lands, bank accounts, leisure. They are boats, cars, and luxuries. They are bombs and ships and armaments. We bow down to the god of mammon, the god of luxuries, the god of dissipation" (in Conference Report, October 1961, p. 33).

Once the Saints were no longer sacrificing their all for the building of the temple in Kirtland, many of them bowed down to the god of mammon. They began looking to themselves, and soon their personal religion was no longer a religion of spiritual power and progression. Again quoting Brother Nibley: "In ancient times, apostasy never came by renouncing the gospel but always by corrupting it. No one renounces it today, and so we have the strange paradox of people stoutly proclaiming beliefs and ideals that they have no intention of putting into practice. . . . The great apostasy in the time of the apostles was not a renouncing of the faith but its corruption and manipulation . . . [a] redirect[ion of] the gospel light . . . for convenience" (Hugh Nibley, *Temple and Cosmos,* edited by Don E. Norton [Provo and Salt Lake City: Foundation for Ancient Research and Mormon Studies and Deseret Book Company, 1992], p. 395).

As time passed, and as this gospel of convenience increased its hold in the hearts and minds of Latter-day Saints, fewer and fewer of them had power to bring to pass and enjoy such spiritual experiences as had occurred in Kirtland—and this despite the fact that they had been endowed with that power from on high. Truly had their spiritual progression been slowed or in some cases even stopped altogether.

The next step, of course, was that angelic ministrations and other manifestations of the Lord's Spirit quite literally went out of fashion. Those who continued to seek and enjoy such rich spiritual blessings hesitated to discuss them or bear witness of them for fear of ridicule and outright scorn, and so their numbers grew fewer and fewer.

And the scorners? Besides the apostates and the anti-Christs, they grew to include good, well-meaning people, especially members of the Church, who had never sought such transcendent experiences, had never sacrificed the things of the world in order to experience them, and who doubted that ordinary people such as themselves could ever see, hear, feel, and know such things. And so they mocked and scorned or shook their heads in sorrow and pity that so-and-so could be so deluded as to think *he* or *she* had actually seen and spoken with an angel.

An Enoch or a Moses People Today

Sadly, the situation has not improved. As was pointed out in chapter 1, a spirit of worldliness or faithlessness permeates not only the world but also many of our modern Church members. Despite covenants to the contrary, too many of us choose to live a gospel of convenience rather than one of sacrifice, and the scorners and doubters of things spiritual reign supreme. Again quoting Brother Nibley: "We are granted enough time on earth to serve only one master. Every day of our lives we have to make a choice, a choice that will show where our real interests and desires lie. From the very beginning of the world the choice was provided as a test for each of us during this time of probation. Satan is allowed to try and tempt us in his way, and God is allowed in his: as Moroni puts it, 'The devil . . . inviteth and enticeth to sin, and to do that which is evil *continually*. But behold, that which is of God inviteth and enticeth to do good *continually*' (Moroni 7:12–13). It is going on all the time, the ancient doctrine of the Two Ways. The point is that we *cannot* choose both ways. They go in opposite directions" (*Approaching Zion*, p. 125).

We as a people are no different today than we were in early Kirtland, and we ought to enjoy the same gifts. As Orson Pratt testified: "God was there [in Kirtland], his angels were there, the Holy Ghost was in the midst of the people, the visions of the Almighty were opened to the minds of the servants of the living God; the veil was taken off from the minds of many; they saw the heavens opened; they beheld the angels of God; they heard the voice of the Lord; and they were filled from the crown of their heads to the soles of their feet with the power and inspiration of the Holy Ghost. . . . The people were blessed as they never had been blessed for generations and generations that were passed and gone" (*Journal of Discourses*, 18:132; spelling standardized).

Yet we *can* experience them. As the Prophet Joseph once said: "God hath not revealed anything to Joseph, but what He will make known unto the Twelve, and even the least Saint *may know all things as fast as he is able to bear them*" (*History of the Church*, 3:380; emphasis mine).

The key here is found in the words "may know . . . as fast as he is able." In other words, experiencing the things Joseph experienced is not automatic. If obtained at all, they must be sought for as diligently as he sought them, through mighty prayer, and the person must be adequately prepared, through ever-increasing personal righteousness, to receive them. As the Prophet said on another occasion: "The things of God are of deep import; and time, and experience, and careful and ponderous and solemn thoughts can only find them out. Thy mind, O man! if thou wilt lead [thy] soul unto salvation, must stretch as high as the utmost heavens, and search into and contemplate the darkest abyss, and the broad expanse of eternity—thou must commune with God" (*Teachings of the Prophet Joseph Smith*, selected by Joseph Fielding Smith [Salt Lake City: Deseret Book Company, 1938], p. 137; hereafter referred to as *Teachings*).

Finally, consider the implications of this statement of Joseph's: "We again say, search the revelations of God; study the prophecies, and rejoice that God grants unto the world Seers and Prophets. They are they who saw the mysteries of godliness; they saw the flood before it came; they saw angels ascending and descending upon a ladder that reached from earth to heaven; they saw the stone cut out of the mountain, which filled the whole earth; they saw the Son of God come from the regions of bliss and dwell with men on earth; they saw the deliverer come out of Zion, and turn away ungodliness from Jacob; they saw the glory of the Lord when he showed the transfiguration of the earth on the mount; they saw every mountain laid low and every valley exalted when the Lord was taking vengeance upon the wicked; they saw truth spring out of the earth, and righteousness look down from heaven in the last days, before the Lord came the second time to gather his elect; they saw the end of wickedness on earth, and the Sabbath of creation crowned with peace; they saw the end of the glorious thousand years, when Satan was loosed for a little season; they saw the day of judgment when all men received according to their works, and they saw the heaven and the earth flee away to make room for the city of God, when the righteous receive an inheritance in eternity. *And, fellow sojourners upon earth, it is your privilege to purify yourselves and come up to the same glory, and see for yourselves, and know for yourselves. Ask, and it shall be given you; seek and ye shall find; knock, and it shall be opened unto you"* (*Teachings*, p. 12; emphasis mine).

It is the indisputable right of mortals to experience such things. Unfortunately, too many modern Latter-day Saints will not be so blessed because the things of the world continue to mean more to us than the things of the Spirit, and so we choose the wrong way. And this is a tragedy that Joseph took personally. Heber C. Kimball declared: "The greatest torment [Joseph] had and the greatest mental suffering was because this people *would not live up to their privileges*. There were many things he desired to reveal that we have not learned yet, but he could not do it. He said sometimes that he felt pressed upon and as though he were pent up in an acorn shell, and all because *the people did not and would not prepare themselves* to receive the rich treasures of wisdom and knowledge that he had to impart. He could have revealed a great many things to us if we had been ready; but he said there were many things that we could not receive because we lacked that diligence and faithfulness that were necessary to entitle us to those choice things of the kingdom" (in *Journal of Discourses*, 11:167; emphasis mine).

And so I wonder, for I cannot help it. Have we become an Enoch people or a Moses people? Do we seek after the face of the Lord and the things of His Spirit, or do we harden our hearts against them? And how does the glorified Joseph feel about the course many members of the Church he restored are following now?

I wonder.

To Be
Born Again

CHAPTER

5

Seven Levels of Spiritual Progression

When my brother Brenton and I wrote *Spiritual Survival in the Last Days,* we included a list of seven different levels of spiritual development. If we are serious about advancing our own spirituality by coming to Christ, then it seems appropriate that these be reconsidered here. But remember, they have nothing to do with ecclesiastical offices within the Church. Rather, they are guidelines for us to use as we chart our own spiritual progression.

Beginning at the lowest level, or the level that is furthest from God, these spiritual levels are:

1. *Enemy to God.* These people resist all enticements from the Holy Spirit within their own lives, and they do all within their power to halt or thwart the work of God within the lives of those around them. As Abinadi said to the wicked Noah and his priests: "Remember that he that persists in his own carnal nature, and goes on in the ways of sin and rebellion against

God, remaineth in his fallen state and the devil hath all power over him. Therefore, he is as though there was no redemption made, being an enemy to God; and also is the devil an enemy to God" (Mosiah 16:5; see also James 4:4; Mosiah 2:37).

2. *Stranger and foreigner.* While not actively campaigning against God and his work, these people have no knowledge of Him. Usually it is not common for them to have a burning desire to find out about God unless something (such as contact with the missionaries or the Book of Mormon) motivates them (see Ephesians 2:19). Of course, even people who are diligently seeking the gospel remain strangers and foreigners until after they are united by baptism with the Church.

3. *Fellow citizen with the Saints.* These people are members of the Lord's earthly church but, for one reason or another, are not actively involved in building the kingdom of God. This may be simply because of their youthfulness, either in age or in church membership, or because they don't want to be involved or to be active (see Ephesians 2:20). Usually such people will have little understanding of the things of the Spirit.

4. *Servant or handmaiden of God.* All mortals who are called to serve by other mortals holding proper priesthood authority become servants of God. These people are actively involved, through various callings, assignments, and personally generated efforts, in building the kingdom of God on the earth. The scriptures state: "In the last days, saith God, I will pour out of my Spirit upon all flesh: and your sons and your daughters shall prophesy, and your young men shall see visions, and your old men shall dream dreams: *and on my servants and on my handmaidens* I will pour out in those days of my Spirit; and they shall prophesy" (Acts 2:17–18; emphasis mine. See also Luke 1:38; D&C 1:38; 90:28; 35:17; 50:26; 93:46; 133:30, 32).

Such individuals wield great authority for the Lord.

Servants of God do a mighty work and are therefore entitled to incredible blessings at the hand of God. These would include the gifts of the Spirit as well as angelic ministrations. However, such individuals may or may not have an understanding of spiritual things and may or may not progress spiritually, depending on whether their true interests are worldly or spiritual.

5. *Son or daughter of Jesus Christ.* These people have experienced the magnificent baptisms of water *and* of the Holy Ghost. Being dramatically changed in the inner man, they have been adopted into the family of Jesus Christ: "Behold, I am he who was prepared from the foundation of the world to redeem my people. Behold, I am Jesus Christ. I am the Father and the Son. In me shall all mankind have life, and that eternally, even they who shall believe on my name; and they shall become *my sons and my daughters*" (Ether 3:14; emphasis mine. See also Mosiah 5:7; 15:10–12; Moroni 7:19).

Such people, having obtained their callings as sons or daughters of Christ but not yet their elections as heirs of God and members of the church of the Firstborn, are granted the privilege of enjoying spiritual experiences and trials such as will most quickly bring them closer to Christ their Father.

6. *Elect of God.* These are those who, once they have become sons or daughters of Christ, "hear [the Lord's] voice and harden not their hearts" (D&C 29:7; see also D&C 33:6). In other words, the elect of God are those who continue to press forward steadfastly, no matter the opposition they might encounter. Elder Bruce R. McConkie says: "The elect of God comprise a very select group, an inner circle of faithful members of The Church of Jesus Christ of Latter-day Saints. They are the portion of church members who are striving with all their hearts to keep the fulness of the gospel law in this life so that they can become inheritors of the fulness of gospel rewards in the life to come. . . . To gain this

elect status they must be endowed in the temple of the Lord (D. & C. 95:8), enter into that 'order of the priesthood' named 'the new and everlasting covenant of marriage' (D. & C. 131:1–4), and overcome by faith until, as the sons [and daughters] of God, they merit membership in the Church of the Firstborn. (D. & C. 76:50–70, 94–96.)" (*Mormon Doctrine*, pp. 217–18).

While not yet sealed up unto eternal life, these men and women, as the elect of God, are declared Christ's friends as well as His family. The Lord says to them: *"Ye are my friends, if ye do whatsoever I command you.* Henceforth I call you not servants; for the servant knoweth not what his lord doeth: but I have called you friends; for all things that I have heard of my Father I have made known unto you" (John 15:14–15; emphasis mine; see also D&C 84:77; 93:45–46; James 2:23).

Thus, when people pursue righteousness until they become the Lord's friends, then by that election of grace they are counted worthy to stand among the members of the Lord's heavenly Church of the Firstborn and to labor with such heavenly beings as they prepare for the day when their own calling and election will be made sure.

7. Joint heir with Jesus Christ. Having overcome all, these people have their exaltation assured while still in mortality and so have become joint heirs with Christ in receiving all the blessings the Father can bestow upon them. As the scriptures state: "The Spirit itself beareth witness with our spirit, that we are the children of God: And if children, then heirs; heirs of God, and *joint-heirs with Christ;* if so be that we suffer with him, that we may be also glorified together" (Romans 8:16–17; emphasis mine; see also Galatians 4:7).

President John Taylor said: "The atonement, having restored man to his former position before the Lord, has . . . made it possible for him to obtain that exaltation and glory which it would have been impossible for him to have received without it; even to become a son of God by adoption; and being a son, then an heir of God, and a joint heir with Jesus Christ" (*The Gospel Kingdom*, edited by G. Homer Durham [Salt Lake City: Bookcraft, 1987], p. 119).

We become joint heirs with Christ of all that the Father has only after we have made our calling and election a sure thing. And that can come to us only after we have thoroughly forsaken the world, dedicated our lives to God and Christ, and then proven that dedication through absolute repentance and lengthy, diligent service to the kingdom. Joseph Smith taught: "To become a joint heir of the heirship of the Son, one must put away all his false traditions" (*Teachings*, p. 321). Then, through diligent righteousness, we can make our calling and election a sure thing. As the Apostle Peter wrote: "Give diligence to make your calling and election sure: for if ye do these things, ye shall never fall: for so an entrance shall be ministered unto you abundantly into the everlasting kingdom of our Lord and Saviour Jesus Christ" (2 Peter 1:10–11).

Setting Up Stakes

While the vast majority of "active" Latter-day Saints have reached the fourth level of spiritual progression and become servants or handmaidens of God, far fewer have gone on to the fifth, sixth, and seventh levels spoken of above. Yet if we wish to enjoy the sort of glorious spiritual progression experienced by the Kirtland Saints, we must do so.

But remember, while scriptures and history seem to lump people together into groups, the issue of spiritual progression remains today, as it always has, entirely personal. The Church has already been established, the ordinances of the priesthood are in place, and we have been given access to them. The question that must be answered, therefore, is simply, "What am I doing about it? Because I alone have the capacity to bring spiritual progression to myself and cannot depend upon the strength of the Church to do it for me. Therefore, what am I doing about advancing my own spiritual state?"

Joseph Smith taught that we all have agency to go as far as we want toward the celestial kingdom but that most, including the angels, would "set up stakes" or personal limitations and say, "I cannot go any further." Nor would we, because we have so decided (see *Words*, pp. 244–47, 256).

The great Book of Mormon prophet Abinadi, in speaking of those unfortunates who would be delivered over to the devil after the resurrection, declared their damnation: "*Having gone according to their own carnal wills and desires;* having never called upon the Lord while the arms of mercy were extended towards them; for the arms of mercy were extended towards them, and they would not; they being warned of their iniquities and yet they would not depart from them; and they were commanded to repent *and yet they would not repent*" (Mosiah 16:12; emphasis mine).

In other words, these people, singly and individually, absolutely refused to repent. They became a group only because so many of them made the same tragic decision. A repentant Alma the Younger, now filled with a burning desire to proclaim the word of God to all the earth, continues this theme: "*I know that [God] granteth unto men according to their desire,* whether it be unto death or unto life; yea, I know that he allotteth unto men, yea, decreeth unto them decrees which are unalterable, *according to their wills,* whether they be unto salvation or unto destruction" (Alma 29:4; emphasis mine).

Like it or not, each of us will be given what we want most—according to our desires. If our wants are worldly, or world-centered rather than spiritually centered, then of course those things will be our reward, and we will never in mortality know the thrill and eternal joy of spiritual progression.

Being Damned or Stopped

Let us consider, for example, those who are in the fourth level of the above list—servants or handmaids of God. All who are granted the wondrous blessing of becoming servants of God should remain so throughout their lives, at least in terms of rendering service to the kingdom and their fellow-beings. Sadly, however, many Latter-day Saints choose to remain at this level *spiritually.*

While usually partaking of the sealing ordinances in the temple and setting the stage for far greater blessings for themselves and their families, they choose by the way they live to remain spiritually dormant or immature, never partaking of the power of the endowment. They have obtained the gift of the Holy Ghost, but rarely do they exercise that gift or enjoy the fruits thereof. These people choose never to offer up mighty prayer unto complete repentance and the obtaining a remission of sins, which are required to move on.

Thus they cannot open the heavens and are never certain of their position before the Lord. Though they might serve diligently all their lives and receive blessings for such service, in their spiritual growth they have effectively "set up stakes" for themselves. Put another way, they have damned or stopped themselves from significant spiritual progression here in mortality.

Is This Wrong?

A legitimate question might be, "Am I being bad or wicked if I don't want to push ahead with being more spiritual? After all, many good people have lived and died without seeing angels or having superlative spiritual experiences. In fact, numerous good Latter-day Saints have probably passed through mortality without ever fully being born again. Is that such a bad thing?"

The answer would be, "It depends on who we want to be." President Ezra Taft Benson states: "In the usual sense of the term, *Church membership* means that a person has his or her name officially recorded on the membership records of the Church. By that definition, we have more than [eight] million members of the Church.

"But the Lord defines a member of His Kingdom in quite a different way. In 1828, through the Prophet Joseph Smith, He said, 'Behold, this is my doctrine—whosoever repenteth and cometh unto me, *the same is my church*' (D&C 10:67; italics added.) To Him whose Church this is, membership involves far more than simply being a member of record" ("A Mighty Change Of Heart," *Ensign*, October 1989, p. 2).

If membership in the Lord's spiritual kingdom is wanted, rather than simply mortal Church membership, then setting up stakes is not only wrong but incredibly foolish. To understand that, we must keep in mind that Jesus Christ lived, suffered, and died so that each of us might have the capacity to repent of our sins, obtain a remission of them through baptisms of water and fire, and begin our return to Him. This is His gospel, which in His kindness and mercy He has restored to the earth through modern prophets (see 3 Nephi 27:20–21; D&C 39:6). He has given us scriptures, both ancient and modern, so that we might know *how* to return to His presence. And finally He has restored the highest or Melchizedek priesthood with its ordinances and keys so that we might *have the power*, as members of an eternally sealed family unit, to open the heavens and thus return to His presence (see D&C 84:19–22).

In all of this, Christ's whole aim is to see that we obtain not only salvation but also exaltation—the privilege of becoming as He is. Nowhere has He given us encouraging instructions on how to become telestial beings, or terrestrial beings, or even celestial beings who are ministering servants for those who are worthy of exaltation.

Rather, every doctrine we are taught, every scripture we read, every ordinance performed in our behalf is designed expressly to lead us to exaltation in the presence of God, and that in as direct and rapid a manner as possible.

That is why putting off repenting and obtaining a remission of sins and the other aspects of spiritual progression, for whatever reason, is the same as choosing to remain *in* our sins. Thereby we are ignoring the will of Christ and placing our eternal futures in jeopardy. Paul urges the Hebrew Saints, "Let us go on unto perfection; not laying *again* the foundation of repentance . . . and of faith . . . " (Hebrews 6:1; emphasis mine).

In other words, it's time to get off the fence! It's time to stop our half-completed and constantly repeated repentance. Instead of wandering around and around the mountain for forty years like the frightened and recalcitrant children of Israel, we need to climb the slopes ourselves and discover the very thing that Moses discovered—that we, too, can stand in the presence of God. As Paul put it, having "tasted of the heavenly gift, . . . the good word of God, and the powers of the world to come" (Hebrews 6:4–5), they could no longer delay their own spiritual progression lest they lose the promise. Paul warns: "Be not slothful, but followers of them who through faith and patience inherit [are inheriting] the promises" (Hebrews 6:12).

These promises referred to by Paul were explained by the Lord to Joseph Smith when He declared: "Sanctify yourselves that your minds become single to God, and the days will come

61

that you shall see him; for he will unveil his face unto you, and it shall be in his own time, and in his own way, and according to his own will. *Remember the great and last promise which I have made unto you*" (D&C 88:68–69; emphasis mine).

By setting up stakes or being slothful about our own spiritual progression, we not only prolong and make more difficult what we must one day accomplish if we truly want exaltation, but also, not having obtained the promise, we may well end up not receiving it at all.

6

The Need for Faith

In what is now known as the Wentworth Letter, Joseph Smith proclaimed to Mr. Charles Wentworth of Chicago: "We believe that the first principles and ordinances of the Gospel are: first, Faith in the Lord Jesus Christ; second, Repentance; third, Baptism by immersion for the remission of sins; fourth, Laying on of hands for the gift of the Holy Ghost" (Article of Faith 4).

When we begin the process of spiritual progression, we are quickly brought to the realization that we must begin at the beginning; we must learn to exercise faith. Why? Because true spiritual progression must be accompanied by personal revelation; we must learn how to ask and receive for ourselves. And that requires faith.

John Taylor related: "I well remember a remark that Joseph Smith made to me upwards of forty years ago. Said he, 'Elder Taylor, you have been baptized, you have had hands laid upon your head for the reception of the Holy Ghost, and you have been ordained to the holy Priesthood. Now, if you will continue to follow the leadings of that spirit, it will always lead you right. Sometimes it might be contrary to your judgment; never mind that, follow its dictates; *and if you be true to its whisperings it will in time become in you a principle of revelation, so that you will know all things"* (*Journal of Discourses*, 19:153–54; emphasis mine).

Joseph Smith stated: "The Spirit of Revelation is in connection with these blessings. A person may profit by noticing the first intimation of the spirit of revelation; for instance, when you feel pure intelligence flowing into you, it may give you sudden strokes of ideas, so that by noticing it, you may find it fulfilled the same day or soon; (i.e.,) those things that were presented unto your minds by the Spirit of God, will come to pass; *and thus by learning the Spirit of God and understanding it, you may grow into the principle of revelation, until you become perfect in Christ Jesus* (*Teachings*, p. 151; emphasis mine).

In other words, we apparently have something akin to spiritual muscles that can be strengthened only through proper "exercise." Once this exercise, which amounts to faithfully seeking after God, is begun, then we can begin to progress, to "grow into the principle of revelation, until [we] become perfect in Christ Jesus."

Ingredients of Mighty Prayer

Let us consider what constitutes such an exercise of faith, that which begins our quest for personal revelation and spiritual growth. One day as Joseph prayed in behalf of Martin Harris, the Lord said: "Behold, I say unto him, *he exalts himself* and does not humble himself sufficiently before me; but if he will bow down before me, and *humble himself in mighty prayer and faith,* in the sincerity of his heart, then will I grant unto him a view of the things which he desires to see" (D&C 5:24; emphasis mine).

Mighty prayer and faith, then, which lead to personal revelation, begin with complete humility. If we are exalting ourselves in any way, our prayers will not be mighty, and we will obtain nothing from the Lord.

But there is more to mighty prayer than humility. As Amulek declared to the poor of the Zoramites: "May God grant unto you, my brethren, that ye may begin to exercise your *faith unto repentance,* that ye begin to call upon his holy name, that he would have mercy upon you" (Alma 34:17; emphasis mine).

For our prayer to be mighty in faith, therefore, it must also be unto repentance, which can only be accomplished through humility. This is exemplified by Amulek's next directive: "Cry unto him for mercy; for he is mighty to save. Yea, humble yourselves, and continue in prayer unto him" (Alma 34:18–19). If we are humble enough to repent of our sins, then what we are actually doing is crying out to God for mercy. In effect we are saying, "O God, I know I have chosen to sin, even when I knew better. For this I humbly apologize, and ask that in thy tender mercy thou wilt lift the burden of these sins from off my heart. Though I am unworthy, wilt thou allow the suffering of Christ, wherein He shed great drops of blood in agony caused at least in part by my willful actions, to redeem me that I might be free of sin and have peace of conscience once again."

If we say something like this, continuing in prayer until divine relief is obtained, then our prayer has been mighty in faith unto repentance.

Amulek continues: "Cry unto him when ye are in your fields, yea, over all your flocks. Cry unto him in your houses, yea, over all your household, both morning, mid-day, and evening. Yea, cry unto him against the power of your enemies.

Yea, cry unto him against the devil, who is an enemy to all righteousness. Cry unto him over the crops of your fields, that ye may prosper in them. Cry over the flocks of your fields, that they may increase.

"But this is not all; ye must pour out your souls in your closets, and your secret places, and in your wilderness. Yea, and when you do not cry unto the Lord, let your hearts be full, drawn out in prayer unto him continually for your welfare, and also for the welfare of those who are around you" (Alma 34:20–27).

Praying at least three times daily concerning our families must be added next (see Alma 34:21) if our prayers are to be mighty in faith. And to those things must be added a willingness to pray over every facet and aspect of our lives, just as Amulek declares. Stated another way, there is no aspect of our lives that our Heavenly Father considers unimportant or inconsequential. He is concerned about everything we think, feel, do, say, or associate with in any manner whatsoever, and He commands us to rehearse all these issues before Him in our daily prayers. Then will all these aspects of our lives be consecrated to the welfare of our souls. As Nephi put it: "I perceive that ye ponder still in your hearts; and it grieveth me that I must speak concerning this thing. For if ye would hearken unto the Spirit which teacheth a man to pray ye would know that ye must pray; for the evil spirit teacheth not a man to pray, but teacheth him that he must not pray. But behold, I say unto you that *ye must pray always, and not faint; that ye must not perform any thing unto the Lord save in the first place ye shall pray unto the Father in the name of Christ, that he will consecrate thy performance unto thee, that thy performance may be for the welfare of thy soul*" (2 Nephi 32:8–9; emphasis mine).

All these things combined—faith, repentance, humility,

crying out for mercy, praying continually, praying three times daily, and praying over all aspects of our lives—all these together begin to constitute mighty prayer and faith. Anything less will not have power sufficient to open the heavens and begin the process of learning to receive personal revelation.

But according to Amulek, there is another aspect to mighty prayer, and it cannot be ignored any more than what we have already discussed. He says: "Do not suppose that this is all; for after ye have done all these things, if ye turn away the needy, and the naked, and visit not the sick and afflicted, and impart of your substance, if ye have, to those who stand in need—I say unto you, if ye do not any of these things, behold, your prayer is vain, and availeth you nothing, and ye are as hypocrites who do deny the faith" (Alma 34:28).

Charity, therefore, or the pure love of Christ (manifesting for all others the same love that Christ manifests for us at all times and in all places), is the final ingredient spoken of here for a prayer to become mighty. And only after our prayers become mighty in all of these respects will we be empowered to progress spiritually.

7

True and Complete Repentance

The second principle of the gospel of Jesus Christ is repentance, which is repentance only if it is true and complete. Anything less is not really repentance at all. So how can we truly repent and give up all our sins?

Pockets Full of Sins

As a boy I played hundreds of games of marbles, as I remember with some success. I had my favorite "taw," a couple of "steelies," some "clayies," and a huge "cat's eye" glass marble that wouldn't budge if hit by an opponent's "taw." These were my favorites, and I carried them around in my back pocket, separate from the other marbles I used in normal situations. I did that because they were mine, I didn't want to give away or lose any of them, and I truly enjoyed owning them.

Many of us seem to treat our sins the same way I treated

my marbles. Our repentance is sufficient to get rid of most of our sins, those we consider the "big" ones. Yet because we enjoy them so, and because they are not what we think of as "big," and besides cannot possibly hurt anyone but ourselves, we take our half-dozen or so favorite "little" sins and place them in our back pockets or our handbags. There we keep them safe and secure, ready to be pulled out and indulged in at a moment's notice, with no one but ourselves the wiser and no one but ourselves hurt by them.

Put this way, such a practice sounds awfully silly. Yet what else can be said about the active priesthood holder who, whenever he thinks himself alone, exposes his mind to pornography or lustful fantasies or crude stories? Or the Relief Society sister who indulges in romantic or even lustful fantasizing because she is bored or her life is not all she had dreamed it would be? Or the practicing Latter-day Saint who lies or gossips because it is "politically" or "socially" correct? Nephi was surely speaking of such people when he said, "There shall . . . be many which shall say: Eat, drink, and be merry; nevertheless, fear God—he will justify in committing *a little sin*; yea, lie a little, take the advantage of one because of his words, dig a pit for thy neighbor; there is no harm in this; and do all these things, for tomorrow we die; and if it so be that we are guilty, God will beat us with a few stripes, and at last we shall be saved in the kingdom of God. Yea, and there shall be many which shall teach after this manner, false and vain and foolish doctrines, and shall be puffed up in their hearts, and shall seek deep to hide their counsels from the Lord; and their works shall be in the dark" (2 Nephi 28:8–9; emphasis mine).

Such people, no matter how "active" they are in the Church, are not repentant. Therefore they cannot possibly be progressing spiritually or enjoying the blessings of the Spirit.

They cannot possibly exercise mighty prayer unto the opening of the heavens. In fact, because they mock spiritual progression and deny the spirit of prophecy and revelation within themselves, then like the Nephite members of the Church described in Helaman, they are left to muddle their way through mortality on their own strength.

As Mormon wrote: "It was because of the pride of their hearts, because of their exceeding riches, yea, it was because of their oppression to the poor, withholding their food from the hungry, withholding their clothing from the naked, and smiting their humble brethren upon the cheek, *making a mock of that which was sacred, denying the spirit of prophecy and of revelation,* murdering, plundering, lying, stealing, committing adultery, rising up in great contentions, and deserting away [from the Church]—and because of this their great wickedness, and their boastings in their own strength, *they were left in their own strength; therefore they did not prosper, but were afflicted and smitten*" (Helaman 4:12–13; emphasis mine).

When life finally got difficult enough, the Nephites began to examine themselves, to see where the fault of their troubles might lie, and they were startled to discover "that they had been a stiffnecked people, and that they had set at naught the commandments of God. And that they had altered and trampled under their feet the laws of [God]; and they saw that their laws had become corrupted, and that they had become a wicked people, insomuch that they were wicked even like unto the Lamanites. *And because of their iniquity the church had begun to dwindle; and they began to disbelieve in the spirit of prophecy and in the spirit of revelation;* and the judgments of God did stare them in the face" (Helaman 4:21–23; emphasis mine).

Even the sins we think of as little and private—maybe especially such sins—must be utterly abandoned if we are to

70

accomplish any sort of spiritual progression. Otherwise we are left unto ourselves and there can be none. The resurrected Christ stated: "No unclean thing can enter into his kingdom; therefore nothing entereth into his rest save it be those who have washed their garments in my blood, because of their faith, and the repentance of *all their sins,* and their faithfulness unto the end" (3 Nephi 27:19; emphasis mine).

Understanding the Nature of Sin

Perhaps if we clearly understood the nature of sin, we would be more anxious to have it purged from our souls and left in the wake of our spiritual progression. To do that, however, we must also understand the nature of blessings and curses and the relationship between the two.

Blessings and Curses

Brigham Young declared: "There is one principle I would like to have the Latter-day Saints perfectly understand—that is, of blessings and cursings" (*Journal of Discourses,* 10:335). Knowing that both blessings and cursings exist, we must remember that any blessing we obtain is predicated upon obedience to a specific law of God. As the Lord explained to Joseph Smith: "There is a law, irrevocably decreed in heaven before the foundations of this world, upon which all blessings are predicated—and when we obtain any blessing from God, it is by obedience to that law upon which it is predicated" (D&C 130:20–21).

The Law of Blessings

For example, those who pay their tithing will not be burned at the Lord's coming (see D&C 64:23), and those who keep the Word of Wisdom are promised "health in their navel and marrow to their bones; and shall find wisdom and great treasures of knowledge, even hidden treasures; and shall run and not be weary, and shall walk and not faint. And . . . the destroying angel shall pass by them, as the children of Israel, and not slay them" (D&C 89:18–21).

All God's laws have specific blessings attached to them that come to those who obey. That is the law of blessings.

The Law of Curses

Frequently the Lord spoke to His ancient prophets about curses, which are judgements that follow disobedience (see Moses 7:10, 15; Joshua 8:34; Proverbs 3:33; Jeremiah 11:3). Brigham Young taught: "We read that war, pestilence, plagues, famine, etc., will be visited upon the inhabitants of the earth; but if distress through the judgements of God comes upon this people, it will be because the majority have turned away from the Lord. Let the majority of the people turn away from the Holy Commandments which the Lord has delivered to us, and cease to hold the balance of power in the Church, and we may expect the judgments of God to come upon us; but while six-tenths or three-fourths of this people will keep the commandments of God, *the curse* and judgments of the Almighty will never come upon them, though we will have trials of various kinds, and the elements to contend with—natural and spiritual elements" (*Journal of Discourses,* 10:335; emphasis mine).

God's laws have curses as well as blessings attached to them, which curses fall upon those who choose to disobey. Mormon declares that "repentance is unto them that are under condemnation and *under the curse of a broken law*" (Moroni 8:24; emphasis mine), and Malachi proclaims: "From the days of your fathers ye are gone away from mine ordinances, and have not kept [them]. Return unto me, and I will return unto you, saith the Lord of hosts. But ye said, Wherein shall we return?

"Will a man rob God? Yet ye have robbed me. But ye say, Wherein have we robbed thee? In tithes and offerings. *Ye are cursed with a curse:* for ye have robbed me, even this whole nation.

"Bring ye all the tithes into the storehouse, that there may be meat in mine house, and prove me now herewith, saith the Lord of hosts, if I will not open you the windows of heaven, and pour you out a blessing, that there shall not be room enough to receive it. And I will rebuke the devourer for your sakes, and he shall not destroy the fruits of your ground; neither shall your vine cast her fruit before the time in the field, saith the Lord of hosts" (Malachi 3:7–11; emphasis mine).

According to Malachi, three things bring this particular curse upon a member of the house of Israel. One, going away from, or not living, God's ordinances, which would include baptismal and temple covenants; two, robbing God by not paying an honest tithe; and three, not offering up an offering of a broken heart and a contrite spirit (see 3 Nephi 9:20; D&C 59:8). If we are guilty of *any one* of these three categories of sin (and it is interesting that all of them have to do with sincere temple worship), then we will be cursed by something called "the devourer," which has power to destabilize and even destroy our economic lives.

And how is the curse removed? By returning to the Lord in all three areas—repenting. Then the Lord will rebuke the devourer, and the curse will be removed so that God can pour out blessings upon us. Otherwise the curse must apparently run its course to a full end, and until then the blessings are withheld.

That is especially significant in light of the Lord's word to

Joseph Smith about those who have been endowed in His holy temples. "If you build a house unto my name, and do not do the things that I say, I will not perform the oath which I make unto you, neither fulfil the promises which ye expect at my hands, saith the Lord. For *instead of blessings, ye, by your own works, bring cursings,* wrath, indignation, and judgments upon your own heads, by your follies, and by all your abominations, which you practise before me, saith the Lord" (D&C 124:47–48; emphasis mine).

Since both of these scriptures about curses pertain to integrity in temple worship, the conclusion is inescapable: Whenever the Lord's people have had the blessings of the temples but have not lived up to all they have covenanted to do therein, then with their sins they have brought upon themselves cursings rather than blessings. These curses bring upon them wrath, indignation, and the judgments of God.

We see, then, that curses are placed upon people by their own actions, in consequence of their sins, and those curses must be endured until they are fully ended or removed through the redemptive power of the Savior, which comes through repentance (see Galatians 3:13).

Sins Are Bonds of Iniquity

In the scriptures the Lord also uses other terms to describe sins and their curses or consequences, terms that are even more graphic. Alma the elder calls sins the "bonds of iniquity," implying that they take away a person's freedom: "Even so I desire that ye should stand fast in this liberty wherewith ye have been made free." (Mosiah 23:13). He also stated that his people were *"bound with the bands of iniquity"* (Mosiah 23:12; emphasis mine), which evokes images of rope-bound captives of the devil, images I am certain he was trying to convey.

His son Alma declared following complete repentance: "My soul hath been redeemed from the gall of bitterness and *bonds of iniquity*" (Mosiah 27:29; emphasis mine). Years later, when speaking to his own son, he stated: "All men that are in a state of nature, or I would say, in a carnal state, are in the gall of bitterness and in the *bonds of iniquity;* they are without God in the world, and they have gone contrary to the nature of God; therefore, they are in a state contrary to the nature of happiness" (Alma 41:11; emphasis mine). Thus, at least a portion of the curse placed upon all sin, of whatever nature, is a loss of happiness and a removal from God.

Nor is this wickedness all ancient. Moroni writes of conditions in our day: "There shall be great pollutions upon the face of the earth; there shall be murders, and robbing, and lying, and deceivings, and whoredoms, and all manner of abominations; when there shall be many who will say, Do this, or do that, and it mattereth not, for the Lord will uphold such at the last day. But *wo unto such, for they are in the gall of bitterness and in the bonds of iniquity*" (Mormon 8:31; emphasis mine).

Curses Are Yokes of Bondage

On the other hand, Paul, writing to those who had received a remission of their sins through Christ, encouraged them to "stand fast therefore in the liberty wherewith Christ hath made [them] free, and be not entangled again with *the yoke of bondage*" (Galatians 5:1; emphasis mine).

That is slightly different imagery, and it pertains to the consequences of sins—their attached curses—rather than to the sins themselves. That is what the Lord means when He tells us that "the yoke of bondage may begin to be broken off from the house of David" (D&C 109:63). Jeremiah declared that anciently the Lord had "broken thy yoke, and burst thy bands" from

75

Israel, but they had turned again to their wickedness, bringing back upon themselves the yoke of bondage He had suffered to remove (see Jeremiah 2:20).

And Nephi wrote that the ultimate purpose of the great and abominable church was to: *"[yoke the people] with a yoke of iron, and bringeth them down into captivity"* (1 Nephi 13:5; emphasis mine).

The captivity spoken of here is the captivity of the devil, "a yoke of iron," which, as Isaiah proclaims again and again, can be removed only by the Savior: "In that day, . . . his burden shall be taken away from off thy shoulder, *and his yoke* from off thy neck, and *the yoke shall be destroyed because of the anointing"* (Isaiah 10:27; emphasis mine). "Is not this the fast that I have chosen," Christ asks, "to loose the bands of wickedness, to undo the heavy burdens, and to let the oppressed go free, and that ye *break every yoke?"* (Isaiah 58:6; emphasis mine). And Paul wrote, "Christ hath redeemed us from the curse of the law" (Galatians 3:13).

Therefore, the bonds or bands of iniquity refer to sins, and yokes of bondage refer to the curses thereof. Bonds of iniquity, when repented of, are removed or forgiven quickly by the Savior. But yokes of bondage, which are the curses or consequences of sin, can be removed before their time only through the laws and ordinances of the priesthood—being born of the water and the Spirit, which brings a remission of sins.

The Purpose of the Priesthood

That is the grand purpose of the priesthood, which is without beginning of days or end of years, for from eternity to all eternity it is designed to provide the sacred ordinances through which Christ redeems the souls of the repentant from their sins—and the curses from their sins—and restores them to the

Father. As Mormon explained to his son Moroni: "Repentance is unto them that are under condemnation and under *the curse of a broken law*. And the *first fruits of repentance is baptism;* and baptism cometh by faith unto the fulfilling the commandments; and the *fulfilling the commandments bringeth remission of sins*" (Moroni 8:24–25; emphasis mine).

Therefore, "every one that hearkeneth to the voice of the Spirit cometh unto God, even the Father. And the Father teacheth him of the covenant [of the priesthood] which he has renewed and confirmed upon you, which is confirmed upon you for your sakes, and not for your sakes only, but for the sake of the whole world. And the whole world lieth in sin, and groaneth under darkness and under *the bondage of sin*. And by this you may know they are under the bondage of sin, because they come not unto me. *For whoso cometh not unto me is under the bondage of sin*" (D&C 84:47–51; emphasis mine).

That means the whole world (the inhabitants of the earth and not the earth itself; see *Words,* p. 25, footnote 9) is cursed, especially those who know the will of God and do not do it. The people of the world are bound by strong bonds of iniquity and groan under heavy yokes of bondage, insomuch that the devil has great power over them. Neither can the Lord stretch forth His hand to lift them up in their carnal state, for He is a God of law and must abide by all the precepts of the law He has established. Thus those who are cursed are left unto themselves insofar as they are cursed, and they can prosper and progress only as their own mortal limitations allow.

Forgiveness Is Not Always a Remission of Sins

So, there can be a difference between being forgiven and obtaining a remission of sins. If we commit a particular sin and then feel bad enough to confess it in humility and ask forgiveness of the Lord, we are freely forgiven of that sin (the bond of iniquity is removed). As the Psalmist exclaimed: "Thou, Lord, art good, and ready to forgive; and plenteous in mercy unto all them that call upon thee" (Psalm 86:5). John the Beloved wrote, "If we confess our sins, he is faithful and just to forgive us our sins" (1 John 1:9). Through Alma the Lord stated that as often as His people repented, he would forgive them (see Mosiah 26:30), and Moroni added that as often as we repent and seek forgiveness with real intent, we are forgiven (see Moroni 6:8). In our day the Lord has said: "I, the Lord, forgive sins unto those who confess their sins before me and ask forgiveness" (D&C 64:7).

Interestingly, this forgiveness seems to be granted even though we may be committing other sins at the time (remember the issue of our favorite marbles?). Thus one who enjoys lusting may at the same time repent of and obtain forgiveness for stealing or lying. Or one who gossips may repent of and obtain forgiveness for immorality.

Unfortunately, such individuals, while blessed with forgiveness for all the sins they choose to repent of, nevertheless persist in their own carnal nature because they are intentionally going on in the ways of sin and rebellion against God (see JST James 2:10). Because they have not repented of *all* their sins, they "remaineth in [their] fallen state and the devil hath all power over [them]" (Mosiah 16:5). In other words, they remain "entangled . . . with *the yoke of bondage*" (Galatians 5:1; emphasis mine), which means that even though they have been forgiven of some things, they continue to suffer the effects of the curses their iniquitous ways have incurred. "Therefore, they are as though there was no redemption made, being enemies to God; and also is the devil an enemy to God" (Mosiah 16:5). As Enoch declared: "Satan hath come among the children of men, and tempteth them to worship him; and men have become carnal, sensual, and devilish, *and are shut out from the presence of God"* (Moses 6:49; emphasis mine).

That is why forgiveness of some or even most of our sins is not sufficient. Even though we are blessed for having repented of some things, we are not granted the peace and joy of a complete remission of our sins! We are not redeemed and brought back into the presence of God! That is why the Psalmist pleaded: "Look upon mine affliction and my pain; and forgive *all* my sins" (Psalm 25:18; emphasis mine). And why Samuel the Lamanite could declare: "If ye believe on his name ye will repent of *all* your sins, that thereby ye may have a remission of them through his merits" (Helaman 14:13; emphasis mine).

Therefore, if we want to enjoy a complete remission of our sins rather than simply forgiveness for some of them, we must give them *all* up! We must become as King Lamoni's father, who prayed after being taught by Aaron, one of the sons of Mosiah: "O God, Aaron hath told me that there is a God; and if there is a God, and if thou art God, wilt thou make thyself known unto me, and *I will give away all my sins to know thee"* (Alma 22:18; emphasis mine).

But remember: Such a remission can be accomplished only through being born again, which redeems us not only from our sins but also from their effects. Thus could Alma proclaim: "The Lord said unto me: Marvel not that all mankind, yea, men and women, all nations, kindreds, tongues and people, *must be born again;* yea, born of God, *changed from their carnal and fallen state, to a state of righteousness,* being *redeemed of God,* becoming his sons and daughters" (Mosiah 27:25; emphasis mine).

Once we are changed from our carnal and fallen state to a state of righteousness through the remission of all our sins or bonds of iniquity, then the yokes of bondage are lifted by the

Lord, and Satan loses his power over us. Then we are not only worthy but also able to become sons and daughters of God. Mormon joyfully explains: "The remission of sins bringeth meekness, and lowliness of heart; and because of meekness and lowliness of heart cometh the visitation of the Holy Ghost, which Comforter filleth with hope and perfect love, which love endureth by diligence unto prayer, until the end shall come, when all the saints shall dwell with God" (Moroni 8:26).

Stirred Up unto Repentance

Still, reaching the point where we are willing to give up all our sins remains a difficult proposition. Few of us seem to have the courage to simply stand forth and do it. Because the Lord understands that weakness in our natures, He has provided an interesting form of help. To Oliver Cowdery He said, "The world is ripening in iniquity; and it must needs be that the children of men are *stirred up unto repentance,* both the Gentiles and also the house of Israel" (D&C 18:6; emphasis mine).

To progress spiritually beyond having faith, therefore, most of us must be "stirred up" unto true and complete repentance. And how might we be "stirred up"? In any number of ways. Some of the Zoramites were stirred up unto repentance by their poverty. Zeezrom was stirred up unto repentance by the testimony of Alma and Amulek. Enos was stirred up unto repentance by the words of his father and because he felt no joy or peace in his life. Alma was stirred up unto repentance by the words of an angel. There seem to be almost as many ways of being stirred up unto repentance as there are people.

Though usually painful or stressful, these stirrings up are gifts from a loving Father to help us soften and open our hearts to the promptings of the Holy Ghost. If we receive them rather than murmur and complain about them, and if we exercise mighty prayer in faith as we seek understanding and guidance, then the Holy Ghost will begin to bear witness of our sins and iniquities so that we can know what we need to repent of and feel godly sorrow for it.

And that, too, is according to divine design. Apparently, because of bad memory, faulty judgment, and so forth, we do not always remember or see clearly our own sins and weaknesses. But the Lord will make them known to us by the power of the Holy Ghost, who as the Spirit of Truth communicates the truthfulness of all things directly to our spirits (see Romans 8:16; 1 John 5:6; Moroni 10:5).

To William E. McLellin the Lord said: "You are clean, but not all; repent, therefore, of *those things which are not pleasing in my sight,* saith the Lord, *for the Lord will show them unto you*" (D&C 66:3; emphasis mine). And to his apostles Christ said: "It is expedient for you that I go away: for if I go not away, *the Comforter* will not come unto you; but if I depart, I will send him unto you. And when he is come, *he will reprove the world of sin*" (John 16:7–8; emphasis mine).

For us to obtain this oftentimes painful but significant revelation through the power of the Holy Ghost, we must open the heavens with complete humility and sincerity in mighty prayer, asking the Lord to reveal our sins to us: "If men come unto me I will show unto them their weakness" (Ether 12:27).

So that we can obtain this revelation, we are also instructed to pray for the companionship of the Holy Ghost, not just once but as often as we need to until we feel his presence. Christ declares: "Ask the Father in my name, in faith believing that you shall receive, and you shall have the Holy Ghost, which manifesteth all things which are expedient unto the children of men" (D&C 18:18).

Once that is done, the Lord will make known to us every

sin for which we have never repented. We will then have an accurate picture of our position before the Lord, and we will no doubt begin to feel remorseful about how we have lived.

Godly Sorrow

However, it is not enough to simply remember our sins or even to feel remorse for them. The Lord wants a change of heart rather than just a change of behavior, which is all that simple remorse would bring. Therefore we must feel godly sorrow.

President Ezra Taft Benson has said: "Godly sorrow is a gift of the Spirit. It is a deep realization that our actions have offended our Father and our God. It is the sharp and keen awareness that our behavior caused the Savior, He who knew no sin, even the greatest of all, to endure agony and suffering. Our sins caused Him to bleed at every pore. This very real mental and spiritual anguish is what the scriptures refer to as having a 'broken heart and a contrite spirit' (3 Ne. 9:20; Moro. 6:2; D&C 20:37; 59:8; Psalms 34:18; 51:17; Isa. 57:15). Such a spirit is the absolute prerequisite for true repentance" (*Ensign*, October 1989, p. 4).

Again, how is godly sorrow manifested in our lives? As President Benson reminds us, through having a broken heart and a contrite spirit. To the Nephites the Lord explained that this was actually a sacrifice we must make if we desire to further our spiritual progression (see 3 Nephi 9:20). And in confirmation that this doctrine remains true for our day, the Lord declared through Joseph Smith: "Thou shalt offer a sacrifice unto the Lord thy God in righteousness, even that of a broken heart and a contrite spirit" (D&C 59:8).

Having a broken heart means that we have reached the point where we are so heartbroken over the fact that we have sinned, that we have taken part in wounding Christ, that we are willing and anxious to repent and obtain forgiveness. And having a contrite spirit means that we are humble enough to be teachable in all things, either by those who preside over us or by the Lord through the Holy Ghost. It is these two qualities that indicate we are truly repentant.

If our godly sorrow is manifested by a broken heart and a contrite spirit, then we will be absolutely willing to repent of whatever the Lord reveals to us about our sins, no matter how embarrassing or painful the process might be. That is true and complete repentance. If we do not completely repent once the Lord has revealed our sins to us, we will be in a position of knowing but doing nothing, and we will be under condemnation. King Benjamin, in teaching his people the doctrines given him by an angel, said: "*Wo, wo unto him who knoweth that he rebelleth* against God! For salvation cometh to none such except it be through repentance and faith on the Lord Jesus Christ" (Mosiah 3:12; emphasis mine).

Alma adds: "My brethren, I wish from the inmost part of my heart, yea, with great anxiety even unto pain, that ye would hearken unto my words, and cast off your sins, *and not procrastinate* the day of your repentance" (Alma 13:27; emphasis mine).

To know must be to do. If our hearts are adequately broken through godly sorrow and our spirits are sufficiently contrite, then through the power of the Holy Ghost we will be enabled to truly and completely repent of all our sins. That is the beginning of spiritual progression. President Joseph F. Smith stated: "God has not and will not suffer the gift of the Holy Ghost to be bestowed upon any man or woman, *except through compliance with the laws of God.* Therefore, no man can obtain a remission of sins; no man can obtain the gift of the Holy Ghost; no man can obtain the revelations of God; no man can obtain the Priesthood, and the rights, powers and privileges thereof; no man can become an heir of God and a joint heir with Jesus Christ, except through compliance with the requirements of heaven" (*Gospel Doctrine*, 5th ed. [Salt Lake City: Deseret Book Company, 1939], p. 49–50; emphasis mine).

Once we are in compliance with the principles of faith and repentance, we will begin to feel after these words of the great prophet Moroni, who wrote: "I would commend you to seek this Jesus of whom the prophets and apostles have written" (Ether 12:41). "Yea, come unto Christ, and be perfected in him, and deny yourselves of all ungodliness; . . . then are ye sanctified in Christ by the grace of God, through the shedding of the blood of Christ, which is in the covenant of the Father unto the remission of your sins, that ye become holy, without spot" (Moroni 10:32–33).

That is why, with Nephi and my friend whose letter was quoted earlier, we "talk of Christ, we rejoice in Christ, we preach of Christ, we prophesy of Christ, and we write according to our prophecies, that our children may know to what source they may look for a remission of their sins" (2 Nephi 25:26).

CHAPTER

8

Being Born Again

For those servants or handmaidens of Christ who have offered up mighty prayer in faith and are willing to give up all their sins through complete repentance, receiving a full remission of sins is the next step in their spiritual progression. For this, however, a mighty change of heart is required; they must be born of water and the Spirit and so become a new creature. As Jesus said to an inquiring Nicodemus: "Except a man be born again, he cannot see the kingdom of God. Nicodemus saith unto him, How can a man be born when he is old? can he enter the second time into his mother's womb, and be born? Jesus answered, Verily, verily, I say unto thee, Except a man be born of water and of the Spirit, he cannot enter into the kingdom of God. That which is born of the flesh is flesh; and that which is born of the Spirit is spirit. Marvel not that I said unto thee, Ye must be born again" (John 3:3–7). And the Prophet Nephi declared: "The gate by which ye should enter is repen-

85

tance and baptism by water; and then cometh a remission of your sins by fire and by the Holy Ghost" (2 Nephi 31:17).

Alma stated the necessity of being born again when he said: "The Lord said unto me: Marvel not that *all mankind,* yea, men and women, all nations, kindreds, tongues, and people, must be born again; yea, born of God, changed from their carnal and fallen state, to a state of righteousness, being redeemed of God, becoming his sons and his daughters; and thus they become new creatures; and unless they do this, they can in nowise inherit the kingdom of God" (Mosiah 27:25–26). And: "Ye must repent, and be born again; for the Spirit saith if ye are not born again ye cannot inherit the kingdom of heaven" (Alma 7:14).

As the Prophet Joseph put it: "Except a man be born again, he cannot see the kingdom of God. This eternal truth settles the question of all men's religion. A man may be saved, after the judgment, in the terrestrial kingdom, or in the telestial kingdom, but he can never see the celestial kingdom of God, without being born of water and the Spirit" (*Teachings,* p. 12).

And emphasizing this doctrine, the Savior said to Joseph Smith: "This is my gospel—repentance and baptism by water, and then cometh the baptism of fire and the Holy Ghost, even the Comforter, which showeth all things, and teacheth the peaceable things of the kingdom" (D&C 39:6).

Two Steps to Being Born Again

These scriptures teach us that, to be born again, we must experience two separate events—baptism of water and baptism of the Spirit. This is confirmed by the Prophet Joseph, who said: "You might as well baptize a bag of sand as a man, if not done in view of the remission of sins and getting of the Holy Ghost. Baptism by water is but half a baptism, and is good for nothing without the other half—that is, the baptism of the Holy Ghost" (*Teachings*, p. 314).

Baptized by Water

Thus, the first step to being born again is being baptized by water, which is for the remission of sins unto all who have kept the law by repenting and coming unto Christ. Because we baptize children who have arrived at the age of accountability as well as adults, let us consider each of these separately.

Little children are alive in Christ (see Moroni 8:12) and cannot sin. That is, they are not held accountable by God for the things they do until they have reached the age of accountability (see D&C 29:47), which is eight years of age (see D&C 68:25). Then, they must simply humble themselves and be baptized. As they do so, all they have done wrong as they have learned accountability (see D&C 29:47) is remitted, and they stand clean before the Lord, fully worthy to receive the gift of the Holy Ghost.

For adults, who, because of accountability, are able to repent, which "repentance is unto them that are under condemnation and under the curse of a broken law" (Moroni 8:24), being baptized for a remission of sins is more arduous. Therefore the Lord has declared "by way of commandment to the church concerning the manner of baptism—All those who humble themselves before God, and desire to be baptized, and come forth with broken hearts and contrite spirits, and witness before the church that they have truly repented of all their sins, and are willing to take upon them the name of Jesus Christ, having a determination to serve him to the end, and truly manifest by their works that they have received of the Spirit of Christ unto the remission of their sins, shall be received by baptism into his church" (D&C 20:37). Put another way, baptismal candidates must exercise faith in Christ sufficient to repent and desire baptism, which "cometh by faith unto the fulfilling the commandments; and the fulfilling the commandments bringeth remission of sins" (Moroni 8:25) through receiving "of the Spirit of Christ unto the remission of their sins" (D&C 20:37). These, then, are worthy to have the gift of the Holy Ghost confirmed upon them by the laying on of hands. As Mormon writes: "The remission of sins bringeth meekness, and lowliness of heart; and because of meekness and lowliness of heart cometh the visitation of the Holy Ghost" (Moroni 8:26).

Joseph Smith taught: "Baptism is a sign to God, to angels, and to heaven that we do the will of God, and there is no other way beneath the heavens whereby God hath ordained for man to come to Him to be saved, and enter into the Kingdom of God, except faith in Jesus Christ, repentance, and baptism for the remission of sins, and any other course is in vain; then you have the promise of the gift of the Holy Ghost" (*Teachings*, p. 198).

Baptized by Fire

Because receiving the gift of the Holy Ghost is not the same as being born of the Spirit, and because all of us continue to commit sins even after baptism, much repentance remains necessary. That is why being baptized by water for the remission of sins is only half the ordinance of being born again. Elder Bruce R. McConkie writes: "Mere compliance with the formality of the ordinance of baptism does not mean that a person has been born again. No one can be born again without baptism, but the immersion in water and the laying on of hands to confer the Holy Ghost do not of themselves guarantee that a person has been or will be born again. The new birth takes place only for those who actually enjoy the gift or companionship of the Holy Ghost, only for those who are fully converted, who have given themselves without restraint to the Lord. Thus Alma addressed himself to his 'brethren of the church,' and pointedly asked them if they had 'spiritually been born of God,' received the Lord's image in their countenances, and had the 'mighty change' in their hearts which always attends the birth of the Spirit (Alma 5:14–31.)" (*Mormon Doctrine*, p. 101).

As baptized members of the Church sin and then, following the promptings of the Holy Ghost, repent of those sins, they are freely forgiven. This continues until they go before the Lord in mighty faith and prayer, manifesting a broken heart and a contrite spirit, being willing in all things to submit to the will of the Father. Then are they visited with fire and the Holy Ghost. Then are their sins remitted again, and also the curses thereof (see Moroni 8:24), and they stand once again clean before the Lord. Then have they been born again. Lehi taught: "[Christ] offereth himself a sacrifice for sin, to answer the ends of the law, unto all those who have a broken heart and a contrite spirit; and unto none else can the ends of the law be answered" (2 Nephi 2:7).

As the Savior declared: "Repent and be baptized, every one of you, for a remission of your sins; yea, be baptized even by water, *and then cometh the baptism of fire and of the Holy Ghost*" (D&C 33:11; emphasis mine). "Thou shalt declare repentance and faith on the Savior, and remission of sins by baptism, and by fire, yea, even the Holy Ghost" (D&C 19:31).

The second part of being born again, then, is the baptism of fire and of the Holy Ghost. This is also called being born of the Holy Ghost and being born of the Spirit. Apparently these terms are interchangeable and refer to the action of the Holy Ghost upon people when their sins are burned or purged from their souls.

But what happens to those who, no matter their age, present themselves for baptism having been fully converted and having fulfilled all the requirements necessary to be born again? Such people, manifesting godly sorrow for their sins through a broken heart and a contrite spirit, and expressing a complete willingness to obey God's commandments and serve Him to the end, are visited immediately with fire and the Holy Ghost unto a complete remission of their sins. Thus, when they receive the Holy Ghost through the laying on of hands, they are also born again and made free of the curses of their sins. Elder McConkie writes: "When converted persons are baptized for the remission of sins, the sacred baptismal ordinance is designed to free them from past and future sins. Those sins committed after baptism are forgiven whenever members of the Church, by full compliance with the law of forgiveness, again get themselves in the same state of righteousness and purity previously attained in connection with their baptisms" (*Mormon Doctrine*, p. 296).

All of the adult Saints in Kirtland were converts. No doubt most of them had manifested godly sorrow for their sins through a broken heart and a contrite spirit. And expressing a complete willingness to obey God's commandments and serve Him to the end, they were visited immediately with fire and the Holy Ghost unto a complete remission of their sins. Therefore, when they received the Holy Ghost through the laying on of hands, they were also born again and made ready for the further spiritual growth and progression their history reveals they experienced.

A Witness from the Father

After John the Baptist had baptized Jesus, he saw that "the heavens were opened, and the Holy Ghost descended upon [Jesus] in the form of a dove, and sat upon him, and there came a voice out of heaven saying: This is my beloved Son" (D&C

93:15). The Father bore this same testimony to Peter, James, and John on the mount of transfiguration (see Matthew 17:5) and to Joseph Smith in the Sacred Grove (see Joseph Smith–History 1:17).

For most of us, however, the Father bears testimony of the Son in a slightly different way. The resurrected Christ said to the Nephites, "Whoso believeth in me believeth in the Father also; and unto him will the Father bear record of me, for he will visit him with fire and with the Holy Ghost. And thus will the Father bear record of me" (3 Nephi 11:35–36).

All who are born of the Spirit are being witnessed to by the Father, who is bearing record of the divinity of the life and atonement of His Beloved Son, the Lord Jesus Christ.

The Blessing of the Sacrament

The Lord instituted the ordinance of the sacrament of the Lord's Supper to help us retain a remission of our sins. As Elder McConkie explains: "Precisely and identically this same covenant is made by persons who partake of the sacrament. In other words, if they have been baptized (thus making the covenant of baptism), and if they then partake of the sacrament, they are renewing or making again the very covenant which brought remission of sins to them. Each time baptized members of the Church partake of the bread and water of the Lord's Supper, they most solemnly promise: 1. To remember the body of the Son of God which was crucified for them; 2. To take upon them the name of the Son; and 3. To 'always remember him and keep his commandments which he has given them.' In return, as his part of the covenant, the Lord promises: 1. That the saints shall 'have his Spirit to be with them'; and 2. That they shall have 'eternal life . . . at the last day.' (D. & C. 20:75–79; John 6:54.)" (*Mormon Doctrine*, p. 297).

Knowing this, is it any wonder the resurrected Lord, each time He appeared among the Nephites, administered the sacrament to them? (see 3 Nephi 26:13).

Why These Baptisms Are Likened to a Natural Birth

Anciently the Prophet Enoch explained why baptism by immersion and baptism by the Holy Spirit is likened to physical birth. He declared the word of God as follows: "By reason of transgression cometh the fall, which fall bringeth death, and inasmuch as ye were born into the world by water, and blood, and the spirit, which I have made, and so became of dust a living soul, even so ye must be born again into the kingdom of heaven, of water, and of the Spirit, and be cleansed by blood, even the blood of mine Only Begotten; that ye might be sanctified from all sin, and enjoy the words of eternal life in this world, and eternal life in the world to come, even immortal glory" (Moses 6:59).

As natural birth must be a complete process if we are to live, so is it with being born again. If the process is not completed, then we cannot live spiritually as we have been foreordained to do.

Feelings as Being Born of the Spirit Occurs

The scriptures inform us that if we sincerely seek this new birth, we can expect the following feelings and emotions:

1. A godly sorrow for all sin (2 Corinthians 7:10).

2. An unending desire to repent and to be made clean (Alma 29:4).

3. An understanding that this cleanliness cannot be self-induced (1 Corinthians 15:3; Alma 5:27).

4. A fixed determination to purify ourselves until such cleanliness has been granted (Alma 5:21; D&C 121:45).

5. A profound willingness to live so that such pain and sorrow as is being experienced will never come upon us again (Acts 17:30; 2 Nephi 9:23; 3 Nephi 11:32; D&C 133:16).

6. An understanding that all sins, even favorite little ones, are a source of great pain to the Savior (Matthew 5:19; Alma 45:16).

7. A recognition that it was we ourselves who, by our own bad choices, drove the nails that day on Golgotha (Hebrews 6:6).

8. A willingness to apologize to Christ for choosing to wound Him (Mosiah 26:29–30).

9. An unending anxiety to cry forth the plea that Christ, through the spilling of His precious blood, will remove the burden of pain from us, allowing us to be finally and forever free of our guilt (Mosiah 27:24–26; Alma 36:13–21; 38:8).

10. A burning desire to sing the song of redeeming love (Alma 5:26).

If we have not yet felt all these, but if we are nevertheless willing to persist in the quest for internal peace and a knowledge that we have been made clean every whit through the blood of Christ, and persist for as many days, weeks, months, or years as the Lord requires of us, then the promise is that God will finally grant our petitions.

Being Born Again Brings a Complete Remission of Sins

The Prophet Nephi taught: "Do the things which I have told you I have seen that your Lord and your Redeemer should do; for, for this cause have they been shown unto me, that ye might know the gate by which ye should enter. For the gate by which ye should enter is repentance and baptism by water; and *then cometh a remission of your sins by fire and by the Holy Ghost*" (2 Nephi 31:17; emphasis mine).

Owned by Christ

While my dictionary's first definition of *remission* is a forgiveness or pardon, as of sins or crimes, the second definition is a cancellation or release from a debt. That is interesting in light of the fact that the Lord has referred to His atonement as the act of buying us (Isaiah 43:24; 52:3; 1 Corinthians 6:20). Peter declared: "Ye were not redeemed with corruptible things, as silver and gold . . . but with the precious blood of Christ, as of a lamb without blemish and without spot" (1 Peter 1:18–19).

Since, by the price of His precious blood we are Christ's, it stands to reason that we are under strict obligation to do all that He says—that is, to keep His commandments. After all, He owns us. Yet each time we keep his commandments, He rewards or pays or blesses us commensurate with what we have done, keeping the ledger balanced always in His favor. As King Benjamin taught: "He doth require that ye should do as he hath commanded you; for which if ye do, he doth immediately bless you; and therefore he hath paid you. And ye are still indebted unto him, and are, and will be, forever and ever" (Mosiah 2:24).

Each time we do not keep His commandments, however, each time we sin, we incur a debt that, since we are not our own, we cannot pay. Only our owner, the Lord Jesus Christ, can pay this debt for us. And He will, but only on condition of repentance. Otherwise, because of our unsatisfied debt, we must be delivered over for judgement, which will be far worse than we can imagine. As Jesus said: "I command you to repent—repent, lest I smite you by the rod of my mouth, and by my wrath, and by my anger, and your sufferings be sore—how sore you know not, how exquisite you know not, yea, how hard to bear you know not. For behold, I, God, have suffered these things for all, that they might not suffer if they would

94

repent; but if they would not repent they must suffer even as I; which suffering caused myself, even God, the greatest of all, to tremble because of pain, and to bleed at every pore, and to suffer both body and spirit—and would that I might not drink the bitter cup, and shrink—Nevertheless, glory be to the Father, and I partook and finished my preparations unto the children of men" (D&C 19:15–19).

Acknowledging the ownership of our Lord Jesus Christ, and willingly accepting all the conditions of that ownership, allows us to repent of all our sins and thus obtain their remission through the baptism of fire and the Holy Ghost (see 2 Nephi 31:17), which means that we will be miraculously relieved of the burden of our indebtedness to Christ. All guilt will be swept away in an incredibly sweet experience with the Holy Ghost (see Mosiah 27:24–26; Alma 36:12–21). We will then be born of the Spirit (see John 3:7). We will have experienced the baptism of fire (see Matthew 3:11; 2 Nephi 31:13–14). We will have experienced the mighty change (see Mosiah 5:2; Alma 5:12–14). Finally, we will be privileged to enjoy the companionship of the Holy Ghost more and more frequently until His companionship becomes constant in our lives (see D&C 121:46).

Another definition of the word *remission* is a relatively prolonged lessening or disappearance of a thing. Thus, when cancer is in remission, its growth is slowed or stopped, though it has not necessarily gone away.

If remission of sins is thought of in this way, then we realize why King Benjamin spoke so forcefully about *retaining* a remission of our sins (see Mosiah 4:11–30), and why Alma quizzed those who had received a remission of their sins about whether that remission yet remained with them (see Alma 5:26–31).

If those who have had their sins fully remitted, through being born again, intentionally return to their former wickedness, then their remission of sins is canceled and they are burdened again with their bonds of iniquity as well as Satan's iron yoke of bondage. It is to such people that the Lord declares: "Go your ways and sin no more; but unto that soul who sinneth shall the former sins return" (D&C 82:7).

Being Born Again Brings a Complete and Mighty Change

We need not return to our former wickedness, however. In fact, God gives divine assistance through the Holy Spirit so that we will not. Thus, those who have paid the price to obtain the baptism of fire and remission of sins will also experience a fundamental change of heart, which leaves them disinclined toward their former wicked ways. This is called in scripture *the mighty change* (see Mosiah 5:2; Alma 5:14).

To illustrate the magnitude of this change, consider the words of Samuel the Lamanite: "As many of [the Lamanites] as are brought to the knowledge of the truth, and to know of the wicked and abominable traditions of their fathers, and are led to believe the holy scriptures, yea, the prophecies of the holy prophets, which are written, which leadeth them to faith on the Lord, and unto repentance, *which faith and repentance bringeth a change of heart unto them . . .* " (Helaman 15:7; emphasis mine).

If the Lamanites could make such a change, then surely the Holy Ghost can also bring about a mighty change within us. President Benson adds: "When you choose to follow Christ, you choose to be changed. 'No man,' said President David O. McKay, 'can sincerely resolve to apply to his daily life the teachings of Jesus of Nazareth without sensing a change in his own nature. The phrase *born again* has a deeper significance than many people attach to it. This *changed feeling* may be indescribable, *but it is real.* . . . ' Our Lord told Nicodemus that 'except a man be born again, he cannot see the kingdom of God' (John 3:3). Of these words President Spencer W. Kimball said: 'This is the simple total answer to the weightiest of all questions. . . . To gain eternal life there must be a rebirth, a transformation.' . . . President McKay said that Christ called for 'an entire revolution' of Nicodemus's 'inner man.' President McKay said that 'His manner of thinking, feeling, and acting with reference to spiritual things would have to undergo a fundamental and permanent change'" (*The Teachings of Ezra Taft Benson* [Salt Lake City: Bookcraft, 1988], pp. 77–78).

Such people have "no more disposition to do evil, but to do good continually" (Mosiah 5:2). "They, after being sanctified by the Holy Ghost, having their garments made white, being pure and spotless before God, [can]not look upon sin save it [is] with abhorrence" (Alma 13:12). And "their hearts [have] been changed; that they [have] no more desire to do evil" (Alma 19:33).

Again, how is such a change brought to pass? Only through the power of God, who sheds forth His Spirit upon the completely repentant through the power of the atonement. Thus the resurrected Christ could declare to the Nephites: "The Father . . . raised me up unto you first, *and sent me to bless you in turning away every one of you from his iniquities;* and this because ye are the children of the covenant" (3 Nephi 20:26; emphasis mine).

Throughout the history of Adam's family, righteous men and women have born testimony to the truthfulness of the Savior's words. Through His matchless power they are literally turned from their sins and so become new creatures. As the scripture says of King Benjamin's people: "They all cried with one voice, saying: Yea, we believe all the words which thou hast spoken unto us; and also, we know of their surety and truth, because of *the Spirit of the Lord Omnipotent, which has wrought a mighty change in us, or in our hearts"* (Mosiah 5:2; emphasis mine).

The issue, as always, comes back to us. As Alma frankly asked: "My brethren of the Church, have ye spiritually been born of God? Have ye received his image in your countenances? Have ye experienced this mighty change in your hearts?" (Alma 5:14).

President Benson's plea to all of us is, "May we be convinced that Jesus is the Christ, choose to follow Him, be changed for Him, captained by Him, consumed in Him, and born again" (*The Teachings of Ezra Taft Benson,* p. 13–14).

Clearing Up a Misunderstanding

Many assume that phrases such as "no more disposition to do evil, but to do good continually" (Mosiah 5:2) mean that those who are born again must thereafter remain perfect and without sin. That is not so. When people have no more disposition to do evil, they simply have no more *desire* to sin. Because their hearts have undergone a mighty change through the power of God, and because they understand the suffering of Jesus Christ in their behalf, those who have been born of water and of the Spirit do their best to remain steadfast in avoiding intentional sin.

However, that does not mean they never sin. As long as men and women remain in mortality, even though they have been born again, they are subject to the vicissitudes of the flesh, which means they will make mistakes and struggle with the weaknesses common to mortality.

They are also deeply ingrained with old habits and genetically induced tendencies or weaknesses, all of which must ultimately be faced, dealt with, and laid upon the altar of Christ before they can be overcome (Ether 12:27). But this honest facing of self is a process, not an event, and it occurs, usually with thankfully diminishing relapses, over an extended period of time. In other words, weaknesses are being turned, through the grace of Christ, into strengths. Yet these relapses are still sins.

Sanctified and Justified

Once such changed individuals discover that they have sinned, however, unlike the rest of the world, they repent immediately. They also begin an instant campaign within their own hearts to see that such sins do not occur again. Moreover, they begin a diligent process of mighty prayer wherein they plead before the Lord for that particular weakness or sin to be taken from them or made a strength unto them. It is because of this righteous approach to their own spiritual progression that those who have been born again are sanctified and justified.

Justification

There are two parts to this aspect of our spiritual progression, Christ's part and our part. According to the scriptures, the Savior's part has to do with what is called justification. On the day the Church was organized, Joseph Smith declared, "Justification through the grace of our Lord and Savior Jesus Christ is just and true" (D&C 20:30). To Moses the Lord said: "By the water ye keep the commandment; by the Spirit ye are justified, and by the blood ye are sanctified" (Moses 6:60). And to Joseph Smith the Lord said: "All kingdoms have a law given . . . and unto every kingdom is given a law; and unto every law there are certain bounds also and conditions. All beings who abide not in those conditions are not justified" (D&C 88:36, 38–39). Justification and its necessity are also spoken of at great length by the Apostle Paul and other New Testament writers, who all declare that it is a gift from Christ, reserved only for the righteous (see Luke 18:14; Acts 13:39; Romans 2:13; 4:16; 5:1, 9; 8:30; Galatians 2:16–17; 3:24–29).

Justification is part of the law of justice. In that law the Lord says that for every obedience to law there is a blessing, while for every disobedience of the law there is a punishment (see D&C 130:20–21). In other words, we receive joy from obedience, misery from disobedience. So we should always be obedient to all God's laws, for then the law of justice would demand that we have pure joy. The trouble is, however, that no one keeps all the laws of God perfectly. That is why Lehi taught that "by the law no flesh is justified" (2 Nephi 2:5). In other words, because of the law of justice we will never make it on our own merits. On our own, we could never know true joy, because we have experienced our own personal fall from premortal purity!

But that does not mean we should give up in despair. Lehi says: "Redemption [from our personal sins] cometh in and through the Holy Messiah" (2 Nephi 2:6). Simply put, we are condemned by the law but redeemed by the Messiah, Jesus Christ, "who is full of grace and truth" (ibid.). These, grace and truth, are the ingredients that give Christ the enabling power to become our Redeemer. And who enjoys this great redemption brought about by Christ's enabling power? Only those "who have a broken heart and a contrite spirit; and unto none else can the ends of the law be answered" (2 Nephi 2:7). In other words, only those who have brought forth true repentance through faith and godly sorrow until they have experienced the mighty change of heart and been born of the Spirit—these will be justified by Christ's sacrifice and atonement.

Jesus says: "Listen to him who is the advocate with the Father, who is pleading your cause before him—saying: Father, behold the sufferings and death of him who did no sin, in whom thou wast well pleased; behold the blood of thy Son which was shed, the blood of him whom thou gavest that thyself might be glorified; wherefore, Father, spare these my brethren that believe on my name, that they may come unto me and have everlasting life" (D&C 45:3–5).

As a modern example of this, consider the words of the Lord concerning the Prophet Joseph Smith: "*After* it was truly manifested unto this first elder that *he had received a remission of his sins, he was entangled again in the vanities of the world;* but after repenting, and humbling himself sincerely, through faith, God ministered unto him by an holy angel, whose countenance was as lightning, and whose garments were pure and white above all other whiteness; and gave unto him commandments which inspired him; and gave him power from on high" (D&C 20:5–8; emphasis mine).

Clearly, no matter our spiritual status or ecclesiastical callings, we are all mortal and are all under the obligation of constant, sincere repentance as we continue the process of overcoming the world and coming to Christ. "There is no flesh that can dwell in the presence of God, save it be through the merits, and mercy, and grace of the Holy Messiah, who layeth down his life according to the flesh, and taketh it again by the power of the Spirit, that he may bring to pass the resurrection of the dead, being the first that should rise. Wherefore, he is the firstfruits unto God, inasmuch as he shall make intercession for all the children of men; and they that believe in him shall be saved" (2 Nephi 2:8–9).

Stated again, the law of justification is simply that those who have gone through godly sorrow until their sins have been forgiven are acquitted of their sinful natures. They are still prone to mortal weaknesses, but because they no longer sin intentionally, God justifies them and allows them almost instant repentance and forgiveness. Of course, such people ask for forgiveness instantly and do all within their power to avoid making the same mistakes again. Thus they are justified and are allowed to progress onward toward sanctification and, ultimately, perfection, all of it through Jesus Christ (see D&C 129:3, 6).

Sanctification

Bruce R. McConkie writes: "To the saints the continual cry of the gospel is: *Sanctify yourselves.* (D.&C. 39:18; 43:9, 11, 16; 133:4; Lev. 11:44; 1 Pet. 3:15.) This is accomplished by obedience to the 'law of Christ' (D.&C. 88:21, 34–35) and is possible because of his atoning sacrifice. (D.&C. 76:41.)" (*Mormon Doctrine*, p. 675).

Becoming sanctified is the first great personal reward granted to those who have become justified and then gone to work for the Lord. Where justification comes strictly through Christ's great efforts rather than our own (see 2 Nephi 25:23), sanctification is granted us through the Holy Ghost based upon *our own* efforts.

According to Brigham Young: "Sanctification . . . consists in overcoming every sin and bringing all into subjection to the law of Christ. God has placed in us a pure spirit; when this reigns predominant . . . and triumphs over the flesh and rules and governs and controls as the Lord controls the heavens and the earth, this I call the blessing of sanctification" (*Journal of Discourses*, 10:173). Such Saints have become "pure and spotless before God," being unable to "look upon sin save it were with abhorrence" (Alma 13:12).

President Spencer W. Kimball stated that the attitude basic to sanctification "is that the former transgressor must have reached a 'point of no return' to sin wherein there is not merely a renunciation but also a deep abhorrence of the sin—where the sin becomes most distasteful to him and where the desire or urge to sin is cleared out of his life" (*The Miracle of Forgiveness* [Salt Lake City: Bookcraft, 1969], pp. 354–55).

Put simply, then, sanctification is the process of becoming pure and spotless before God through the power of the sanctifier, who is the Holy Ghost, through true and constant repentance and a love of that which is good.

9

Called as Sons
and Daughters of Christ

Those who have been born again have achieved what we called the fifth level of spiritual progression—they are called as sons and daughters of Christ. To the Nephites following his resurrection, Christ said: "Behold, I am Jesus Christ the Son of God. . . . *As many as have received me, to them have I given to become the sons of God;* and even so will I to as many as shall believe on my name" (3 Nephi 9:15, 17; emphasis mine).

Concerning this calling into the family of our God, who is Jesus Christ, King Benjamin said to his people: "*Ye shall be called the children of Christ, his sons and his daughters;* for behold, this day he hath spiritually begotten you; for ye say that your hearts are changed through faith on his name; therefore ye are born of him and have become his sons and his daughters (Mosiah 5:7; emphasis mine).[1] And to nineteen-year-old Orson Pratt the Lord declared that He "so loved the world that he gave his own life, that as many as would believe might become the sons of God. Wherefore [Orson] you are my son" (D&C 34:3).

This doctrine of being called as children of Christ through a personal covenant and mighty works is expounded upon elsewhere. James E. Talmage wrote: "By the new birth—that of water and the Spirit—mankind may become children of Jesus Christ, being through the means by Him provided 'begotten sons and daughters unto God' (D.&C. 76:24). This solemn truth is further emphasized in the words of the Lord Jesus Christ given through Joseph Smith in 1833: 'And now, verily I say unto you, I was in the beginning with the Father, and am the Firstborn; And all those who are begotten through me are partakers of the glory of the same, and are the church of the Firstborn' (D.&C. 93:21, 22). . . . An analogous instance of sonship attained by righteous service is found in the revelation relating to the order and functions of Priesthood, given in 1832: 'For whoso is faithful unto the obtaining these two priesthoods of which I have spoken, and the magnifying their calling, are sanctified by the Spirit unto the renewing of their bodies. They become the sons of Moses and of Aaron and the seed of Abraham, and the church and kingdom, and the elect of God' (D.&C. 84:33, 34)" (James E. Talmage, *The Articles of Faith*, 12th ed. [Salt Lake City: The Church of Jesus Christ of Latter-day Saints, 1924], p. 470, foot-notes).

Moses says: "[Adam] heard a voice out of heaven, saying: Thou art baptized with fire, and with the Holy Ghost. This is the record of the Father, and the Son, from henceforth and for-ever; And thou art after the order of him who was without beginning of days or end of years, from all eternity to all eter-nity. *Behold, thou art one in me, a son of God; and thus may all become my sons*" (Moses 6:66–68; emphasis mine). Then Moroni pleads: "Search diligently in the light of Christ that ye may know good from evil; and if ye will lay hold upon every good thing, and condemn it not, ye certainly will be *a child of Christ*" (Moroni 7:19; emphasis mine).

To the wicked King Noah, Abinadi declared that through obedience to the words of the prophets, men and women would become Christ's seed or posterity. "When his [Christ's] soul has been made an offering for sin he shall see his seed. And now what say ye? And who shall be his seed? Behold I say unto you, that whosoever has heard the words of the prophets, yea, all the holy prophets who have prophesied concerning the coming of the Lord—I say unto you, that all those who have hearkened unto their words, and believed that the Lord would redeem his people, and have looked forward to that day for a remission of their sins, I say unto you, that these are his seed, or they are heirs of the kingdom of God. For *these are they whose sins he has borne; these are they for whom he has died, to redeem them from their transgressions. And now, are they not his seed?*" (Mosiah 15:10–12; emphasis mine).[2]

And finally, in his introductory remarks to the Brother of Jared upon the mount Shelem after He had revealed His spirit body, Jesus Christ declared: "Behold, I am he who was prepared from the foundation of the world to redeem my people. Behold, I am Jesus Christ. I am the Father and the Son. In me shall all mankind have life, and that eternally, even they who shall believe on my name; and *they shall become my sons and my daughters*" (Ether 3:14; emphasis mine).

In other words, those who have been born again are, by the purity granted them through the power of the Holy Ghost, worthy to be made members of Jesus Christ's personal eternal family.

Blessings of Being a Member of the Family of Christ

As members of this royal family, those who are being sanctified and justified by the Holy Spirit, and who set up no stakes or limitations for themselves by choosing to sin and remain in sin by not repenting, will be given permission and the power to go on and obtain all the blessings mentioned by the Prophet Joseph Smith when he said: "After a person has faith in Christ, repents of his sins, and is baptized for the remission of his sins and receives the Holy Ghost, (by the laying on of hands), which is the first Comforter, then let him continue to humble himself before God, hungering and thirsting after righteousness, and living by every word of God, and the Lord will soon say unto him, Son, thou shalt be exalted" (*Teachings*, p. 150).

Sons and daughters of Christ are allowed to progress until they become the elect of God. Also known as friends of Christ, they will be elected or sustained to membership in the Church of the Firstborn, which is Christ's heavenly church (see D&C 76:50–70, 94–96); his ordinances will all be sealed upon them by the Holy Spirit of Promise (see D&C 132:7–8); and finally they will be joint heirs with Christ, to inherit with Him all that the Father has promised throughout all eternity.

Having been born of the water and the Spirit, they have been called as sons and daughters of Jesus Christ, and having become the elect of God, they are elected to or chosen for membership in the heavenly Church of the Firstborn. It is this calling and election that must, at a later date, be made sure (see *Teachings*, p. 150; 2 Peter 1:1–19).

---

1. Benjamin makes an interesting promise here. He states that those who strive for righteousness until they become sons and daughters of Christ will be found on the right hand of God (as is Christ), and shall be called by the name of Christ, thus becoming joint heirs with Him in eternity. This is granted them because they have been "steadfast and immovable, always abounding

in good works, that Christ, the Lord God omnipotent, may seal [them] his, that [they] may be brought to heaven, that [they] may have everlasting salvation and eternal life" (see Mosiah 5:15).

2. In an interesting sequel to this thought of seeds, the resurrected Lord declared to the Nephites that only the humble and righteous (the seed of Christ) would be allowed to sprout and have eternal roots and branches, which obviously has reference to dwelling with eternal families (see 3 Nephi 25:1–2), which is called a "continuation of the seeds forever and ever" (D&C 132:19).

10

Conclusions about
Being Born of the Spirit

Throughout the scriptures, accounts exist of individuals and groups who have been born of the Spirit and undergone the mighty change. Some of these accounts are of Enos (see Enos 1), Alma the Younger (see Alma 36), Paul (see Acts 9), King Benjamin's people (see Mosiah 1–5), and a specific group of Lamanites to which the Savior referred (see 3 Nephi 9:20; Helaman 5). In considering these scriptural accounts, as well as what we have previously discussed, several aspects of the mighty change become apparent. Among these are some that seem very significant, and some that seem less so.

Significant Aspects

1. The birth of the Spirit usually occurs after we have been stirred up unto repentance of all our sins, usually through uncomfortable circumstances of some sort. There was some sort of stirring up in all the accounts listed above.

2. We must have been taught of Christ's atonement prior to the experience and have a sincere desire to believe in it.

3. We must show forth godly sorrow for our sins, which sorrow is manifested as a broken heart and a contrite spirit.

4. The birth of the Spirit occurs only after we cry out to the Lord for mercy in mighty prayer, which is exercising faith in Christ unto repentance.

5. As the experience concludes, we will feel our guilt swept away as we receive a remission of our sins through the power of the Holy Ghost. This is the baptism of fire and the Holy Spirit, which some in modern times have described as a sensation of incredible warmth that sweeps over the body in a cleansing action that is otherwise indescribable.

6. We feel complete peace of conscience for all our past sins. This feeling is so wonderful that, in an instant, as it were, all sin becomes abhorrent to us, we have no more disposition to do evil, and we resolve never intentionally to sin again. However, that does not mean we will never sin again, only that we will no longer sin intentionally. Nor does it mean that we forget our sins. As a matter of fact, it seems that memory is left until the resurrection so that learning will occur. Witness Alma's detailed memory of his own wickedness that he shared with his son Helaman (see Alma 36:6–27) and Benjamin's commandment to his people to remember what they had been through. However, with guilt being swept away through the atonement of Christ, the memory of our sins is no longer painful, and it will ever after be useful for instruction of self and others. That is why Benjamin said to "remember, and perish not" (Mosiah 4:30).

7. Once the experience is over, we are filled with the burning desire to acquaint others with what we have discovered about Christ and His power to deliver from sins so that they might enjoy the same peace and happiness we have found.

8. From this point forward, hopefully throughout our lives, we will strive for a closer relationship with the Spirit and with our Savior. We will do this through intensive study, righteous living, constant repentance, and diligent service to those around us. In doing so we will be manifesting the image of Christ in our countenances.

9. We have now been born witness to, by the Father, that Christ's suffering and dying have been the gifts of God, and that those gifts have wrought an at-one-ment in our lives, making us one with, or bringing us into the family of, the Lord Jesus Christ.

Less Significant Aspects

1. While we may be harrowed up a long time by the realization and comprehension of our sins, as Paul and Alma were for three days, the experience might also occur quickly, as it did with Benjamin's people.

2. During this period of total repentance we may or may not suffer some sort of physical malady, again like Paul and Alma. Perhaps this and the length of time mentioned above might be related to the degree of our wickedness before our repentance.

3. During the experience, we may or may not hear the voice of the Lord (either audibly or in our minds) as did Enos, and we may or may not have the eyes of our spirits opened to visions, as did Paul and Alma.

4. We may or may not know what is happening to us when this experience occurs. Either way, we are entitled to all the blessings enjoyed by those who have been born again and are diligently laboring to retain a remission of their sins, including personal spiritual progression.

If We Don't Know

To the Nephites the resurrected Lord said: "Ye shall offer for a sacrifice unto me a broken heart and a contrite spirit. And whoso cometh unto me with a broken heart and a contrite spirit, him will I baptize with fire and with the Holy Ghost, even as the Lamanites, because of their faith in me at the time of their conversion, were baptized with fire and with the Holy Ghost, *and they knew it not*" (3 Nephi 9:20; emphasis mine).

By the same token, there may be many among us today who, for one reason or other, do not know that they have been baptized by fire and received a remission of their sins. Yet their righteous works follow them, Saints everywhere are blessed by them, and in the Lord's own time they will be informed of their significant spiritual progression. Meanwhile, they are fully entitled to all the blessings of inner joy and peace that come to those who have been called as sons and daughters of Jesus Christ.

An Additional Blessing

Though this is not specifically mentioned in the accounts we have discussed, those who have been born again and are filled with the Holy Ghost will have the scriptures opened to their understanding to a degree that would have been unimaginable prior to their experience.

Joseph Smith wrote: "Immediately on our coming up out of the water after we had been baptized, we experienced great and glorious blessings from our Heavenly Father. No sooner had I baptized Oliver Cowdery, than the Holy Ghost fell upon him, and he stood up and prophesied many things which should shortly come to pass. And again, so soon as I had been baptized by him, I also had the spirit of prophecy, when standing up, I prophesied concerning the rise of this church, and many other things connected with the Church, and this generation of the children of men. We were filled with the Holy Ghost, and rejoiced in the God of our salvation.

"Our minds being now enlightened, we began to have the Scriptures laid open to our understandings, and the true meaning and intention of their more mysterious passages revealed unto us in a manner which we never could attain to previously, nor ever before had thought of" (*History of the Church*, 1:42–43; emphasis mine).

How the Holy Ghost Is Manifested in Us

As a final thought on being born again, consider the words of President Brigham Young, who asked: "How shall I know [if the mighty change] has occurred?" He then answered his own question: "By the Spirit that shall come unto you through obedience, which will make you feel like little children, and cause you to delight in doing good, to love your Father in Heaven and the society of the righteous. Have you malice and wrath, then? No, it is taken from you, and you feel like the child in its mother's lap. You will feel kind to your children, to your brothers and sisters, to your parents and neighbors, and to all around you; you will feel a glow, as of fire, burning within you; and if you open your mouths to talk you will declare ideas which you did not formerly think of; they will flow into your mind, even such as you have not thought of in years. The Scriptures will be opened to you, and you will see how clear and reasonable everything is which this or that Elder teaches you. Your hearts will be comforted, you can lie down and sleep in peace, and wake up with feelings as pleasant as the breezes of summer. This is a witness to you" (*Discourses of Brigham Young*, selected and arranged by

John A. Widtsoe [Salt Lake City: Deseret Book Company, 1954], p. 331).

President Ezra Taft Benson adds in more contemporary terms: "Yes, Christ changes men, and changed men can change the world. Men changed for Christ will be captained by Christ. Like Paul they will be asking, 'Lord, what wilt thou have me do?' (Acts 9:6). Peter stated they will 'follow his steps.' (1 Peter 2:21) John said they will 'walk, even as he walked.' (1 John 2:6).

"Finally men captained by Christ will be consumed in Christ. To paraphrase President Harold B. Lee, they set fire in others because they are on fire. (Harold B. Lee, *Stand Ye In Holy Places*, Salt Lake City, Deseret Book Co., 1974, p. 192).

"Their will is swallowed up in his will. (See John 5:30.) They do always those things that please the Lord. (See John 8:29.) Not only would they die for the Lord, but, more important, they want to live for Him.

"Enter their homes, and the pictures on their walls, the books on their shelves, the music in the air, their words and acts reveal them as Christians. They stand as witnesses of God at all times, and in all things, and in all places. (See Mosiah 18:9.) They have Christ on their minds, as they look unto Him in every thought. (See D&C 6:36.) They have Christ in their hearts as their affections are placed on Him forever. (See Alma 37:36.)

"Almost every week they partake of the sacrament and witness anew to their Eternal Father that they are willing to take upon them the name of His Son, always remember Him, and keep His commandments. (See Moroni 4:3.)

"In Book of Mormon language, they 'feast upon the words of Christ' (2 Ne. 32:3), 'talk of Christ' (2 Ne. 25:26), 'rejoice in Christ' (2 Ne. 25:26), 'are made alive in Christ' (2 Ne. 25:25), and 'glory in [their] Jesus' (2 Ne. 33:6). In short, they lose themselves in the Lord and find eternal life. (See Luke 17:33.)" ("Born of God," *Ensign*, July 1989, p. 5).

If we find that such descriptions are of us, then we may be assured that we have been born again.

Into the Wilderness

11

The School
of the Wilderness

Once we have been born again and experienced the mighty change of heart, are we finished? Not according to the Prophet Joseph, who said: "After a person has faith in Christ, repents of his sins, and is baptized for the remission of sins and receives the Holy Ghost, (by the laying on of hands), which is the first Comforter, then let him continue to humble himself before God, hungering and thirsting after righteousness, and living by every word of God, and the Lord will soon say unto him, Son, thou shalt be exalted" (*Teachings*, p. 150). Then we will "come unto Mount Zion, and unto the city of the living God, the heavenly Jerusalem, and to an innumerable company of angels; to the general assembly and Church of the Firstborn, which are written in heaven, and to God the judge of all, and to the spirits of just men made perfect, and to Jesus the Mediator of the new covenant" (*Teachings*, p. 12).

A large percentage of the Saints in Kirtland, following

Joseph's counsel of hungering and thirsting after righteousness and living by every word of God, experienced for themselves the progressive spiritual blessings he promised. But it required effort, for Joseph's words indicate that, having been born again, we have only started with our spiritual progression. Nephi agrees, explaining that repentance and a remission of our sins "by fire and by the Holy Ghost" take us through the gate and place us at the beginning of the "strait and narrow path which leads to eternal life" (2 Nephi 31:17–18). King Benjamin went to great lengths to teach his followers what was expected of them once they had experienced the mighty change. "As ye have come to the knowledge of the glory of God, or if ye have known of his goodness and have tasted of his love, and have received a remission of your sins, which causeth such exceedingly great joy in your souls, even so I would that ye should remember, and always retain in remembrance, the greatness of God, and your own nothingness, and his goodness and long-suffering towards you, unworthy creatures, and humble yourselves even in the depths of humility, calling on the name of the Lord daily, and standing steadfastly in the faith of that which is to come, which was spoken by the mouth of the angel. And behold, I say unto you that if ye do this ye shall always rejoice, and be filled with the love of God, and always retain a remission of your sins; and ye shall grow in the knowledge of the glory of him that created you, or in the knowledge of that which is just and true" (Mosiah 4:11–12).

Benjamin then instructed his people to (1) live peaceably and kindly with each other; (2) give diligent attention to the spiritual and temporal needs of their children; (3) teach their children the peaceable way of Christ; (4) impart freely of their substance to any who stood in need of it, "every man according to that which he hath, such as feeding the hungry, clothing the naked, visiting the sick and administering to their relief, both spiritually and temporally, according to their wants"; (5) never take advantage of another by borrowing and not returning; (6) always watch their thoughts, words, and deeds, observing the commandments of God, and "continue in the faith of what ye have heard concerning . . . our Lord, even unto the end of your lives" (Mosiah 4:13–30).

These are all things that we must do if we are to retain a remission of our sins. But at the same time we must not neglect our own spiritual growth and progression. That is what Nephi meant when he said that we "must press forward with a steadfastness in Christ, having a perfect brightness of hope, and a love of God and of all men. Wherefore, if ye shall press forward, *feasting upon the word of Christ,* and endure to the end, behold, thus saith the Father: Ye shall have eternal life (2 Nephi 31:20; emphasis mine).

If we are willing to do as Benjamin, Nephi, and Joseph Smith counsel us, then truly we are ready to embark on the most exciting and glorious journey of discovery any of us have ever imagined—a heaven-directed course of study, granted with the intent of bringing to pass absolute trust and purity. There is ample evidence to suggest that the Lord calls this divine tutelage His school of the wilderness.

Jesus went fasting into the wilderness for forty days so He could learn directly from the Father; Moses did the same. Adam called his wilderness experience being driven into the lone and dreary world, and Lehi called his experience the wilderness of his affliction. Both Ether and Moroni were well acquainted with wilderness schooling, and John the Baptist received his preparation there. The Lord has always required of those who desire to be His people a withdrawal from the world and its telestial ways. If we so desire, we can have the same sanctifying experience.

12

Leaving the Things
of the World Behind

For many of us, one of the most difficult aspects of entering into the Lord's wilderness school is the requirement that we leave behind the world and its attractions. In ancient times, both Jesus and Moses went through their wilderness school fasting, with nothing of the world in their pockets or backpacks. Elijah was allowed to eat only what was brought him by ravens (see 1 Kings 17:4–6). Lehi left his house, the land of his inheritance, and "his gold, and his silver, and his precious things, and took nothing with him, save it were his family, and provisions, and tents, and departed into the wilderness" (1 Nephi 2:1–4, 11). All else was left behind, according to the commandment of the Lord.

For the Kirtland Saints, the wilderness of frontier Ohio was a land of poverty and privation. Not only had they given up most of their worldly goods just to get there, but once they arrived they had to sacrifice even further as they struggled to build their magnificent temple.

Coming Out of Babylon

The Lord has asked us to come out of the worldliness of Babylon. To the Prophet Joseph He declared: "Go ye out of Babylon; gather ye out from among the nations, from the four winds, from one end of heaven to the other" (D&C 133:7). "What is Babylon?" Brigham Young asked. "It is the confused world: come out of her then, and cease to partake of her sins, for if you do not you will be partakers of her plagues" (*Journal of Discourses*, 12:282). And Hugh Nibley writes: "I could quote a hundred scriptures to show that Babylon is nothing but the inverse image of Zion. Babylon is a state of mind, as Zion is, with its appropriate environment. Just like Zion, Babylon is a city. 'Babylon the great is fallen, is fallen' (Revelation 18:2). The great world center of commerce and business, 'the kings of the earth have committed fornication with her, and the merchants of the earth are waxed rich through the abundance of her delicacies' (Revelation 18:3). Indeed, 'thy merchants were the great men of the earth; for by thy sorceries were all nations deceived' (Revelation 18:23). Babylon's economy is built on deceptions. Babylon is described fully in Revelation 18: She is rich, luxurious, immoral, full of fornications, merchants, riches, delicacies, sins, merchandise, gold, silver, precious stones, pearls, fine linens, purples, silks, scarlets, thyine wood, all manner of vessels, ivory, precious wood, brass, iron, marble, and so on. She is a giant delicatessen, full of wine, oil, fine flour, wheat; a perfume counter with cinnamon, odors, ointments, and frankincense; a market with beasts and sheep. It reads like a savings stamp catalog or a guide to a modern supermarket or department store. Horses and chariots and all manner of services are available; slaves in the souls of men. These are 'the fruits thy soul lusted after . . . and all things which were dainty and goodly' (Revelation 18:14). And it is all for sale. 'O virgin daughter of Babylon, . . . thou hast laboured . . . [with] thy merchants, from thy youth' (Isaiah 47:1, 15). In her power and affluence she is unchallenged. 'For thou hast trusted in thy wickedness: thou hast said, None seeth me. Thy wisdom and thy knowledge, it hath perverted thee; and thou hast said in thine heart, I am, and none else beside me' (Isaiah 47:10). Babylon is number one. She dominates the world. Her king is equated to Lucifer, who says, 'I will be like the most High' (Isaiah 14:14). And all the nations are weakened at her expense. He was the man that 'made the earth to tremble, that did shake kingdoms; that made the world as a wilderness' (Isaiah 14:16–17). The 'lady of kingdoms' who rules over polluted lands and says, 'I shall be a lady forever' (Isaiah 47:5, 7)—she leads the world. 'The nations have drunken of her wine; therefore the nations are mad' (Jeremiah 51:7). 'Babylon the great, all nations have drunk of the wine of the wrath of her fornication' (Revelation 18:3). And when Babylon falls, all the world is involved: 'At the noise of the taking of Babylon the earth is moved, and the cry is heard among the nations' (Jeremiah 50:46). And 'at Babylon shall fall the slain of all the earth' (Jeremiah 51:49). Her clever, experienced, and unscrupulous men will be helpless. She thinks she can get away with anything, and says, 'None seeth me.' But 'thy wisdom and thy knowledge, it hath perverted thee' (Isaiah 47:10). 'And I will make drunk her men; and they shall sleep a perpetual sleep' (Jeremiah 51:57). Her military might is helpless: 'A sound of battle is in the land, and of great destruction. How is the hammer of the whole earth cut asunder and broken!' (Jeremiah 50:22–23)" (*Approaching Zion*, pp. 14–16).

Training in the Ways of the Lord

No wonder Brigham Young said that Babylon, or the world, is confusing. With all the worldliness Brother Nibley describes, who wouldn't be confused? Or enticed? Or even led astray? Isn't it far better to allow the Lord to lead us into a spiritual wilderness, a place of simplicity where, without distraction, we can receive training in His ways? And all of us need training in His ways before we can be brought into His presence.

Concerning the need for such divine instruction, Joseph Smith stated: "We consider that God has created man with a mind capable of instruction, and a faculty which may be enlarged in proportion to the heed and diligence given to the light communicated from heaven to the intellect; and that the nearer man approaches perfection, the clearer are his views, and the greater his enjoyments, till he has overcome the evils of his life and lost every desire for sin; and like the ancients, arrives at that point of faith where he is wrapped in the power and glory of his Maker and is caught up to dwell with Him. But we consider that this is a station to which no man ever arrived in a moment: he must have been instructed in the government and laws of that kingdom by proper degrees, until his mind is capable in some measure of comprehending the propriety, justice, equality, and consistency of the same. For further instruction we refer you to Deut. [32], where the Lord says, that Jacob is the lot of His inheritance. *He found him in a desert land, and in the waste[d], howling wilderness; He led him about, He instructed him, He kept him as the apple of His eye,* etc.; which will show the force of the last item advanced, that it is necessary for men to receive an understanding concerning the laws of the heavenly kingdom, before they are permitted to enter it: we mean the celestial glory" (*Teachings,* p. 51; emphasis mine).

Brother Hugh Nibley writes: "The Israelites always looked

back upon the days of their wandering in the wilderness as the true schooling of the Chosen People and the time when they were most nearly fulfilling the measure of their existence. The concept of man as a wanderer and an outcast in a dark and dreary world is as old as the records of the human race. The desert has always had two aspects, that of refuge and asylum on the one hand, and of trial and tribulation on the other; in both respects it is a place where God segregates and tests his people. Throughout the history of Israel zealous minorities among the people have gone out into the wilderness from time to time in an attempt to get back to the ways of the patriarchs and to live the old Law in its purity, fleeing from Idumea, or the wicked world" (*An Approach to the Book of Mormon* [Provo and Salt Lake City, Foundation for Ancient Research and Mormon Studies and Deseret Book Company, 1988], p. 145).

For those who desire to continue their spiritual growth, wilderness schooling is as essential as ever, though today it will likely be more spiritual than physical. Elder William J. Critchlow, Jr., taught: "We live in a wicked world like unto Babylon of old. Our latter-day prophets, like the prophets of old, have cried, 'Come out, come out of Babylon.' To come out physically presents a problem, but spiritually it is possible, and spiritually we must come out if we are to prosper in the land" (in Conference Report, October 1961, p. 56).

The Lord exclaimed to the Prophet Joseph: "That which you hear is as the voice of one crying in the wilderness—in the wilderness, because you cannot see him—my voice, because my voice is Spirit; my Spirit is truth; truth abideth and hath no end; and if it be in you it shall abound. And if your eye be single to my glory, your whole bodies shall be filled with light, and there shall be no darkness in you; and that body which is filled with light comprehendeth all things. Therefore, sanctify yourselves that your minds become single to God, and the days will come that you shall see him; for he will unveil his face unto you, and it shall be in his own time, and in his own way, and according to his own will" (D&C 88:66–68).

Clearly the Lord is saying that as we give up the world (as our eyes become single to God's glory), we learn to hear the voice of God crying out of the wilderness. And by hearing His voice, we are preparing ourselves for the day when we will behold His face. That is the entire point of the wilderness journey upon which those who have been born again are invited to embark.

Deliverance into the Wilderness

Every time the Lord's people have been led into the wilderness, it has been as a means of delivering them from evil or danger. Of the Jaredites we are told that they and their friends were delivered from having their language confounded (see Ether 1:35–43). Moses and the Children of Israel were delivered from the Egyptians (see Exodus 13–14). And Nephi and his family were delivered not only from the hands of the people of Jerusalem (see 1 Nephi 2:1) but also from the destruction of Jerusalem at the hands of the Babylonians (see 1 Nephi 1:18).

Later, Nephi had his own wilderness deliverance after he and his father's family had arrived in the Promised Land. Nephi records, "The Lord did warn me, that I, Nephi, should depart from [my brothers] and flee into the wilderness, and all those who would go with me" (2 Nephi 5:5).

Concerning the deliverance of Alma, a later Book of Mormon prophet, Mormon records: "Alma, having been warned of the Lord that the armies of king Noah would come upon them, and having made it known to his people, therefore they gathered together their flocks, and took of their grain, and departed into the wilderness before the armies of king Noah" (Mosiah 23:1).

Even the little-known Mulekites were granted a wilderness deliverance, which was discovered when Mosiah found "that the people of Zarahemla came out from Jerusalem at the time that Zedekiah, king of Judah, was carried away captive into Babylon. And they journeyed in the wilderness, and were brought by the hand of the Lord across the great waters, into the land where Mosiah discovered them; and they had dwelt there from that time forth" (Omni 1:15–16).

The final account of deliverance and being led into the wilderness that we will consider is that of Abraham. He records: "I, Abraham, saw that it was needful for me to obtain another place of residence" (Abraham 1:1) "[because] the priests laid violence upon me, that they might slay me" (Abraham 1:12). Therefore, "as they lifted up their hands upon me, that they might offer me up and take away my life, behold, I lifted up my voice unto the Lord my God, and the Lord hearkened and heard, and he filled me with the vision of the Almighty, and the angel of his presence stood by me, and immediately unloosed my bands; And his voice was unto me: Abraham, Abraham, behold, my name is Jehovah, and I have heard thee, and have come down to deliver thee, and to take thee away from thy father's house, and from all thy kinsfolk, into a strange land which thou knowest not of" (Abraham 1:15–16).

Modern Application

Clearly, in each of the instances mentioned above, deliverance was granted, after which those who had been delivered were commanded to depart into the wilderness. The first part of the school of the wilderness, then, is that we can enter it only after deliverance has been sought and granted by the Lord—whether from danger or evil, it must also include deliverance from sin—which means being born again and experiencing the mighty change, wherein we are redeemed from our personal sins.

Deliverance from Sin Must Occur before the Wilderness Experience

Nephi the son of Helaman declared, "Except ye repent of all your iniquities, and cry unto the Lord, ye will in no wise be delivered" (3 Nephi 3:15). Alma taught "that all men shall reap a reward of their works. . . . If they have been righteous they shall reap the salvation of their souls, according to the power and deliverance of Jesus Christ" (Alma 9:28). Zeezrom learned the hard way that "his many . . . sins did harrow up his mind until it did become exceedingly sore, having no deliverance" (Alma 15:3). And to Joseph Smith the Lord declared: "Whom I love I also chasten that their sins may be forgiven, for with the chastisement I prepare a way for their deliverance in all things out of temptation, and I have loved you" (D&C 95:1).

Having been delivered from our sins through being born again, if we desire with all our hearts to be delivered from our enemies (including the worldliness that surrounds us), then we have but to ask in faith and it will be done. We will be admitted into the wilderness of the Lord, where we will be forged, refined, and purified by the Lord Jesus Christ, who is "like a refiner's fire, and like fullers' soap," and who will "purify the [wilderness wanderers], and purge them as gold and silver, that they may offer unto the Lord an offering in righteousness" (Malachi 3:2–3).

Frequently the Lord appears willing to help us give up worldly things by allowing such things as severe financial reversals, thus bringing to pass loss of homes, cars, and incomes; personal and corporate bankruptcy; and so forth. A severe loss of health or the death of a loved one can do the same thing by making worldly things unattractive or meaningless. All such things can be a means of helping us leave behind the things of this world, a means for which we should rejoice.

We must also remember that once worldliness has been left behind, we must not return to it. That does not mean we will not prosper, for the Lord always prospers the righteous. What it means is that our hearts and spirits must remain pure and without greed and avarice. That was a difficult lesson for the Nephites, who seemed to plummet into destruction as often as the Lord prospered them. On the rare occasions when they succeeded, however, it was because "they did not send away any who were naked, or that were hungry, or that were athirst, or that were sick, or that had not been nourished; and they did not set their hearts upon riches; therefore they were liberal to all, both old and young, both bond and free, both male and female, whether out of the church or in the church, having no respect to persons as to those who stood in need" (Alma 1:30).

While many in Kirtland maintained this same Christlike attitude, Eliza R. Snow wrote: "Prosperity was dawning upon them . . . and many who had been humble and faithful . . . were getting haughty in their spirits, and lifted up in the pride of their hearts. As the Saints drank in the love and spirit of the world, the Spirit of the Lord withdrew from their hearts, and they were filled with pride and hatred toward those who maintained their integrity" (*History of the Church*, 2:487–88, footnotes). These are valuable lessons to consider.

13

A Separation
from Worldly People

Ancient wilderness travelers frequently found it necessary to temporarily separate themselves spiritually from friends, associates, and even beloved family members who chose to remain attached to the wickedness of the world. Why? Because the Lord required the wilderness traveler's heart and soul to plumb new depths of spiritual understanding, which others, including loved ones, are frequently unwilling to consider.

Jesus "said unto another, Follow me. But he said, Lord, suffer me first to go and bury my father. Jesus said unto him, Let the dead bury their dead: but go thou and preach the kingdom of God. And another also said, Lord, I will follow thee; but let me first go bid them farewell, which are at home at my house. And Jesus said unto him, No man, having put his hand to the plow, and looking back, is fit for the kingdom of God" (Luke 9:59–62).

Elder Bruce R. McConkie explained what Jesus meant by

these statements: " 'I have called you; forsake the things of this world and seek for those of a better. What is the life or death of family or friends to those who are taking life and salvation to a dying world? Let those who are spiritually dead bury those in whose bodies the breath of life no longer dwells. Go thou; preach the gospel of the kingdom; proclaim faith, repentance, baptism, and the gift of the Holy Ghost. Bring souls unto me, and you shall have rest with them in the kingdom of my Father' "(*The Mortal Messiah* [Salt Lake City: Deseret Book Company, 1980], 2:274).

As Abraham found, leaving behind loved ones can be a difficult but necessary experience. He wrote: "My fathers, having turned from their righteousness, and from the holy commandments which the Lord their God had given unto them, unto the worshiping of the gods of the heathen, utterly refused to hearken to my voice" (Abraham 1:5). "Accordingly a famine prevailed throughout all the land of Chaldea, and my father was sorely tormented because of the famine, and he repented of the evil which he had determined against me, to take away my life" (Abraham 1:30). "Now the Lord had said unto me: Abraham, get thee out of thy country, and from thy kindred, and from thy father's house, unto a land that I will show thee. Therefore I left the land of Ur, of the Chaldees, to go into the land of Canaan; and I took Lot, my brother's son, and his wife, and Sarai my wife; and also my father followed after me, unto the land which we denominated Haran. And the famine abated; and my father tarried in Haran and dwelt there, as there were many flocks in Haran; and my father turned again unto his idolatry, therefore he continued in Haran. But I, Abraham, and Lot, my brother's son, prayed unto the Lord, and the Lord appeared unto me, and said unto me: Arise, and take Lot with thee; for I have purposed to take thee away out of Haran, and to make of thee a minister to bear my name in a strange land which I will give unto thy seed after thee for an everlasting possession, when they hearken to my voice" (Abraham 2:3–6).

Nephi's experience was similar. "As we journeyed in the wilderness, behold Laman and Lemuel, and two of the daughters of Ishmael, and the two sons of Ishmael and their families, did rebel against us; yea, against me, Nephi, and Sam, and their father, Ishmael, and his wife, and his three other daughters. And it came to pass in the which rebellion, they were desirous to return unto the land of Jerusalem" (1 Nephi 7:6–7).

These people wanted nothing to do with a wilderness experience. In their rebelliousness they had never repented and been born again, and so to them the wilderness meant nothing more than pain and difficulty. Despite all the evidence of the hand of God in their affairs, they were blind to it and murmured and schemed constantly about how to return to the world.

"I, Nephi, being grieved for the hardness of their hearts, therefore I spake unto them, saying, yea, even unto Laman and unto Lemuel: Behold ye are mine elder brethren, and how is it that ye are so hard in your hearts, and so blind in your minds, that ye have need that I, your younger brother, should speak unto you, yea, and set an example for you? How is it that ye have not hearkened unto the word of the Lord? How is it that ye have forgotten that ye have seen an angel of the Lord? Yea, and how is it that ye have forgotten what great things the Lord hath done for us, in delivering us out of the hands of Laban, and also that we should obtain the record?

"Yea, and how is it that ye have forgotten that the Lord is able to do all things according to his will, for the children of men, if it so be that they exercise faith in him? Wherefore, let us be faithful to him. And if it so be that we are faithful to him, we shall obtain the land of promise" (1 Nephi 7:8–13).

As Nephi points out, those who desire to live the law of the wilderness must learn not to murmur when things become painful—even in the face of death. Thus: "We were about to be swallowed up in the depths of the sea. And after we had been driven back upon the waters for the space of four days, my brethren began to see that the judgments of God were upon them, and that they must perish save that they should repent of their iniquities; wherefore, they came unto me, and loosed the bands which were upon my wrists, and behold they had swollen exceedingly; and also mine ankles were much swollen, and great was the soreness thereof. Nevertheless, I did look unto my God, and I did praise him all the day long; and I did not murmur against the Lord because of mine afflictions" (1 Nephi 18:15–16).

For obvious reasons, righteous parents suffer excruciatingly when their children choose to separate themselves because of a hardened heart. Of his own parents' experience, Nephi wrote: "My father, Lehi, had said many things unto [my unrighteous brothers], and also unto the sons of Ishmael; but, behold, they did breathe out much threatenings against anyone that should speak for me; and my parents being stricken in years, and having suffered much grief because of their children, they were brought down, yea, even upon their sick-beds. Because of their grief and much sorrow, and the iniquity of my brethren, they were brought near even to be carried out of this time to meet their God; yea, their grey hairs were about to be brought down to lie low in the dust; yea, even they were near to be cast with sorrow into a watery grave" (1 Nephi 18:17–18).

But in spite of their parents' suffering, Nephi's brothers continued to harden their hearts against Nephi and the other righteous members of his family. Therefore, the Lord directed that Nephi split the family in half and separate himself from his brothers: "The Lord did warn me, that I, Nephi, should depart from them and flee into the wilderness, and all those who would go with me. Wherefore, it came to pass that I, Nephi, did take my family, and also Zoram and his family, and Sam, mine elder brother and his family, and Jacob and Joseph, my younger brethren, and also my sisters, and all those who would go with me. And all those who would go with me were those who believed in the warnings and the revelations of God; wherefore, they did hearken unto my words. And we did take our tents and whatsoever things were possible for us, and did journey in the wilderness for the space of many days. And after we had journeyed for the space of many days we did pitch our tents" (2 Nephi 5:5–7).

Modern Application

For those who would enter the wilderness of the Lord, a separation of sorts must occur as they leave behind those who do not wish, for whatever reasons, to travel where they are going. In our day this separation will usually be more spiritual and emotional than physical, but it will be just as real and difficult as a physical separation might be. It will usually mean that world-oriented loved ones will have less and less in common with the wilderness travelers, conversations about things of the Spirit will decrease as the wilderness travelers' knowledge concerning the things of God increases, and the wilderness sojourners' increasing sense of responsibility for the spiritual welfare of their loved ones will often be unappreciated.

Wilderness travelers must look forward to a certain amount of loneliness. If they talk of their experiences with others who are not fellow travelers (and truthfully there never seem to be many), they will either be misunderstood or, worse, maligned and mocked. One or two such encounters, and they soon learn

135

to keep their mouths closed and to lean wholly upon the strength of the Lord for companionship. Thus does their journey become private and even occasionally secret.

Hugh Nibley writes: "'He leadeth away the righteous into precious lands, and the wicked he destroyeth, and curseth the land unto them' (1 Nephi 17:38). Such was always the Lord's way. When he brought Lehi out of Jerusalem, 'no one knew about it save it were himself and those whom he brought out of the land.' Exactly so did the Lord bring Moses and the people in secret out of the wicked land of Egypt, and Abraham fled by night and secretly from Ur of the Chaldees as Lot did from Sodom and Gomorrah, and so was the city of Enoch removed suddenly to an inaccessible place. And in every case, the wicked world thus left behind is soon to be destroyed, so that those who leave the flesh-pots and the 'precious things' behind and lose all for a life of hardship are actually losing their lives to save them. It would be hard to say whether this pattern is more clearly set forth in the Old Testament or the New, but certainly it is most fully exemplified in the Book of Mormon" (*An Approach to the Book of Mormon,* p. 139).

The separation we have been speaking of, whether actual or not, must also be considered as temporary. That is because the Lord invariably expects His successfully graduated wilderness students to carry the things they have learned back to others. That is as it should be, for the closer the wilderness travelers draw to the Lord, the more filled with charity or pure love they become, and the more anxious they are to share their joyous knowledge. Of the repentant sons of Mosiah the record states: "They were desirous that salvation should be declared to every creature, for they could not bear that any human soul should perish; yea, even the very thoughts that any soul should endure endless torment did cause them to quake and tremble.

And thus did the Spirit of the Lord work upon them" (Mosiah 28:3–4).

Both Jesus and Moses eagerly returned to teach the very people they were originally led away from, and Enos and Alma left vivid descriptions of their lifelong efforts to bring the message of Christ to the people they called enemies—those they loved who had chosen the things of Babylon over the things of God. Alma declared concerning the success of his life's work: "The Lord doth give me exceedingly great joy in the fruit of my labors; for because of the word which he has imparted unto me, behold, many have been born of God, and have tasted as I have tasted, and have seen eye to eye as I have seen; therefore they do know of these things of which I have spoken, as I do know; and the knowledge which I have is of God. And I have been supported under trials and troubles of every kind, yea, and in all manner of afflictions; yea, God has delivered me from prison, and from bonds, and from death; yea, and I do put my trust in him, and he will still deliver me. And I know that he will raise me up at the last day, to dwell with him in glory; yea, and I will praise him forever" (Alma 36:25–28).

14

Traveling Only
as the Lord Directs

All who travel in the Lord's wilderness are required to go only where He directs that they go. Any minor deviation simply adds time and additional trials to the wilderness experience, while major deviations may bring it to a halt altogether.

The Lord told Abraham: "I will lead thee by my hand, and I will take thee . . . unto a land that I will show thee" (Abraham 1:18; 2:3). Of the Jaredites, Mormon records: "They did travel in the wilderness, and did build barges, in which they did cross many waters, being directed continually by the hand of the Lord" (Ether 2:6).

Lehi's obedience was chronicled as follows: "The Lord commanded my father, even in a dream, that he should take his family and depart into the wilderness. And . . . he was obedient unto the word of the Lord, wherefore he did as the Lord commanded him . . . and . . . departed into the wilderness" (1 Nephi 2:2–4).

Moses, who led the recalcitrant children of Israel into their wilderness experience, said: "We turned, and took our journey into the wilderness by the way of the Red sea, as the Lord spake unto me" (Deuteronomy 2:1; see also Exodus 13:17–18). Later, the Lord directed that they circle a certain mountain again and again until a particular lesson had been learned. Only then would He allow them to proceed along their very specific course (see Deuteronomy 2:1–7).

Modern Application

For those who would travel the Lord's wilderness, this lesson seems to be one of the most difficult to grasp. For some reason, we want to stand independent above all other creatures, God included, as we forge our own way forward through life, learning for ourselves what is right and what is wrong. But such pride is not to be part of the Lord's wilderness. He is in charge of the school, and He will provide for our needs in His own time and manner. As Moses declared to Israel: "The Lord thy God . . . knoweth thy walking through this great wilderness: these forty years the Lord thy God hath been with thee; thou hast lacked nothing" (Deuteronomy 2:7).

President Kimball warned: "You probably think you have found a new freedom: to think wholly for yourself, to make wholly your own determinations, to criticize and decide for yourself what is right and wrong. That was decided eternities ago. Right and wrong are not to be determined by you or me. Those elements were decided for us before our birth. We have the free agency to do the right or do the wrong, but who are we to alter those changeless things? We can scoff at sacred things, express our own little opinions, but remember that millions of men and women with keener minds than ours, with more erudite training than yours and mine, have said things and done things more startling, more ugly, more skeptical than you or I could think of. . . . They have all come to grief or will ultimately. Shall the violin say to Tony Stradivarius, 'You did not make me?' Shall the created thing question the creator?" (*The Teachings of Spencer W. Kimball,* edited by Edward L. Kimball [Salt Lake City: Bookcraft, 1982], p. 160).

Absolute Obedience Leads to Knowledge of God

What the Lord asks of wilderness wanderers is nothing less than absolute trust, absolute faith, absolute obedience. Why? Because only in that way does one gain godly, godlike knowledge. Joseph Smith taught: "A man is saved no faster than he gets knowledge, for if he does not get knowledge, he will be brought into captivity by some evil power in the other world, as evil spirits will have more knowledge, and consequently more power than many men who are on the earth. Hence [we] need revelation to assist us, and give us knowledge of the things of God" (*Teachings,* p. 217).

Only with this righteous knowledge can we come fully to Christ. Elder Neal A. Maxwell puts it this way: "Jesus' divinity is not only a reality; it is a very directing and drawing reality. We are to 'feast upon the words of Christ; for behold, the words of Christ will tell [us] all'—*all,* not some—of the things we should do. And, so often, 'what' we are to do is to be learned from the 'what' of the Lord we worship. So the truly Christ-centered life is one in which—without being incantational—'we talk of Christ, we rejoice in Christ, we preach of Christ, we prophesy of Christ' . . .

"Yet *He cannot fully receive us until we fully follow Him.* His love for us is unconditional and perfect, but ours for Him is clearly not. Being just, He cannot deviate from His standards by giving us blessings without our obedience to the laws upon which such blessings are predicated. His devotion to truth is such that even in His mercy, He cannot lie, including to Himself, about our readiness. He knows our weaknesses, but, mercifully, He also knows how to succor us as we seek to cope with them. And whatever weaknesses remain in us, He will tutor us and train us to exculpate these, if we will but let Him" (*Even As I Am* [Salt Lake City: Deseret Book Company, 1982], p. 33; emphasis mine).

Understanding God's Thoughts and Ways

Lest we forget the goal here, the purpose of the Lord's wilderness school is to train us to think as He does, in all things, at all times, and in all places—not an easy task, by any means. The Lord says: "My thoughts are not your thoughts, neither are your ways my ways. . . . For as the heavens are higher than the earth, so are my ways higher than your ways, and my thoughts than your thoughts" (Isaiah 55:8–9).

Still, the only way we can successfully graduate from the Lord's school is by manifesting through our own behavior the Lord's thoughts and ways. It is this knowledge Joseph the Prophet was speaking of earlier when he declared, "A man is saved no faster than he gets knowledge." That is why, as was revealed through the Prophet Joseph, "the Lord requireth the heart and a willing mind" (D&C 64:34), as we "becometh as a child, submissive, meek, humble, patient, full of love, willing to submit to all things which the Lord seeth fit to inflict upon [us], even as a child doth submit to his father" (Mosiah 3:19). Only by developing such attributes do we learn of God. And such saving knowledge can come in no other way.

This willing mind is made manifest first by our not complaining or wavering no matter the circumstances; and second, by our never making a decision or pursuing some goal without first obtaining the mind and will of the Lord concerning it. In other words, we exercise our agency by choosing to obey. As Brigham Young put it: "Does it follow that a man is deprived of his rights, because he lists in his heart to do the will of God? Must a man swear to prove that he has an agency? I contend there is no necessity for that, nor for stealing, nor for doing any wrong. I can manifest to the heavens and to the inhabitants of the earth that I am free-born, and have my liberty before God, angels and men, when I kneel down to pray, certainly as much as if I were to go out and swear. I have the right to call my family together at certain hours for prayer, and I believe that this course proves that I am a free agent, as much as if I were to steal, swear, lie, and get drunk" (*Journal of Discourses,* 10:333).

Following the Brethren

Once the Lord's mind and will is obtained, of course, there should be no deviation from strict obedience to what He has directed. And how do we know what He has directed? By following His prophets and by following His Spirit, which are absolutely interrelated acts of obedience. Elder Neal A. Maxwell writes: "Among the requirements that God has laid upon us is to pay heed to His living prophets. In our dispensation this has been described as 'following the Brethren.' It is a dimension of obedience that has been difficult for some in every dispensation. It will be particularly hard in ours, the final dispensation. Secularly, every form of control, except self-control, seems to be increasing, and yet obedience rests on self-control. . . .

"Elder Marvin J. Ashton of the Council of the Twelve warned of another consequence of not heeding: 'Any Church member not obedient to the leaders of this Church will not have the opportunity to be obedient to the promptings of the Lord'

(*Munich Area Conference Report,* August 1973, p. 24). A lack of obedience to the leaders will, therefore, mean that we will not have the precious promptings of the Spirit, which we need personally—so much and so often. This potential loss would be reason enough for us to be obedient to the prophets, for apparently we cannot have one without the other. Vital as the words of the prophets are, these come to us only periodically. We need the directions of the Spirit daily, even hourly" (*All These Things Shall Give Thee Experience* [Salt Lake City: Deseret Book Company, 1980], pp. 101, 104).

Traveling through the wilderness only as the Lord directs, then, is nothing more nor less than an exercise in obedience and humility. And for most of us it will be a difficult exercise "Unless—unless, through humility and obedience, we can transform feeling owned into a grand sense of belonging, and being purchased into gratitude for being rescued, and dependency into appreciation for being tutored by an omniscient God, which He does in order that we might become more dependable and have more independence and scope for service in the future" (ibid., p. 24).

CHAPTER

15

The Difficulty of
the Wilderness Experience

As they passed through the wilderness, all of the Lord's highly favored experienced great difficulties. Lehi wasn't just being trite when he called his own experience "the wilderness of mine afflictions" (2 Nephi 3:1) and spoke of "the days of my tribulation in the wilderness" (2 Nephi 2:1). Rather than simply handing them everything as they needed it, the Lord required them to work, to think, to use their own creativity, as a means of solving their difficult problems. Yet always the Lord was near, neither taking away agency nor denying opportunities for needed lessons, but ready nevertheless to help in whatever manner He could.

Hugh Nibley writes: "God has more to offer those who break with the world than 'wearying in a land of sands and thorns.' The wilderness is only a transition, a difficult exercise of disengaging from the fashion of the world: 'He did straiten them in the wilderness with his rod' (1 Nephi 17:41). Besides the 'mysteries of God,' there was more awaiting the faithful: 'Ye shall prosper, and be led to a *land of promise* . . . which I have prepared for you; yea, even a land which is choice above all other lands' (1 Nephi 2:20). 'He leadeth away the righteous into precious lands, and the wicked he destroyeth, and curseth the land unto them for their sakes' (1 Nephi 17:38)" (Hugh Nibley, *The Prophetic Book of Mormon* [Provo and Salt Lake City, Foundation for Ancient Research and Mormon Studies and Deseret Book Company, 1989], p. 504).

Thus with hard work under difficult circumstances the Lord prepares His people for the blessings He desires to impart. As Moroni wrote concerning the work the Jaredites were required to perform: "And the Lord said: Go to work and build, after the manner of barges which ye have hitherto built. And it came to pass that the brother of Jared did go to work, and also his brethren. . . . And it came to pass that the brother of Jared cried unto the Lord, saying: O Lord, I have performed the work which thou hast commanded me, and I have made the barges according as thou hast directed me" (Ether 2:16, 18).

All this was well and good. But suddenly the Jaredites perceived a problem. This voyage was going to last many days (344, as it turned out), and would therefore require more air than the vessels would ordinarily hold. Additionally, the barges were dark, and it was discomforting to think of traveling so long in total darkness. Wishing to be obedient, and yet not knowing how to solve this dilemma, the Brother of Jared again approached the Lord.

Interestingly, the Lord gave a solution for the problem of air, instructing them to make a hole in the top and bottom of each barge, through which air could be replenished when they were above water (see Ether 2:19–21). However, He left the problem of light for the Brother of Jared to solve, though He did more thoroughly explain the parameters. "And the Lord said unto the brother of Jared: What will ye that I should do that ye may have light in your vessels? For behold, ye cannot have windows, for they will be dashed in pieces; neither shall ye take fire with you, for ye shall not go by the light of fire. For behold, ye shall be as a whale in the midst of the sea; for the mountain waves shall dash upon you. Nevertheless, I will bring you up again out of the depths of the sea; for the winds have gone forth out of my mouth, and also the rains and the floods have I sent forth. And behold, I prepare you against these things; for ye cannot cross this great deep save I prepare you against the waves of the sea, and the winds which have gone forth, and the floods which shall come. Therefore what will ye that I should prepare for you that ye may have light when ye are swallowed up in the depths of the sea?" (Ether 2:23–25).

Rather than answering the Lord immediately, the Brother of Jared apparently withdrew and gave the matter some very careful thought. An inspired plan formed in his mind, and he set out immediately to put that plan into action.

"And it came to pass that the brother of Jared, (now the number of the vessels which had been prepared was eight) went forth unto the mount, which they called the mount Shelem, because of its exceeding height, and did molten out of a rock sixteen small stones; and they were white and clear, even as transparent glass; and he did carry them in his hands upon the top of the mount, and cried again unto the Lord" (Ether 3:1).

Mahonri Moriancumer's prayer, recorded in the scriptures, is beautiful. But the beauty lies more in the incredible faith and confidence it manifests, than in the poetic nature of the words themselves. As a result of that faith and confidence in the Lord, the Brother of Jared received the blessing he was seeking. "And it came to pass that when the brother of Jared had said these words, behold, the Lord stretched forth his hand and touched the stones one by one with his finger" (Ether 3:6).

The Nephites experienced a similar thing as they were required to build a ship (see 1 Nephi 17:8), which was to be constructed after the manner of the Lord rather than the manner of man. Adding to the difficulty of this undertaking was the necessity of smelting ore with which to manufacture tools. Yes, the Lord revealed the location of the ore, but the labor was left up to Nephi, who had no choice but to go to work and get it done (see 1 Nephi 17:10–11, 16).

For Nephi the difficulties did not end there, for he had to endure the scorn and wrath of his rebellious brothers, who would not step forth to help. After attempting to teach them, they were desirous of murdering him. Yet at this juncture the Lord stepped forth, as he had done by touching the stones of the Brother of Jared, and filled Nephi with His Spirit to such a degree that Laman and Lemuel could not stand before him, but were shocked by the force of the Lord's power (see 1 Nephi 17:17–55). Therefore they agreed to help with the ship, and the labor was accomplished.

Murmuring Is Unrighteous

But there was another sort of difficulty in passing through the wilderness that affected many travelers. It was the difficulty of emotional trauma and turmoil—the despair of believing that all was hopeless, and that there could be no positive end to the experience.

Both Lehi and Sariah found some of the trials of the wilderness to be almost more than they could bear. They each murmured, repented, and then bore powerful testimonies as to the goodness of God in allowing them to enter their wilderness (see 1 Nephi 5:1–3, 16:20).

Modern Application

For those who would pass through the Lord's wilderness school, it is vital that we develop the faith and confidence in God necessary to go forth with full equanimity of spirit, no matter how difficult what we have been commanded to do seems to be. The Lord will not do for us what we can do for ourselves, but will require labor at our hands. Elder Boyd K. Packer says that even when our gospel roots are firm, "some things won't seem to change a great deal. You will still have to work for what you get. You won't be immune to illness or death. You will still have problems to solve, but you will have great strength, and you will be prompted by the Spirit of the Lord in the solution of these problems" (in Conference Report, October 1962, p. 49).

Thus, even in the labor that is required of us, the Lord will always inspire us, instruct us, grant us the necessary raw materials to accomplish what He has asked, and even step forward with miraculous solutions when we have reached the limits of our abilities.

The Law of Sacrifice

Frequently it requires great sacrifice to accomplish without murmur or complaint the labor God has asked of us. This is the law of sacrifice, and only by living this law to the fullest extent possible will our wilderness experience produce the hoped-for results.

Joseph Smith taught the law of sacrifice in these words: "For a man to lay down his all, his character and reputation, his honor, and applause, his good name among men, his houses, his lands, his brothers and sisters, his wife and children, and even his own life also—counting all things but filth and dross for the excellency of the knowledge of Jesus Christ—requires more than mere belief or supposition that he is doing the will of God; but actual knowledge, realizing that, when these sufferings are ended, he will enter into eternal rest, and be a partaker of the glory of God. . .

"A religion that does not require the sacrifice of all things never has power sufficient to produce the faith necessary [to lead] unto life and salvation; for, from the first existence of man, the faith necessary unto the enjoyment of life and salvation never could be obtained without the sacrifice of all earthly things. It was through this sacrifice, and this only, that God has ordained that men should enjoy eternal life; and it is through the medium of the sacrifice of all earthly things that men do actually know that they are doing the things that are well pleasing in the sight of God. When a man has offered in sacrifice all that he has for the truth's sake, not even withholding his life, and believing before God that he has been called to make this sacrifice because he seeks to do his will, he does know, most assuredly, that God does and will accept his sacrifice and offering, and that he has not, nor will not seek his face in vain. Under these circumstances, then, he can obtain the faith necessary for him to lay hold on eternal life.

"It is vain for persons to fancy to themselves that they are heirs with those, or can be heirs with them, who have offered their all in sacrifice, and by this means obtained faith in God and favor with him so as to obtain eternal life, unless they, in like manner, offer unto him the same sacrifice, and through that offering obtain the knowledge that they are accepted of him. . . . From the days of righteous Abel to the present time, the knowledge that men have that they are accepted in the sight of God is obtained by offering sacrifice. . . .

"Those, then, who make the sacrifice, will have the testimony that their course is pleasing in the sight of God; and those who have this testimony will have faith to lay hold on eternal life; and will be enabled, through faith, to endure unto the end, and receive the crown that is laid up for them that love the appearing of our Lord Jesus Christ. But those who do not make the sacrifice cannot enjoy this faith, because men are dependent upon this sacrifice in order to obtain this faith: therefore, they cannot lay hold upon eternal life, because the revelations of God do not guarantee unto them the authority so to do, and without this guarantee faith could not exist" (*Lectures on Faith,* pp. 58–59).

The Law of the Fast

One of the ways an additional sacrifice can be offered up, when the wilderness traveler feels the need for a particular blessing, is through fasting. This was taught most forcefully by the Savior, whose entire life was proclaimed as a fast. "Is not this the fast that I have chosen? to loose the bands of wickedness, to undo the heavy burdens, and to let the oppressed go free, and that ye break every yoke?" (Isaiah 58:6).

The most common way of fasting is by abstaining from both food and water for a particular period of time—usually 24 hours. This is an effective way of offering up sacrifice, especially when the cautionary instructions of Christ are remembered. "Moreover when ye fast, be not, as the hypocrites, of a sad countenance: for they disfigure their faces, that they may appear unto men to fast. Verily I say unto you, They have their reward. . . . That thou appear not unto men to fast, but unto thy Father which is in secret: and thy Father, which seeth in secret, shall reward thee openly" (Matthew 6:16, 18). We should also remember that in fasting our joy should be full, for "Verily, *this is fasting and prayer, or in other words, rejoicing and prayer"* (D&C 59:14; emphasis mine).

But not always does fasting mean going without food and water for a specific period of time. President Joseph F. Smith explained: "The Lord has instituted the fast on a reasonable and intelligent basis, and none of his works are vain or unwise. His law is perfect in this as in other things. Hence, those who can are required to comply thereto; it is a duty from which they cannot escape; but let it be remembered that the observance of the fast day by abstaining twenty-four hours from food and drink is not an absolute rule, it is no iron-clad law to us, but it is left with the people as a matter of conscience, to exercise wisdom and discretion. Many are subject to weakness, others are delicate in health, and others have nursing babies; of such it should not be required to fast" (*Gospel Doctrine*, 5th ed., p. 244).

Scripturally we read of at least two alternatives to the typical fast used by most of us today. The first is what I call the Daniel fast. "In those days I Daniel was *[fasting] three full weeks. I ate no pleasant bread, neither came flesh nor wine in my mouth, neither did I anoint myself at all, till three whole weeks were fulfilled"* (Daniel 10:2–3; emphasis mine).

The second alternative fast was proclaimed by Moses as a way of preparing the children of Israel to enter into the presence of the Lord. "And [Moses] said unto the people, Be ready against the third day: *come not at your wives"* (Exodus 19:15). In other words, in this case a brief abstinence from sexual intimacy was a way of fasting for purity before the Lord.

Scripturally we learn that righteous fasts are offered up to express joy in the Lord (see Alma 45:1); to obtain humility and faith (see Helaman 3:35); to do missionary work (see Alma 6:6); to obtain the spirit of prophecy and revelation (see Alma 17:3);

and to teach with the power and authority of God (see Alma 17:3).

As Brother McConkie put it: "Fasting, with prayer as its companion, is designed to increase spirituality; to foster a spirit of devotion and love of God; to increase faith in the hearts of men, thus assuring divine favor; to encourage humility and contrition of soul; to aid in the acquirement of righteousness; to teach man his nothingness and dependence upon God; and to hasten those who properly comply with the law of fasting along the path to salvation" (*Mormon Doctrine*, p. 276).

To determine when and how they should fast or offer up other sacrifice, wilderness travelers must obtain the mind and will of God. If through that source they are given directions that seem difficult, or that make little sense; and yet if they are certain beyond any doubt concerning the source of their instructions and inspiration, which certainty comes through strict adherence to all the commandments of God every day that they are in the wilderness, then trust and obedience to the whisperings of the Spirit—the only true options—will bring them great blessings and will draw them ever nearer to the veil behind which waits the Lord Jesus Christ.

CHAPTER

16

Discovering
Our Basic Weakness

When the children of Israel first left Egypt, the Lord led them into what the scripture calls the wilderness of Sin (see Exodus 16:1). There, immediately following their miraculous deliverance from Pharaoh, they turned against Moses and the Lord and began to murmur (see Exodus 16:2). In other words, they came face to face with their own carnal natures.

After their miraculous deliverance from the wicked at the tower of Babel, and the Lord's leading them through the wilderness, the Jaredites camped in a lovely valley they called Moriancumer, where they rested for a time—three years, in fact. And there the Brother of Jared, after he had been chastised for three hours by the Lord for not remembering to call on His name, came face to face with his own natural man.

Both of these groups of wilderness travelers had discovered—to their sorrow—that despite their desires to remain free from sin, they were continually beset by it. Thus they seemed to need an inordinate amount of time on their knees repenting, and even more time on their feet as they went about their daily tasks, sometimes castigating themselves and feeling godly sorrow that they were such weak servants of the Lord. Their guilt was made worse by their knowledge of the incredible blessings the Lord had been pouring out upon them, blessings of knowledge and understanding, of spiritual communication, of priesthood power. All these they had probably always assumed were reserved for the totally righteous, and not the spiritual flunkies they now felt themselves to be.

Interestingly, that is exactly the state the great Nephi had reached in his own wilderness of afflictions when he exclaimed: "Notwithstanding the great goodness of the Lord, in showing me his great and marvelous works, my heart exclaimeth: O wretched man that I am! Yea, my heart sorroweth because of my flesh; my soul grieveth because of mine iniquities. I am encompassed about, because of the temptations and the sins which do so easily beset me. And when I desire to rejoice, my heart groaneth because of my sins; nevertheless, I know in whom I have trusted. My God hath been my support; he hath led me through mine afflictions in the wilderness; and he hath preserved me upon the waters of the great deep. He hath filled me with his love, even unto the consuming of my flesh [Nephi's baptism of fire]. He hath confounded mine enemies, unto the causing of them to quake before me. Behold, he hath heard my cry by day, and he hath given me knowledge by visions in the nighttime. And by day have I waxed bold in mighty prayer before him; yea, my voice have I sent up on high; and angels came down and ministered unto me. And upon the wings of his Spirit hath my body been carried away upon exceedingly high mountains. And mine eyes have beheld great things, yea, even too great for man; therefore I was bidden that I should not write them.

"O then, if I have seen so great things, if the Lord in his condescension unto the children of men hath visited men in so much mercy, why should my heart weep and my soul linger in the valley of sorrow, and my flesh waste away, and my strength slacken, because of mine afflictions? And why should I yield to sin, because of my flesh? Yea, why should I give way to temptations, that the evil one have place in my heart to destroy my peace and afflict my soul? Why am I angry because of mine enemy?" (2 Nephi 4:17–27).

Nephi asked some powerful questions, likely parallelling the questions other wilderness sojourners have always been plagued with. Why do we continue to sin, even when we know better?

And we can be thankful that there are answers that allow hope to replace the despair we frequently feel.

Modern Application

To Moroni the Lord declared: "If men come unto me I will show unto them their weakness. I give unto men weakness that they may be humble" (Ether 12:27). Note that the word "weakness" is not plural here and so cannot refer to the multitude of sins we all struggle with. Being singular, it must refer to the aspect of mortality that is also called "the natural man" (see 1 Corinthians 2:14; Mosiah 3:19; Alma 26:21; D&C 67:12) or our "carnal nature" (see D&C 67:12; Mosiah 16:5; Alma 42:10).

Because of this mortal weakness, we all have an inherent tendency to commit sin. That tendency, according to what the Lord told Moroni, was intentionally "given" to us by God. How was it given? Through genetic traits, conditions under which we are raised, the tormentings of Satan and his evil horde, circumstances we are forced to live through, and so forth. And why was it given? To help keep us humble, penitent, and filled with faith.

Tendencies to Personal Sin Limited

But more can be learned about the God-given weakness called the natural man that we all have. If we examine our own behavior closely and prayerfully, we will discover that our weakness is composed of various tendencies to sin. Moreover, those tendencies do not usually entice us to wickedness in every area. Rather, they are more limited, so that the temptations we experience, as well as the sins we commit, generally fall into two or three areas rather than the hundreds that might be possible. For example, while one of us may struggle with alcohol or tobacco, another (who is not troubled with those temptations at all) may do battle daily with dishonesty and lust. Another may struggle with feelings of self-doubt; a fourth may be required to subdue anger, violence, and other abuse; and a fifth must diligently labor to overcome homosexual tendencies.

Having such tendencies does not mean we are evil. Rather, evil occurs as we submit to them and therefore commit sin (see Mosiah 3:19). Remember, God has given us these carnal or natural tendencies so that, by striving to rise above them according to "the enticings of the Holy Spirit," we become humble, penitent, and filled with faith in Christ. And since we as wilderness travelers seek to develop those attributes and to overcome our own "natural man," we must come to a thorough understanding of our personal weakness. By understanding that weakness, we will be better armed to completely overcome it as well as the sins it begets—the sins we battle so constantly.

The Grace of Christ

So, how do we come to understand our weakness and put it behind us? In the same way we learned of all our sins before we had been born again—by going before God and asking for it to be made known in all its ramifications and details. That is why the Lord said, "If men come unto me I will show unto them their weakness." He will! And there is eternal hope in that, for the Lord continues: "My grace is sufficient for all men that humble themselves before me; for if they humble themselves before me, and have faith in me, *then will I make weak things become strong unto them.* Behold, I will show unto the Gentiles their weakness and I will show unto them that faith, hope and charity bringeth unto me—the fountain of all righteousness" (Ether 12:27–28; emphasis mine).

In other words, we must continue our quest to find Christ. Having a knowledge of these things, Nephi concluded his lament by exclaiming: "Awake, my soul! No longer droop in sin. Rejoice, O my heart, and give place no more for the enemy of my soul. Do not anger again because of mine enemies. Do not slacken my strength because of mine afflictions. Rejoice, O my heart, and cry unto the Lord, and say: O Lord, I will praise thee forever; yea, my soul will rejoice in thee, my God, and the rock of my salvation. O Lord, wilt thou redeem my soul? Wilt thou deliver me out of the hands of mine enemies? Wilt thou make me that I may shake at the appearance of sin? May the gates of hell be shut continually before me, because that my heart is broken and my spirit is contrite! O Lord, wilt thou not shut the gates of thy righteousness before me, that I may walk in the path of the low valley, that I may be strict in the plain road! O Lord, wilt thou encircle me around in the robe of thy righteousness! O Lord, wilt thou make a way for mine escape before mine enemies! Wilt thou make my path straight before me! Wilt thou not place a stumbling block in my way—but that thou wouldst clear my way before me, and hedge not up my way, but the ways of mine enemy.

"O Lord, I have trusted in thee, and I will trust in thee forever. I will not put my trust in the arm of flesh; for I know that cursed is he that putteth his trust in the arm of flesh. Yea, cursed is he that putteth his trust in man or maketh flesh his arm. Yea, I know that God will give liberally to him that asketh. Yea, my God will give me, if I ask not amiss; therefore I will lift up my voice unto thee; yea, I will cry unto thee, my God, the rock of my righteousness. Behold, my voice shall forever ascend up unto thee, my rock and mine everlasting God. Amen" (2 Nephi 4:28–35).

CHAPTER

17

The Lord Takes Care
of All Worldly Needs

Ancient wilderness travelers universally discovered that, if they sincerely did their best to be obedient, the Lord would take care of all their worldly needs. As Abraham declared: "[We] dwelt in tents as we came on our way; *therefore, eternity was our covering and our rock and our salvation,* as we journeyed from Haran by the way of Jershon, to come to the land of Canaan" (Abraham 2:15–16; emphasis mine).

To the children of Israel, who were in a barren desert, the Lord revealed His power in a miraculous manner, giving them meat in the form of quail and then a daily portion of manna. That miracle continued, week in and week out, for forty long years until they could finally provide for themselves (see Exodus 16:11–26).

The Nephites were treated differently, being allowed to gather provisions from the land and to hunt for their own food: "We did take our bows and our arrows, and go forth into the wilderness to slay food for our families. . . . We did travel for the space of many days, slaying food by the way, with our bows and our arrows and our stones and our slings" (1 Nephi 16:14–15).

Then Nephi broke his bow, which must have seemed a horrible setback to the people. Thus the Nephites learned that even in the Lord's wilderness there are setbacks and opposition. But through faith and diligence, even these will be made into blessings that are part of the true wilderness experience.

Nephi relates: "We did return without food to our families, and being much fatigued, because of their journeying, they did suffer much for the want of food. . . . And it came to pass that I, Nephi, did make out of wood a bow, and out of a straight stick, an arrow; wherefore, I did arm myself with a bow and an arrow, with a sling and with stones. And I said unto my father: Whither shall I go to obtain food? And it came to pass that he did inquire of the Lord, for they had humbled themselves because of my words; for I did say many things unto them in the energy of my soul. And it came to pass that the voice of the Lord came unto my father; and he was truly chastened because of his murmuring against the Lord, insomuch that he was brought down into the depths of sorrow. . . .

"And it came to pass that I, Nephi, did go forth up into the top of the mountain, according to the directions which were given upon the ball. And it came to pass that I did slay wild beasts, insomuch that I did obtain food for our families" (1 Nephi 16:19, 23–25, 30–31).

As with the children of Israel, miracles were performed for the Nephites. The Nephites were made stronger than normal, and their meat was sweetened so that it could be eaten raw. "And thus we see," Nephi summarizes, "that . . . if it so be that the children of men keep the commandments of God he doth nourish them, and strengthen them, and provide means whereby they can accomplish the thing which he has commanded them; wherefore, he did provide means for us while we did sojourn in the wilderness" (see 1 Nephi 17:3; see also vv. 2, 12–13).

Modern Application

As pupils in the Lord's wilderness school, if we allow our minds to be preoccupied with worry about our temporal needs, then we only prolong the trials of our wilderness experience. As scriptural examples amply testify, God is eager to help provide exactly what we need to survive His wilderness. But the key is sufficiency, not excess. While Elijah was in the wilderness, the Lord commanded him: "Thou shalt drink of the brook; and I have commanded the ravens to feed thee there. So [Elijah] went and did according unto the word of the Lord: for he went and dwelt by the brook Cherith, that is before Jordan. And the ravens brought him bread and flesh in the morning, and bread and flesh in the evening; and he drank of the brook" (1 Kings 17:3–6).

Those may not have been the kinds of meals Elijah would have chosen, yet they seem to have been sufficient, and they were granted in a miraculous manner. After the brook dried up, the Lord commanded Elijah to depart: "Get thee to Zarephath, which belongeth to Zidon, and dwell there: behold, I have commanded a widow woman there to sustain thee. So he arose and went to Zarephath. And when he came to the gate of the city, behold, the widow woman was there gathering of sticks: and he called to her, and said, Fetch me, I pray thee, a little water in a vessel, that I may drink. And as she was going to fetch it, he called to her, and said, Bring me, I pray thee, a morsel of bread in thine hand.

"And she said, As the Lord thy God liveth, I have not a

cake, but an handful of meal in a barrel, and a little oil in a cruse: and, behold, I am gathering two sticks, that I may go in and dress it for me and my son, that we may eat it, and die.

"And Elijah said unto her, Fear not; go and do as thou hast said: but make me thereof a little cake first, and bring it unto me, and after make for thee and for thy son. For thus saith the Lord God of Israel, The barrel of meal shall not waste, neither shall the cruse of oil fail, until the day that the Lord sendeth rain upon the earth. And she went and did according to the saying of Elijah: and she, and he, and her house, did eat many days. And the barrel of meal wasted not, neither did the cruse of oil fail, according to the word of the Lord, which he spake by Elijah" (1 Kings 17:9–16).

As the widow learned, while in the wilderness we will always have sufficient but usually not much more.

Additionally, often that sufficient amount will not come until the last possible moment, which might be called "the law of the true last moment." Why? Because the Lord is not in the business of feeding us and making us wealthy. Rather, He is in the business of teaching us, stretching us, purifying us, and bringing us to the point where our trust in Him is absolute. Only then can we hope to finish His wilderness course with a passing grade.

Thus, in the wilderness, our temporal needs are strictly incidental to our spiritual needs. Like the widow who fed Elijah, our temporal needs will be met only after our faith has been tried sufficiently for spiritual growth to have occurred. And that seems to occur best when circumstances come down to the last possible minute—not our minute but the Lord's—when no meal can possibly be left in the barrel. Hence it is called the law of the *true* last minute.

18

Coming to
the Land Bountiful

After Lehi and his family had been journeying in the wilderness for eight years, the Lord gave them a temporary reprieve from their daily toil and struggles. This reprieve they called the Land Bountiful.

As Nephi records: "We did come to the land which we called Bountiful, because of its much fruit and also wild honey; and all these things were prepared of the Lord that we might not perish. And we beheld the sea, which we called Irreantum, which, being interpreted, is many waters. And it came to pass that we did pitch our tents by the seashore; and notwithstanding we had suffered many afflictions and much difficulty, yea, even so much that we cannot write them all, we were exceedingly rejoiced when we came to the seashore; and we called the place Bountiful, because of its much fruit" (1 Nephi 17:5–6).

Abraham was also granted reprieves—two, in fact—from the terrible famine that pervaded his wilderness experience. He first went to Haran, where "the famine abated" (Abraham 2:4–5; emphasis mine). Later he left Haran and made his way toward the land of Egypt, for though the famine was everywhere else, in Egypt there was plenty, and Abraham prospered there (see Abraham 2:21).

The Jaredites were also led to a "land Bountiful," which they called Moriancumer, after Jared's brother, where they tarried and rested for four years, recouping their strength (see Ether 2:13).

Modern Application

Modern wilderness travelers are also granted occasional periods of rest—lands of Bountiful or Moriancumer where the intensity of the wilderness schooling will be eased. During those times, we are expected to prepare for further wilderness experiences by taking advantage of all the Lord gives us. We are also expected, as were Nephi and the Brother of Jared, to use that time of respite to draw ever nearer to the Lord through fasting and mighty prayer.

CHAPTER

19

The Ministry of Angels

Adam's quest to obtain messengers, once he had entered the lone and dreary world of his wilderness experience, is no idle tale. Beginning with him, all who entered the Lord's wilderness anciently, if they wished to understand the gospel thoroughly, sought for such visitations. And if they remained faithful in gospel study, strict obedience, mighty prayer, and the proper attitude during both the hard times and the Bountifuls, they grew stronger in the Spirit and closer to the Lord until they were blessed with the ministering of angels. Thus, after Adam's profound personal anguish and diligent prayer, an angel finally appeared to him (can his relief even be imagined?) and instructed him in the law of sacrifice and obedience (see Moses 5:6–7). Similarly, an angel delivered Abraham from the sacrificial altar in Ur of the Chaldees (see Abraham 1:15). And Jacob obtained his endowment and his new name (Israel) from an angel (see Genesis 32:24–30).

One of the most singular aspects of the Book of Mormon is

its consistent testimony of the ministry of angels to mortals. In 1 Nephi we learn that an angel visited Nephi and his brothers while they hid in the cavity of a rock (see 1 Nephi 3:29–30). Moreover, an angel as well as the premortal Christ conducted Nephi through his great vision of the history of the world (see 1 Nephi 11–14). King Benjamin was given the words of his final address to his people by an angel of God (see Mosiah 3:2–27), Amulek saw an angel who told him of Alma's coming (see Alma 10:7), Nephi the son of Helaman received the ministrations of angels daily (see 3 Nephi 7:18), and many of King Lamoni's people saw angels (see Alma 19:34).

Alma, Ammon, Aaron, Omner, and Himni were warned of their impending destruction by an angel (see Mosiah 27:11–16). Later the same angel appeared to Alma, complimented him on the righteousness of his repentance, and gave him further instructions about his missionary work (see Alma 8:15). No doubt because of his own experiences, Alma spoke frequently of angels and their missions, saying: "The voice of the Lord, by the mouth of angels, doth declare [the coming of Christ] unto all nations; yea, doth declare it, that they may have glad tidings of great joy; yea, and he doth sound these glad tidings among all his people, yea, even to them that are scattered abroad upon the face of the earth; wherefore [angels] have come unto us. . . . For behold, angels are declaring it unto many at this time in our land; and this is for the purpose of preparing the hearts of the children of men to receive his word at the time of his coming in his glory. And now we only wait to hear the joyful news declared unto us by the mouth of angels, of his coming; . . . and it shall be made known unto just and holy men, by the mouth of angels, at the time of his coming, that the words of our fathers may be fulfilled" (Alma 13:22, 24–26).

"And now, he imparteth his word by angels unto men, yea,

not only men but women also. Now this is not all; little children do have words given unto them many times, which confound the wise and the learned" (Alma 32:23). "Is it not as easy at this time for the Lord to send his angel to declare these glad tidings unto us as unto our children, or as after the time of his coming?" (Alma 39:19). And "by the ministering of angels," Moroni wrote, "and by every word which proceeded forth out of the mouth of God, men began to exercise faith in Christ; and thus by faith, they did lay hold upon every good thing" (Moroni 7:25).

In fact, the words *angel* and *angels* appear 138 times in the Book of Mormon, attesting to the importance the Nephite prophets placed upon angelic ministrations.

Identity of Angels

But who exactly are these angels, and is there a particular order to both them and their ministry? While wrapped in vision with Sidney Rigdon, Joseph Smith declared: "We saw the glory of the celestial, which excels in all things—where God, even the Father, reigns upon his throne forever and ever. . . . They who dwell in his presence are the church of the Firstborn; and they see as they are seen, and know as they are known, having received of his fulness and of his grace; and he makes them equal in power, and in might, and in dominion" (D&C 76:92, 94–95).

The Apostle Paul declared to those Hebrews who had progressed spiritually: "Ye are come unto mount [Z]ion, and unto the city of the living God, the heavenly Jerusalem, and to an innumerable company of angels, to the general assembly and church of the firstborn, which are written in heaven, and to God the Judge of all, and to the spirits of just men made perfect, and to Jesus the mediator of the new covenant" (Hebrews 12:22–24). From these scriptural references we see that angels are members of the heavenly Church of Jesus Christ, which is referred to scripturally as the Church of the Firstborn.

Spiritual Progression in the Hereafter

Earlier we discussed seven levels of spiritual progression in mortality, most of which are part of the earthly Church. There also appear to be various levels in the heavenly Church. These were recognized by President John Taylor when he taught that there were different grades of angels (see *Gospel Kingdom*, p. 31). These levels might look like this:

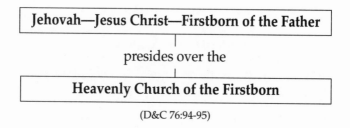

Jehovah—Jesus Christ—Firstborn of the Father

presides over the

Heavenly Church of the Firstborn

(D&C 76:94-95)

Three classes of beings make up this heavenly church. These are:

Resurrected Beings	Spirits of Just Individuals made Perfect	Translated Beings
(D&C 129:1)	(D&C 129:3)	(D&C 7:6)

A fourth class of spirit beings seems to be an integral but peripheral part of the heavenly church. This group is called the

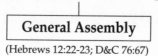

General Assembly

(Hebrews 12:22-23; D&C 76:67)

168

All these beings can be referred to as angels, for all are allowed to interact with mortals and to have communion with members of the mortal church—according to their stewardships. Therefore, under the direction of Christ and by the power of the Holy Ghost, they encourage members of the mortal Church and give the Lord's direction to it.

Resurrected Beings

Resurrected beings seem to be the highest order of beings who make up the heavenly Church of the Firstborn. The Lord has said that these are true angels, resurrected personages who have received their formerly mortal bodies of flesh and bone, just as Jesus did in His resurrection (see D&C 129:1).

Spirits of the Just Who Are Made Perfect

The second order of beings in the heavenly Church is the spirits of the just who are made perfect, they who are not resurrected but inherit the same glory (see D&C 129:1, 3). While resurrected beings can appear as glorious beings or as normal individuals, the spirits of the just who are made perfect can appear only in their glory (see D&C 129:6).

Interestingly, the scriptures make it quite clear that these two kinds of heavenly beings have a specific mission among mortals: to bring messages and blessings *to* them. As D&C 129:4 says: "When a messenger comes saying he has a message from God," and so forth. They are carriers of information.

Always these messages will be delivered through the power of the Holy Ghost and will be the words of Christ. As the prophet Nephi declared: "Angels speak by the power of the Holy Ghost; wherefore, they speak the words of Christ" (2 Nephi 32:3).

Translated Beings

The third group of heavenly beings who are part of the heavenly Church are known as translated beings. As the Lord declared to the Prophet Joseph: "[John the Revelator] has undertaken a greater work; *therefore I will make him as flaming fire and a ministering angel;* he shall minister for those who shall be heirs of salvation who dwell on the earth" (D&C 7:6; emphasis mine).

A careful reading of this verse indicates that at least one mission of translated beings is to minister *for* those mortals who will be heirs of salvation—those who have experienced the mighty change and are diligently striving to bring themselves back into the presence of Christ. In other words, translated beings can interact with and do things for righteous mortals, while angels seem to be more limited in this aspect of their eternal service. Thus translated beings can mingle with righteous mortals and work beside them doing temporal things, while angels and justified spirits usually do not.

General Assembly

Finally, there is a fourth group of spirit beings who are associated with the Church of the Firstborn—the general assembly. The scriptures state: "Ye are come unto mount [Z]ion, and unto the city of the living God, the heavenly Jerusalem, and to an innumerable company of angels, to the general assembly and church of the firstborn, which are written in heaven, and to God the Judge of all, and to the spirits of just men made perfect" (Hebrews 12:22–23). And, "These are they who have come to an innumerable company of angels, to the general assembly and church of Enoch, and of the Firstborn" (D&C 76:67).

Included with but kept separate from the Church of the

Firstborn, these righteous spirit beings in the general assembly have obtained paradise, where they are allowed to rest from the temptations of Satan and the toils and cares of the world while they continue their eternal progression. In this capacity they minister as they are assigned to their own mortal families and loved ones.

These, as well as the ministrations of resurrected beings, translated beings, and the spirits of the just who have been made perfect, all of them working through the power of the Holy Ghost, are what comprise the ministering of angels.

Modern Application

All who enter the Lord's school of the wilderness may be given access by the Lord, if they desire it, to the general assembly and Church of the Firstborn by being allowed to mingle with them.

Concerning this, Joseph Smith said on August 13, 1843: "You have come to an innumerable company of angels [and] to the general assembly and church of the first born. And for [what] were [you] brought thus far? I answer that [you] came to these personages to learn of the things of God and to hear revealed through them the order and glory of the kingdoms of God" (*Words,* p. 240; punctuation standardized).

The Lord states: "The power and authority of the higher, or Melchizedek Priesthood, is to hold the keys of all the spiritual blessings of the church—to have the privilege of receiving the mysteries of the kingdom of heaven, to have the heavens opened unto [you], to commune with the general assembly and church of the Firstborn, and to enjoy the communion and presence of God the Father, and Jesus the mediator of the new covenant. The power and authority of the lesser, or Aaronic Priesthood, is to hold the keys of the ministering of angels" (D&C 107:18–20).

171

Because the ministering of angels requires a lesser amount of power or spiritual preparation than does communing with God and Christ, it follows that angels will come first in the spiritual growth of the wilderness traveler. Thus the Lord has stated: "Ye are not able to abide the presence of God now, neither the ministering of angels; wherefore, continue in patience until ye are perfected" (D&C 67:13). He has also said: "Marvel not at these things, for ye are not yet pure; ye can not yet bear my glory; but ye shall behold it if ye are faithful in keeping all my words that I have given you, from the days of Adam to Abraham, from Abraham to Moses, from Moses to Jesus and his apostles, and from Jesus and his apostles to Joseph Smith, whom I did call upon by mine angels, my ministering servants, and by mine own voice out of the heavens, to bring forth my work" (D&C 136:37).

The Spirits of Elias and Elijah

On Sunday, March 10, 1844, Joseph Smith stood in the Nauvoo Temple and gave an address in which he stated: "The Spirit of Elias is first, Elijah second, and Messiah last. Elias is a forerunner to prepare the way, and the spirit and power of Elijah is to come after, holding the keys of power, building the temple to the capstone, placing the seals of the Melchizedek Priesthood upon the house of Israel and making all things ready. Then Messiah . . . [which] is all power in Heaven and in Earth . . . comes to his temple, which is last of all" (*Words,* pp. 331–32, 336; spelling and punctuation standardized).

While these words have obvious reference to the coming of Moses, Elias, Elijah, and then the Savior to Joseph Smith and Oliver Cowdery in the Kirtland Temple on April 3, 1836, Joseph may also have meant that sequence of heavenly visitations to have a more personal application. In that context, worthy people who have been born again and who have had the mighty change would progress into and through the wilderness, learning divine knowledge through the administrations of selected messengers, whether they were aware of them or not. Each of these messengers would act as an Elias or forerunner until the students of the Lord's school were worthy and ready to receive the ministrations or blessings restored by Elijah. These can be received in their fulness only by making one's calling and election sure. And all this, of course, is preparatory to receiving the Messiah as Second Comforter and being given a fulness of authority over one's individual stewardship by Him.

But back to Elias, or angelic messengers. Brigham Young declared: "What is the sum of the whole of the teachings of Him who has created [the universe]? . . . Simply this—Son, daughter, live before me, so that I can come and visit you; order your lives with that propriety, that I will not be disgraced to come and abide with you for a season; or, when I send my angels or my minister the Holy Ghost to reveal my mind and will to you, or to bless you with abiding comfort, that they may not be disgraced in your society.

"I say, all the revelations of God teach simply this—Son, daughter, you are the workmanship of mine hands: walk and live before me in righteousness; let your conversation be chaste; let your daily deportment be according to my law; let your dealings one with another be in justice and equity; let my character be sacred in your mouth, and do not profane my holy name and trample upon mine authority; do not despise any of my sayings, for I will not be disgraced. *I wish to send one of my servants to visit you.* What for? That you may see and know as others have—that you may see as you are seen—that you may understand those principles pertaining more particularly to the kingdom you are in. You have descended below all things. I

173

have, in my wisdom, reduced you; I have caused that you should drink of the dregs of the bitter cup. I have placed you in the depths of ignorance, and have surrounded you with weakness, to prove you. I have subjected you to all misery, . . . and darkness, and every species of unbelief and wickedness reign, to prove you, that you may understand and know the good from the evil, and be capable of judging between these with a righteous judgment.

"I have caused all this to be done; and now, son and daughter, the *inhabitants* of the *whole earth* that have lived from the days of Adam until now, the first and the last,—the grand aim of all that I, the Lord, have revealed is to instruct you to live so that I can come and visit you, *or send my angels, that they can enter into your habitations, walk and converse with you, and they not be disgraced.* By so doing, you shall be made partakers of all knowledge and wisdom, power and glory that the sanctified, or glorified beings enjoy. And this is, first of all, what the Lord wishes of the people" (*Journal of Discourses*, 6:284–85; emphasis mine).

John Taylor added concerning the mission of angels: "The angels are our watchmen, for Satan said to Jesus: 'He shall give his angels charge concerning thee: and in their hands they shall bear thee up, lest at any time thou dash thy foot against a stone' (Matthew 4:6). It would seem from a careful perusal of the scriptures that the angels, while God has saints upon the earth, stay in this lower world to ward off evil: for the prophet Isaiah has left this testimony on the subject" (see Isaiah 63:7–9).

"The angels that have gone forth at sundry times to execute the decrees of God, fully substantiate this fact: Abraham, Hagar, Jacob, Balaam, Joshua, Gideon, together with the enemies of the Lord, are the witnesses who knew the power and offices of angels on earth.

"But lest we take up too much time on the resurrected bodies, who go and come at the bidding of him who was, and is, and is to come, we will change the theme to the thoughts and witnesses of the heart. The action of the angels, or messengers of God, upon our minds, so that the heart can conceive things past, present, and to come, and revelations from the eternal world, is, among a majority of mankind, a greater mystery than all the secrets of philosophy, literature, superstition, and bigotry, put together. Though some men try to deny it, and some try to explain away the meaning, still there is so much testimony in the Bible, and among a respectable portion of the world, that one might as well undertake to throw the water out of this world into the moon with a teaspoon, as to do away with the supervision of angels upon the human mind. . . . *But, without going into a particular detail of the offices and duties of the different grades of angels,* let us close by saying that the angels gather the elect, and pluck out all that offends. They are the police of heaven and report whatever transpires on earth, and carry the petitions and supplications of men, women, and children to the mansions of remembrance, where they are kept as tokens of obedience by the sanctified, in 'golden vials' labelled 'the prayers of the saints'" (*Gospel Kingdom,* p. 31; emphasis mine).

A clear recognition of the labor of angels, as well as a deepening understanding of the mysteries of Godliness as granted through personal revelation, makes the ministering of angels much easier to comprehend and accept.

Again, all who enter today into the Lord's wilderness, if they remain faithful in gospel study, strict obedience, mighty prayer, and the proper attitude during both the deserts and the Bountifuls, grow stronger and stronger in the Spirit through the ministering of our fellow-servants the angels and thus closer and closer to the Lord and to a perfect understanding of His ways.

A Means of
Daily Revelation Is Given

In His mercy the Lord provided His ancient wilderness travelers with miraculous means of direct communication with Him, which gave them necessary day-to-day information about how to survive His schooling. For example: "The Lord commanded [the Jaredites] that they should go forth into the wilderness, yea, into that quarter where there never had man been. And it came to pass that the Lord did go before them, and did talk with them as he stood in a cloud, and gave directions whither they should travel" (Ether 2:5).

For Abraham, the Lord provided revelatory instruments whose names have become quite famous in the generations since: "I, Abraham, had the Urim and Thummim, which the Lord my God had given unto me, in Ur of the Chaldees" (Abraham 3:1).

At first, Lehi received personal revelation through dreams and open visions. But as his wilderness experience progressed, the Lord gave Lehi and his family a tool through which they could obtain daily revelation about how to survive as they journeyed forward: "The voice of the Lord spake unto my father by night, and commanded him that on the morrow he should take his journey into the wilderness. And it came to pass that as my father arose in the morning, and went forth to the tent door, to his great astonishment he beheld upon the ground a round ball of curious workmanship; and it was of fine brass. And within the ball were two spindles; and the one pointed the way whither we should go into the wilderness" (1 Nephi 16:9–10).

"And it came to pass that the voice of the Lord said unto him: Look upon the ball, and behold the things which are written. And it came to pass that when my father beheld the things which were written upon the ball, he did fear and tremble exceedingly, and also my brethren and the sons of Ishmael and our wives. And it came to pass that I, Nephi, beheld the pointers which were in the ball, that they did work according to the faith and diligence and heed which we did give unto them. And there was also written upon them a new writing, which was plain to be read, which did give us understanding concerning the ways of the Lord; and it was written and changed from time to time, according to the faith and diligence which we gave unto it. And thus we see that by small means the Lord can bring about great things" (1 Nephi 16:26–29).

These examples indicate that the Lord had no one single way of helping his ancient people receive revelation. Whatever worked best for each group was the method He apparently chose to use.

The Scriptures Must Be Studied Dutifully and Prayerfully

Today, part of a successful journey through God's wilderness is accomplished through a constant, careful, and prayerful study of the scriptures. If that is neglected, the wilderness experience will be prolonged.

Nephi records: "Thus far I and my father had kept the commandments wherewith the Lord had commanded us. And we had obtained the records which the Lord had commanded us, and searched them and found that they were desirable; yea, even of great worth unto us, insomuch that we could preserve the commandments of the Lord unto our children. Wherefore, it was wisdom in the Lord that we should carry them with us, as we journeyed in the wilderness towards the land of promise" (1 Nephi 5:20–22).

Abraham was also given the scriptures prior to his journeying into the wilderness, so that he, too, might become familiar with them. By diligent study, therefore, he was enabled to more easily recognize the voice of the Lord. "The records of the fathers, even the patriarchs, concerning the right of Priesthood, the Lord my God preserved in mine own hands; therefore a knowledge of the beginning of the creation, and also of the planets, and of the stars, as they were made known unto the fathers, have I kept even unto this day, and I shall endeavor to write some of these things upon this record, for the benefit of my posterity that shall come after me" (Abraham 1:31).

Brigham Remembers Joseph

For the Lord's modern wilderness travelers, an occasional cursory examination of the scriptures is not sufficient. After all, the scriptures are His voice, which we have been commanded to hearken to and obey. How can we do either if we are not familiar with what He has said? Also, the Holy Ghost is by now enlightening the mind of the wilderness traveler about the meaning of the scriptures in his or her own life. Earlier Joseph Smith was quoted describing how the Holy Ghost enlightened his mind so that the scriptures, including their most mysterious passages, were made plain and simple (see Joseph Smith–History 1:74).

Adding to our information about how this opening of scriptural knowledge was used by Joseph Smith, Brigham Young said: "What is the nature and beauty of Joseph's mission? You know that I am one of his Apostles. When I first heard him preach, he brought heaven and earth together; and all the priests of the day could not tell me anything correct about heaven, hell, God, angels, or devils; they were as blind as Egyptian darkness. When I saw Joseph Smith, he took heaven, figuratively speaking, and brought it down to earth; and he took the earth, brought it up, and opened up, in plainness and simplicity, the things of God; and that is the beauty of his mission. . . . Did not Joseph do the same to your understandings? Would he not take the Scriptures and make them so plain and simple that everybody could understand? Every person says, 'Yes'" (*Journal of Discourses*, 5:332).

Truly the things of God are known only by the power of the Spirit of God (see 1 Corinthians 2). Therefore, the scriptures must become a daily source of inspiration and instruction. In fact, wilderness pilgrims ought to go before the Lord at least daily, seeking direction on where and what to study in the scriptures, simply to obtain His mind and will concerning them for that particular day.

But There Is More

To us who travel in the Lord's wilderness today, the Lord is just as anxious to communicate directions as he was anciently. Therefore we are granted the privilege of receiving personal revelation from him, according to our faith and preparations in righteousness.

Praying for Answers

And how do we receive personal revelation from the Lord?
By learning to open a two-way line of communication with
heaven. To survive the wilderness we must be able to pray, ask
direct questions, and obtain specific, sometimes even immediate, answers. According to President Harold B. Lee: "The fundamental and soul-satisfying step in our eternal quest is to
come in a day when each does know, for himself, that God
answers his prayers. This will come only after 'our soul
hungers,' and after mighty prayer and supplication" (Harold B.
Lee, in Conference Report, April 1969, p. 133). As Joseph Smith
said: "The only way to obtain truth and wisdom, is not to ask it
from books, but to go to God in prayer and obtain divine teaching" (*Words,* p. 77). That is receiving personal revelation.

Revelation—the Order in Heaven

Again according to Joseph Smith: "All men are liars who
say they are of the true Church without the revelations of Jesus
Christ and the priesthood of Melchizedek, which is after the
order of the Son of God. It is in the order of heavenly things that
God should always send [revelations] into the world"
(*Discourses of the Prophet Joseph Smith,* edited by Alma P. Burton
[Salt Lake City, Deseret Book Company, 1965], p. 52.) At another
time Joseph Smith declared: "If any man has the testimony of
Jesus has he not the spirit of prophecy? And if he has the spirit
of prophecy I ask is he not a prophet? And if a prophet he can
receive revelation. Any man that does not receive revelation for
himself must be damned, for the testimony of Jesus is the spirit
of prophecy. For Christ says, ask and you shall receive. And if
he happens to receive anything, I ask, will it not be a revelation?" (*Words,* p. 230; spelling and punctuation standardized).

Because there is such order in all heavenly things (see D&C 129:7; 132:8), there must also be order in the process of praying and of obtaining answers to prayer. In heaven there are laws, rules, regulations, order! Upon these things is our Father's heavenly society based. He abides totally by order, and as we come to learn and follow that same order, we draw closer and closer to the society of God, until finally we are one with Him. As He so eloquently declared to Joseph Smith nearly a hundred and fifty years ago: "All who will have a blessing at my hands shall abide the law which was appointed for that blessing, and the conditions thereof, as were instituted from before the foundation of the world" (D&C 132:5).

Thus, if we truly want to communicate with God through prayer, we have only to abide the eternal laws appointed to prayer, and the conditions thereof, and through the power of the Holy Ghost we will be allowed to receive personal revelation (see D&C 121:46).

Joseph Smith said: "The Lord cannot always be known by the thunder of His voice, by the display of His glory, or by the manifestation of His power, and those that are the most anxious to see these things, are the least prepared to meet them. . . . We would say to the brethren, seek to know God in your closets, call upon him in the fields. Follow the directions of the Book of Mormon, and pray over, and for your families, your cattle, your flocks, your herds, your corn, and all things that you possess; ask the blessing of God upon all your labors, and everything that you engage in. Be virtuous and pure; be men of integrity and truth; keep the commandments of God; and then you will be able more perfectly to understand the difference between right and wrong—between the things of God and the things of men; and your path will be like that of the just, which shineth brighter and brighter unto the perfect day" (*Teachings*, p. 247).

In *Spiritual Survival in the Last Days,* my brother and I listed eight reasons why we should pray over all things and at all times. These reasons apply equally to us as we travail in the Lord's wilderness:

1. Constant praying invokes 'the law of asking.' Simply by asking for divine assistance and guidance, we invoke the heavenly law that allows God to respond openly to our needs (see 3 Nephi 14:7–8). Jesus said: "Ask, and it shall be given unto you; seek, and ye shall find; knock, and it shall be opened unto you. For everyone that asketh, receiveth; and he that seeketh, findeth; and to him that knocketh, it shall be opened" (3 Nephi 14:7–8). To obtain any specific blessing from God, we must initiate the process. We ask—He gives. We seek—He helps us find. We knock—He opens unto us. Once we exercise faith sufficient to initiate the action (pray—ask), then by eternal law God is free to respond to our request (answer). Simple and obvious but true.

2. Constant praying invokes 'the law of consecrated performances.' Simply by humbling ourselves enough to address our Heavenly Father before we do something, we invoke the heavenly law that allows God to consecrate (or count) that particular thing we are doing for our eternal well-being (see 2 Nephi 32:9). Otherwise God must apparently count it as a good deed worthy of mortal blessings but no more.

3. Constant prayer establishes clearly whose side we are on in the eternal struggle between right and wrong, between light and darkness, between Christ and Lucifer (see 2 Nephi 32:8). Only those who are willing to humble themselves in mighty prayer—"with real intent of heart" (Moroni 6:8)—can be enlisted on the side of Christ. Truthfully, this is where all wilderness travelers wish to be.

4. Constant prayer allows us to learn of and then to under-

stand the mysteries of Godliness (see Alma 26:22). These, the peaceable things of the kingdom, are what give us power to return to God's celestial realms (see D&C 42:61) and not to be taken captive by the devil (see Alma 12:9–11).

5. Constant prayer gives us power to be lifted up at the last day (see Alma 37:35–37). That means that we will have come off conqueror in the war against evil and will be made clean so that we can be lifted up to come with Christ in His glory, to rule and reign with Him through all eternity.

6. Constant prayer gives us power to become mighty missionaries, capable of bringing thousands of God's children to a knowledge of the truth (see Alma 26:4, 13). That is one way we have of serving righteously and so retaining a remission of our sins.

7. Constant prayer gives us power to become teachers of eternal truths, revealing "things which never have been revealed" (Alma 26:22).

8. Constant prayer allows us to continue to recognize and then obtain forgiveness for our sins (see 1 Nephi 7:21; D&C 64:7; Ether 12:27).

How to Recognize an Answer

Having obtained the wilderness of the Lord through complete repentance and a remission of sins, we are worthy in all respects to enjoy the companionship and presence of the Holy Ghost. However, while it is the Holy Spirit's responsibility to be with us when we are worthy, it is our responsibility to learn to recognize the manifestations of His presence. If we feel nothing, then it is appropriate to ask God each time we pray, in the name of Christ, to allow the Holy Ghost to fill our hearts and minds until we can feel Him (see 3 Nephi 19:9, 13; D&C 130:22). Then, if all else is in order, we will. And it is these manifestations of the Holy Ghost, or His workings within us, that will first indicate the Lord's answers to our prayers (see Moroni 10:4–5).

But remember, we cannot receive such answers unless we listen—in other words, stay on our knees, asking, waiting, asking, listening or feeling, remaining patiently until we feel something. Being in a hurry, not waiting for an answer, may be one of the major reasons more people don't receive answers to their prayers.

Physical Reactions to the Holy Spirit

Because our spirits are housed in physical bodies, the effect of the Holy Ghost influencing our spirits and minds is almost always accompanied by at least some physical reaction; our bodies feel the workings of the Spirit. When Lehi saw a vision, "he did quake and tremble exceedingly" (1 Nephi 1:6). Joseph Smith once said that his "bones [did] quake" (D&C 85:6) when the Spirit was working with him. Also, many accounts say that Joseph Smith glowed as though a light were within him when the Holy Ghost came upon him. And one man, Philo Dibble, in describing Joseph Smith and Sidney Rigdon receiving what became the 76th section of the Doctrine and Covenants, said that while Joseph sat calmly and looked serene because he was used to such things, Sidney Rigdon, who was not so accustomed to the physical rigors of spiritual experiences, was left weak and limp as a wet rag (see *Juvenile Instructor*, May 15, 1892, p. 304).

The scriptures point out several ways the Holy Ghost affects our feelings and our physical bodies. Let us itemize some of them here, with a little elaboration:

1. A burning in the bosom (see D&C 9:8). This is a warm feeling in the chest or the central area of the body. It might also be a feeling of warmth all over one's body.

2. A quaking frame (see D&C 85:6; 1 Nephi 1:6). This would be a slight trembling of the body, like a chill or a shiver, except that it would not be cold. This might increase with the intensity of the manifestation of the Spirit.

3. A still, small voice (see D&C 85:6). Our mind "hears" a new thought or idea that gives us knowledge or direction. This voice of the Spirit also "whispereth through and pierceth all things" (ibid.). Occasionally this voice even becomes audible to our natural ears.

4. Crying or weeping. People shouldn't be ashamed of this joyful response to the Spirit or judge others harshly when it occurs, for this is truly one of the most common effects of the Spirit upon a physical body.

5. Enlightened minds or sudden strokes of ideas (see D&C 6:15; 11:13). As we know, the Holy Ghost is a spirit and so will communicate directly with our own spirits as we receive answers to our prayers. The overall effect of this Spirit-to-spirit communication is to enlighten our minds. The Lord says: "Blessed art thou for what thou hast done; for thou hast inquired of me, and as often as thou hast inquired thou hast received instructions of my Spirit. If it had not been so, thou wouldst not have come to the place where thou art at this time. Behold, thou knowest that thou hast inquired of me and I did *enlighten thy mind;* and now I tell thee these things that thou mayest know that thou hast been enlightened by the Spirit of truth; yea, I tell thee, that thou mayest know that there is none else save God that knowest thy thoughts and the intents of thy heart" (D&C 6:14–16; emphasis mine).

6. Peace in the mind and heart (see D&C 6:23). No earthly serenity feels like this. It can come in the midst of great turmoil and will remove fear.

7. A constraining or impression not to say or do a specific

thing (see 4 Nephi 1:48). This is where we would be literally prevented from or prompted to avoid doing something the Lord does not want done. This can be a physical constrainment, a verbal constrainment, or even a mental constrainment. Almost always, however, it comes in response to prayers of faith, offered by ourselves or others, for divine direction, protection, or preservation.

8. A stupor of thought (see D&C 9:9). This is an understanding that a decision we have made is not in harmony with God's will. This sensation is best described as a sense of darkness or confusion, a feeling of anxiety that something is not working out no matter how hard we might be trying to bring it to pass. A simple prayer of acceptance of divine will brings this awful feeling to an abrupt halt.

9. Comfort from distress or sorrow (see Alma 17:9–10). If we will only humble ourselves and ask, we will receive this comfort. The Lord says, "Blessed are all they that mourn, for they shall be comforted" (3 Nephi 12:4).

There are, no doubt, other feelings or physical responses to the presence of the Spirit that I have not mentioned, for we will not all react to the Spirit's stimuli in exactly the same way or in the same degree. But we *will* be affected, and that is how we begin receiving personal revelation. Thus Joseph Smith declared: "[The] first Comforter or Holy Ghost has no other effect than pure intelligence. It is more powerful in expanding the mind, enlightening the understanding, and storing the intellect with present knowledge, of a man who is of the literal seed of Abraham, than one that is a Gentile, *though it may not have half as much visible effect upon the body;* for as the Holy Ghost falls upon one of the literal seed of Abraham, it is calm and serene; and his whole soul and body are only exercised by the pure spirit of intelligence; while the effect of the Holy Ghost upon a

Gentile, is to purge out the old blood, and make him actually of the seed of Abraham. . . . In such a case, there may be more of a powerful effect upon the body, and visible to the eye, than upon an Israelite, while the Israelite might at first be far before the Gentile in pure intelligence" (*Teachings*, p. 150; emphasis mine).

Asking Specific Questions

Unfortunately, many times prayers are offered without any questions being asked—no specific questions at all! It is vital that we become specific in our requests of the Lord. Just imagine what would have been the result if the light-seeking Brother of Jared had gone upon the mount Shelem and prayed only in general terms for health, protection, and so forth. The ocean-going Jaredites would certainly have experienced a long, dark passage. Or suppose that Nephi, even though he wanted to see the vision that his father Lehi had seen, had knelt and simply asked in general terms for a good day. He might have been blessed with a good day, but had he not been specific, millions of us would have missed not only the interpretation of Lehi's vision but also the marvelous additional views the Lord granted Nephi. So yes, it is important to be specific in our praises to the Lord and our requests of Him as we seek to have our needs fulfilled.

Keeping Questions Simple

As we grow into the principle of revelation, which is something like starting in kindergarten and graduating upward as our spiritual understanding increases, it is a good idea to learn to keep our questions simple enough that they can be answered with either a yes or a no. That way, when the physical effects of the Spirit are felt in response to a question (and each of us will most always feel the Spirit in our own unique way), we can assume the answer is yes. If we feel nothing or experience a withdrawal, then the answer would be either a no or an invitation to rephrase the question.

Later, as spiritual progression continues, pure knowledge or information will begin to flow into the mind as the Lord elaborates on His yes or no.

Calling Upon the Name of the Lord

One other aspect of the mighty prayers of wilderness travelers ought to be discussed, and that is the necessity of calling upon the name of the Lord (see D&C 133:6). Moroni recorded: "At the end of four years . . . the Lord came again unto the brother of Jared, and stood in a cloud and talked with him. And for the space of three hours did the Lord talk with the brother of Jared, *and chastened him because he remembered not to call upon the name of the Lord*" (Ether 2:14; emphasis mine).

It does not make sense to me that the Brother of Jared had simply stopped praying. That does not seem like him. Rather, I believe he had stopped praying in a particular manner, and this was what brought forth the Lord's chastisement.

In an effort to substantiate this idea, I discovered that almost no scriptural prayers before the coming of Christ, as well as very few since then, have been addressed to the Father or Heavenly Father. Instead, nearly all have been addressed to God or the Lord or the Lord God. In my computer scripture file I discovered that the phrases and the numbers of times these names of God are used in prayer are impressive. They are:

O Lord: 744
O God: 472
O Lord God: 230
O Lord my God: 92

O my God: 178

The Lord my God: 1,146

On the other hand, *O Father* is used only fifty times, and most of these refer to a mortal father rather than a prayerful plea to heaven. The phrase *O My Father* occurs only twenty-two times, and again not all are prayers. *Heavenly Father* is used fourteen times, and *Father in Heaven* or *Father who art/is in Heaven* is used fifty-two times. Again, almost none of these phrases occur until after the mortal advent of Christ, and most of their uses are by Christ personally. To clarify, we are commanded to pray unto the Father in the name of Christ. Therefore, the phrase *calling upon the name of the Lord* means calling upon God the Father.

Interestingly, it appears that regular calling on the name of the Lord is a requirement of those who have been born again. King Benjamin said: "As ye have come to the knowledge of the glory of God, or if ye have known of his goodness and have tasted of his love, and have received a remission of your sins, which causeth such exceedingly great joy in your souls, even so I would that ye should remember, and always retain in remembrance, the greatness of God, and your own nothingness, and his goodness and long-suffering towards you, unworthy creatures, and humble yourselves even in the depths of humility, *calling on the name of the Lord daily,* and standing steadfastly in the faith of that which is to come, which was spoken by the mouth of the angel" (Mosiah 4:11; emphasis mine). And Alma added: "He sent angels to converse with them, who caused men to behold of his glory. *And they began from that time forth to call on his name;* therefore God conversed with men, and made known unto them the plan of redemption, which had been prepared from the foundation of the world; and this he made known unto them according to their faith and repentance and their holy works" (Alma 12:29–30; emphasis mine).

From these passages we see that the righteous are commanded to call on the name of the Lord regularly, and they have been so commanded since the days of Adam.

Blessings Come from Calling on the Name of the Lord

Scripturally, we are informed that diligent "calling on the name of the Lord" brings certain blessings. In the last verse quoted above, we are informed that Adam and his posterity were taught by angels to call upon the name of God, after which men had the plan of salvation revealed to them.

Elsewhere we are promised mercy: "The Lord will be merciful unto all who call on his name" (Alma 9:17). We are told that it is a part of repenting and casting off sins (see Alma 13:27), that calling on the name of the Lord will protect us from being tempted above that which we can bear, and that calling upon the name of God is essential to being led by "the Holy Spirit, becoming humble, meek, submissive, patient, full of love and all long-suffering" (Alma 13:27–28).

Those who call on the name of God are also promised divine protection: "They did rejoice and cry again with one voice, saying: May the God of Abraham, and the God of Isaac, and the God of Jacob, protect this people in righteousness, so long as they shall call on the name of their God for protection" (3 Nephi 4:30). This protection includes, interestingly enough, having the power to recognize and then cast out Satan (see Moses 1:18).

Also, calling upon the holy name of the Lord is essential for those who would "make known his wonderful works among the people" (D&C 65:4) or serve as teachers and missionaries within the kingdom.

190

Never to call upon the name of God is a grievous sin, as is evident from the Brother of Jared's experience with the Lord's severe chastisement.

Ordinances of the Priesthood

In one sense, or on one level, we call upon the name of God daily each time we pray to the Father in the name of Christ. Thus Jesus commanded the Nephites: "Ye must always pray unto the Father in my name" (3 Nephi 18:19).

But is it appropriate to use those particular words, the words and phrases that have been so important to praying men and women from Adam through Joseph Smith and to our day? Yes, if we wish to, in our personal prayers. But more significantly, we always call upon His name in certain ordinances of the priesthood. Thus, each of the sacramental prayers begins with the words, "O God, the Eternal Father" (Moroni 4:3; 5:2). Such words are also used in temple prayer circles, where they help give our prayers greater power to penetrate the heavens than can be experienced in any other way. In a direct reference to such temple worship, Moses recorded in Genesis: "[Isaac] builded an altar there, and called upon the name of the Lord. . . . And the Lord appeared unto him the same night" (Genesis 26:25, 24). In our day the Prophet Joseph declared: "The Great God has a name by which He will be called"[1] (*Words*, p. 64). Then, referring directly to temple ordinances, Joseph continued: "Also in asking have reference to a personage. . . . Now this is [a] key for you to know how to ask and obtain" (ibid.; spelling and punctuation standardized).

Bathsheba W. Smith, wife of apostle George A. Smith,

---

1. The name of God that Joseph Smith gives is *Ahman*. This name, a word from the Adamic language, means "Man of Holiness" or "Holy Man" (see *Mormon Doctrine*, p. 29).

declared: "When speaking in one of our general fast meetings, [Joseph Smith] said that we did not know how to pray to have our prayers answered. But when I and my husband had our endowments . . . , Joseph Smith presiding, he taught us the order of prayer" (*Juvenile Instructor,* June 1, 1892, p. 345; see also *Words,* p. 54, footnote 19).

Thus we see that the highest level of calling upon the name of the Lord is associated with temple prayer and is therefore the most powerful way of praying of which we know. It was for not praying in this manner, I believe, for not participating in temple ordinances upon the mount Shelem, that the Brother of Jared experienced divine chastisement. And this, of course, leads directly to the next requirement for wilderness travelers—diligent temple attendance.

CHAPTER

21

Temples in the Wilderness

The temple is the doorway through which all wilderness travelers must pass to reenter the presence of the Lord. Having lost that presence through birth and our own carnal ways of living, still we yearn after the perfect love we once felt. Thus we are drawn to the temple, where by sacred ordinances the Lord seals His children to Himself and brings them back into His presence. Adam, cast out into the lone and dreary world, searched relentlessly until he found the keys that would open the narrow doorway behind which the Lord was waiting. Abraham, seeking all the blessings of the fathers, embarked on the same quest (see Abraham 1:2–4) until at last and in triumph he exclaimed: "Thy servant has sought thee earnestly; now I have found thee" (Abraham 2:12).

Isaac and Jacob at their sacred altars, Moses on Mount Horeb, Lehi at the Tree, Nephi on the mountaintop, Moriancumer on the mount Shelem—all these wilderness travelers conducted the search that is outlined and empowered for each of us in the temple, gradually increasing the hold, the seal, between themselves and their Lord, until in reality they were brought back into His presence. That was the very quest for which they had sought and obtained a remission of their sins and for which they had entered the Lord's wilderness—to rend the veil of unbelief, stand in the Lord's presence (see JST Genesis 14:30–31; D&C 84:19; 107:19), and be encircled eternally in the arms of His love (see D&C 6:20; 2 Nephi 1:15).

Most of us are familiar with the fact that Isaiah spoke of the temple as the Lord's mountain. That is because, when no structural facility is available, the Lord uses actual mountains as His temple. Isaiah says: "In the last days, the mountain of the Lord's house shall be established in the top of the mountains, and shall be exalted above the hills; and all nations shall flow unto it. And many people shall go and say, Come ye, and let us go up to the mountain of the Lord, to the house of the God of Jacob; and he will teach us of his ways, and we will walk in his paths" (Isaiah 2:2–3). Nephi wrote: "I, Nephi, did go into the mount oft, and I did pray oft unto the Lord; wherefore the Lord showed unto me great things" (1 Nephi 18:3). The Prophet Joseph added: "The keys are certain signs and words by which false spirits and personages may be detected from true, which cannot be revealed to the Elders till the Temple is completed. *The rich can only get them in the Temple, the poor may get them on the mountain top as did Moses*" (*History of the Church*, 4:608; emphasis mine).

Thus, when the Brother of Jared carried his sixteen small stones to the top of the mount Shelem to present them before the Lord (see Ether 3:1), he was obviously doing all he could to get himself closer to the presence of God—he was going to the temple, where he might appropriately ask and receive (see D&C 124:95, 97).

His prayer, too, is interesting, for though he was after light for his peoples' barges, he seems much more concerned about his own and his peoples' inadequacy before the Lord. Probably because of his three-hour chastisement, he feared the anger of the Lord exceedingly. Yet he pressed on past his fear because he knew he had been commanded to do what he was doing (see Ether 3:2–6).

Isaiah, another wilderness traveler, also reported great fear when he realized that he was actually in the presence of the Lord. He cried: "Woe is me! for I am undone; because I am a man of unclean lips, and I dwell in the midst of a people of unclean lips: for mine eyes have seen the King, the Lord of hosts" (Isaiah 6:5).

As the wilderness traveler draws closer and closer to the presence of the Lord, he sees ever more clearly the great contrast between God and his own carnal or mortal nature, even though he has been born again, and he is sorely tempted to shrink back and give up his quest. Many, such as the children of Israel, do shrink, and they spend the remainder of their lives wandering in the wilderness. But those who are determined press boldly on, exercising mighty faith as they penetrate the veil and are brought into the presence of the Lord.

Thus Isaiah pressed on until one of the Lord's seraphim left the altar of the Lord's temple and, coming to Isaiah, declared: "Lo, this hath touched thy lips; and thine iniquity is taken away, and thy sin purged" (Isaiah 6:7). And in the case of the Brother of Jared, "the Lord showed himself unto him, and said: Because thou knowest these things ye are redeemed from the fall; therefore ye are brought back into my presence; therefore I show myself unto you" (Ether 3:13).

What Moriancumer had beheld for so long with the eye of faith was now visually confirmed. He had "[rent] the veil of unbelief" (Ether 4:15) with his persistent efforts, and now he had succeeded. Rather than seeing in order to believe, which is the way of the world, he had believed in order to see, and so on the mountain of the Lord's temple, God had rewarded his righteous faith and efforts.

Temples in this Dispensation

Though we have already shown the significance of the temple in the lives of the early Kirtland Saints, it should be helpful to examine the scriptural history of temple ordinances in this dispensation. By so doing, we will discover why temple worship empowers us to obtain God's presence.

In 1823 Moroni declared to the youthful Joseph Smith, speaking for the Lord: "Behold, I will reveal unto you the Priesthood, by the hand of Elijah the prophet, before the coming of the great and dreadful day of the Lord" (D&C 2:1).

One definition of the word *reveal* means "to explain or empower." So, Elijah's mission was to give specific temple-oriented keys to priesthood holders so that they would have the divine knowledge required to use with power the priesthood they held. It was for this reason that the Lord commanded Joseph early in 1831: "That ye might escape the power of the enemy, and be gathered unto me a righteous people without spot and blameless—Wherefore, for this cause I gave unto you the commandment that ye should go to the Ohio, and there I will give unto you my law; and there you shall be endowed with power from on high" (D&C 38:13, 28–32). Again He says: "I [gave] unto you a commandment that you should build a house, in the which house I design to endow those whom I have chosen with power from on high" (D&C 95:8).

And how was this empowerment accomplished? At least in part through the sealing keys restored to Joseph Smith and

Oliver Cowdery by Elijah, thus planting in the hearts of the children the promises of priesthood rights and responsibilities made to the fathers (which priesthood-oriented promises were also planted in Abraham's heart [see Abraham 1:2–4]), in order that the hearts of the children might turn to their fathers (see D&C 2:2).

In Nauvoo the Saints were commanded to build another temple for the same reason—further priesthood empowerment. The Lord commanded: "Build a house to my name, for the Most High to dwell therein. For there is not a place found on earth that he may come to and restore again that which was lost unto you, or which he hath taken away. . . . For therein are the keys of the holy priesthood ordained, that you may receive honor and glory" (D&C 124:27–28, 34). President Ezra Taft Benson elaborates: "Even though the Aaronic Priesthood and Melchizedek Priesthood had been restored to the earth, the Lord urged the Saints to build a temple to receive the keys by which this order of priesthood could be administered on the earth again, 'for there (was) not a place found on earth that he may come to and restore again that which was lost . . . even the fulness of the priesthood' (D&C 124:28). Again, the Prophet Joseph said: 'If a man gets a fullness of the priesthood of God he has to get it in the same way that Jesus Christ obtained it, and that was by keeping all the commandments and obeying all the ordinances of the house of the Lord' (*Teachings of the Prophet Joseph Smith,* p. 308)" (*The Teachings of Ezra Taft Benson,* p. 249).

The Lord declares: "This greater priesthood administereth the gospel and holdeth the key of the mysteries of the kingdom, even the key of the knowledge of God. Therefore, in the ordinances thereof [and where are most of our ordinances found? Obviously, in the temple], the power of godliness is manifest.

197

And without the ordinances thereof, and the authority of the priesthood, the power of godliness is not manifest unto men in the flesh; for without this no man can see the face of God, even the Father, and live" (D&C 84:19–22).

The Peaceable Things of God

Besides empowering us to perform essential priesthood ordinances both for ourselves and in behalf of our deceased ancestors (see D&C 124, 132), such keys of priesthood empowerment as we have been discussing enhance our ability to commune with God. In a revelation/letter concerning temple work and the revelatory powers of the priesthood as restored by Elijah, Joseph Smith wrote: "The great and grand secret of the whole matter, and the *summum bonum* of the whole subject that is lying before us, consists in obtaining the powers of the Holy Priesthood. *For him to whom these keys are given, there is no difficulty in obtaining a knowledge of facts in relation to the salvation of the children of men, both as well for the dead as for the living*" (D&C 128:11; emphasis mine).

Called the "peaceable things of the kingdom" and "the mysteries of Godliness," a knowledge of these things, according to scripture, is taught by the Holy Ghost through personal revelation (see D&C 36:2). The Lord says: "If thou shalt ask, thou shalt receive revelation upon revelation, knowledge upon knowledge, that thou mayest know the mysteries and peaceable things—that which bringeth joy, that which bringeth life eternal" (D&C 42:61).

Some wilderness travelers might balk at the thought of "delving into the mysteries" of godliness, but that is because they don't understand the difference between them and the mysteries of man. Where the latter lead to confusion and endless arguments and contention, the former actually lead to God.

Thus Joseph Smith said: "I advise all to go on to perfection, and to search deeper and deeper into the mysteries of Godliness" (*Teachings*, p. 364). Why? Because we progress spiritually by gaining Godly knowledge. The great prophet Nephi adds: "He that diligently seeketh shall find; and the mysteries of God shall be unfolded unto them, by the power of the Holy Ghost, as well in these times as in times of old, and as well in times of old as in times to come; wherefore, the course of the Lord is one eternal round" (1 Nephi 10:19). Alma continues: "Yea, he that repenteth and exerciseth faith, and bringeth forth good works, and prayeth continually without ceasing—unto such it is given to know the mysteries of God; yea, unto such it shall be given to reveal things which never have been revealed" (Alma 26:22).

But, as Alma explained to Zeezrom: "It is given unto many to know the mysteries of God; nevertheless they are laid under a strict command that they shall not impart only according to the portion of his word which he doth grant unto the children of men, according to the heed and diligence which they give unto him" (Alma 12:9). And how is the amount of knowledge imparted to be determined? Again Alma answers: "He that will harden his heart receiveth the lesser portion of the word . . . until they know nothing concerning the mysteries . . . and he that will not harden his heart, to him is given the greater portion of the word, until it is given unto him to know the mysteries of God until he know them in full" (Alma 12:10–11).

There are at least a dozen additional scriptural references stating the same thing; each Latter-day Saint, if he or she wants to progress spiritually during mortality, must seek to know and understand the mysteries of Godliness (see Matthew 13:11; Luke 8:10; 1 Nephi 1:1; 2:16; Jacob 4:8; Mosiah 1:5; 2:9; Alma 10:5; 12:9–11; D&C 6:7; 8:11; 63:22–23; 76:5–10). For those of us who wish a successful journey through the Lord's wilderness, such seeking is imperative. And inevitably, such seeking will lead to the temple.

President Benson states: "The temple ceremony was given by a wise Heavenly Father to help us become more Christ-like. The endowment was revealed by revelation and can be understood only by revelation. The instruction is given in symbolic language. The late Apostle John A. Widtsoe taught, 'No man or woman can come out of the temple endowed as he should be, unless he has seen, beyond the symbol, the mighty realities for which the symbol stands' ("Temple Worship," address given in Salt Lake City, 12 October 1920)" (*The Teachings of Ezra Taft Benson*, pp. 250–51).

And how do we gain that understanding? Joseph Smith said: "The endowment you are so anxious about, you cannot comprehend now, nor could Gabriel explain it to the understanding of your dark minds; but strive to be prepared in your hearts, be faithful in all things, [and] be clean every whit. Let us be faithful and silent, brethren, and if God gives you a manifestation, keep it to yourselves; be watchful and prayerful . . . do not watch for iniquity in each other, if you do you will not get an endowment, for God will not bestow it on such. But if we are faithful, and live by every word that proceeds forth from the mouth of God, I will venture to prophesy that we shall get a blessing that will be worth remembering, if we should live as long as John the Revelator" (*Discourses of the Prophet Joseph Smith*, compiled by Alma P. Burton [Salt Lake City: Deseret Book Co., 1977], p. 113).

The Ordinances of the Temple

Concerning how the blessings of the temple were first instituted in our dispensation, the Prophet Joseph wrote on Wednesday, May 4, 1842: "I spent the day in the upper part of the store, that is my private office (so called because in that room I keep my sacred writings, translate ancient records, and receive revelations) and in my general business office . . . in council with General James Adams, of Springfield, Patriarch Hyrum Smith, Bishops Newell K. Whitney and George Miller, and President Brigham Young and Elders Heber C. Kimball and Willard Richards, instructing them in the principles and order of the Priesthood, attending to washings, anointings, endowments and the communication of keys pertaining to the Aaronic Priesthood, and so on to the highest order of the Melchizedek Priesthood, setting forth the order pertaining to the Ancient of Days, and all those plans and principles by which anyone is enabled to secure the fullness of those blessings which have been prepared for the Church of the First Born and come up and abide in the presence of the Eloheim in the eternal worlds. In this council was instituted the ancient order of things for the first time in these last days. And the communications I made to this council were of things spiritual and to be received only by the spiritual minded; and there was nothing made known to these men but what will be made known to all the Saints of the last days, so soon as they are prepared to receive . . . even to the weakest of the Saints. . . . [So let them] wait their time with patience in all meekness, faith, perseverance unto the end, knowing assuredly that all these things referred to in this council are always governed by the principle of revelation (*History of the Church*, 5:1–2; spelling standardized).

President Heber C. Kimball, speaking of temple ordinances at a slightly later date, said: "This is why you are required to be sober, to be honest, that you could ask and receive, knock and it should be opened, and that when you sought for things you should find them. [The endowment] is putting you in possession of those keys by which you can ask for things you need

201

and obtain them. This is the key by which to obtain all the glory and felicity of eternal life. It is the key by which you approach God . . . and be recognized. . . . Now you have been taught how to pray. . . . The principles which have been opened to you are the things which ought to occupy your attention all of your lives. They are not second to anything. You have the key by which, if you are faithful, you will claim on your posterity all the blessings of the priesthood" (in Helen Mar Whitney, "Scenes in Nauvoo, and Incidents from Heber C. Kimball's Journal," *Women's Exponent*, 12:26).

The key phrase in Heber C. Kimball's journal is "if you are faithful." Brigham Young agreed, saying: "The Gospel has brought to us the holy Priesthood. . . . The keys of that Priesthood are here; we have them in our possession; we can unlock, and we can shut up. We can obtain salvation, and we can administer it. . . . But the Lord has so ordained that no man shall receive the benefits of the everlasting Priesthood without humbling himself before Him, and giving Him the glory for teaching him, that he may be able to witness to every man of the truth, and not depend upon the words of any individual on the earth, but know for himself, live 'by every word that proceedeth out of the mouth of God,' love the Lord Jesus Christ and the institutions of His kingdom, and finally enter into His glory. Every man and woman may be a Revelator, and have . . . the spirit of prophecy, and foresee the mind and will of God concerning them" (*Journal of Discourses*, 2:189). President Young taught: "The Priesthood is given to the people, and the keys thereof, and, when properly understood, they may actually unlock the treasury of the Lord, and receive to their fullest satisfaction. But through our own weaknesses, through the frailty of human nature, we are not capable of doing so" (*Journal of Discourses*, 3:192).

Modern Application

All we who sojourn through the Lord's wilderness must recognize the eternal significance of the ordinances of the temple. The endowment we have received is literally a gift of power from God to us. Once that power is obtained, through faithful temple attendance each Saint can obtain knowledge sufficient "to overcome all things" (see *Discourses of the Prophet Joseph Smith*, p. 148; see also D&C 38:32; 95:8; 124:95, 97; 128:11). Brigham Young adds: "Then go on and build the temples of the Lord, that you may receive the endowments in store for you, and possess the keys of the eternal Priesthood, that you may receive every word, sign, and token, and be made acquainted with the laws of angels, and of the kingdom of our Father and our God, and know how to pass from one degree to another, and enter fully into the joy of your Lord" (*Discourses of Brigham Young*, pp. 395–96).

An understanding of these things makes regular and frequent temple attendance essential for all modern wilderness travelers.

CHAPTER

22

Confronting Satan

Part of the reality of this world is Satan. Since the days of Adam he has pretended to rule it, and he has done all in his power to stop righteous men and women from progressing spiritually. As the two accounts that follow relate, he uses both temptation and intimidation in his efforts to make us as miserable as he is.

Jesus in the Wilderness

After Jesus was baptized by water and by the Spirit, he was led into the wilderness by the Holy Ghost to be with God. Combining all the scriptural references on the Savior's wilderness experience, we read: "He was there in the wilderness forty days, *Satan seeking to tempt him;* and was with the wild beasts; and the angels ministered unto him.

"And when he had fasted forty days and forty nights, and had communed with God, he was afterwards an hungered, and *was left to be tempted of the devil.* And when the tempter came to him, he said, If thou be the Son of God, command that these stones be made bread. But [Jesus] answered and said, It is written, Man shall not live by bread alone, but by every word that proceedeth out of the mouth of God.

"And the Spirit brought him to Jerusalem, and set him on the pinnacle of the temple. Then the devil came unto him and said, If thou be the Son of God, cast thyself down, for it is written, He shall give his angels charge concerning thee, and in their hands they shall bear thee up, lest at any time thou dash thy foot against a stone. Jesus said unto him, It is written again, Thou shalt not tempt the Lord thy God.

"And again, Jesus was in the Spirit, and it taketh him up into an exceeding high mountain, and showeth him all the kingdoms of the world and the glory of them. And the devil came unto him again, and said, All these things will I give unto thee, if thou wilt fall down and worship me.

"Then saith Jesus unto him, Get thee hence, Satan: for it is written, Thou shalt worship the Lord thy God, and him only shalt thou serve.

"Then the devil leaveth him, and, behold, angels came and ministered unto him" (Matthew 4:1–11; JST Matthew 4:2, 5–6, 8–9; JST Mark 1:11; Luke 4:1–13; JST Luke 4:2, 5–6, 9; emphasis mine).

Jesus not only accepted the reality of Satan but was also left subject to the evil one's temptations. We all experience these things in mortality, and it is the devil's right to torment us with them (see Moses 4:4, 21).

However, when Satan demanded that he be worshipped rather than God, Jesus drew the line. He knew who was to be worshipped in righteousness, and it was not Lucifer. Neither could Jesus countenance the usurper's vain efforts to overthrow God (see Moses 4:3). That war had already been fought and won. Therefore he commanded him, "Get thee hence," and Satan was gone.

Moses on the Mountain

Of Moses' experience with the devil we read: "The words of God, which he spake unto Moses at a time when Moses was caught up into an exceedingly high mountain, and he saw God face to face, and he talked with him, and the glory of God was upon Moses; therefore Moses could endure his presence. . . .

"And the presence of God withdrew from Moses, that his glory was not upon Moses; and Moses was left unto himself. . . . And it came to pass that . . . Satan came tempting him, saying: Moses, son of man, worship me. And it came to pass that Moses looked upon Satan and said: Who art thou? For behold, I am a son of God, in the similitude of his Only Begotten; and where is thy glory, that I should worship thee? For behold, I could not look upon God, except his glory should come upon me, and I were transfigured before him. But I can look upon thee in the natural man. Is it not so, surely? Blessed be the name of my God, for his Spirit hath not altogether withdrawn from me, or else where is thy glory, for it is darkness unto me? And I can judge between thee and God; for God said unto me: Worship God, for him only shalt thou serve. Get thee hence, Satan; deceive me not; for God said unto me: Thou art after the similitude of mine Only Begotten. And he also gave me commandments when he called unto me out of the burning bush, saying: Call upon God in the name of mine Only Begotten, and worship me. And again Moses said: I will not cease to call upon God, I have other things to inquire of him: for his glory has been upon me, wherefore I can judge between him and thee. Depart hence, Satan.

"And now, when Moses had said these words, Satan cried

with a loud voice, and ranted upon the earth, and commanded, saying: I am the Only Begotten, worship me. And it came to pass that Moses began to fear exceedingly; and as he began to fear, he saw the bitterness of hell. Nevertheless, calling upon God, he received strength, and he commanded, saying: Depart from me, Satan, for this one God only will I worship, which is the God of glory.

"And now Satan began to tremble, and the earth shook; and Moses received strength, and called upon God, saying: In the name of the Only Begotten, depart hence, Satan. And it came to pass that Satan cried with a loud voice, with weeping, and wailing, and gnashing of teeth; and he departed hence, even from the presence of Moses, that he beheld him not. And now of this thing Moses bore record; but because of wickedness it is not had among the children of men" (Moses 1:1–2, 9–10, 12–23).

In Moses' experience Satan does not seem to have wasted much time with temptations of the flesh. Instead he demanded immediate worship, which Moses immediately rejected, bearing testimony to Satan of his devotion to God as he did so. Then Moses commanded him to depart.

Interestingly, Satan went nowhere but only grew angry and threw a temper tantrum. Moses began to fear this devilish display, and as he feared, he saw the bitterness of hell—an interesting commentary on the fate of those who fear the devil. But calling on God, Moses received strength to allay his fear, and finally he rebuked Satan in the name of the Only Begotten, who is Jesus Christ. At that point Satan left.

The scripture continues: "When Satan had departed from the presence of Moses, . . . Moses lifted up his eyes unto heaven, being filled with the Holy Ghost, which beareth record of the Father and the Son; and calling upon the name of God, he beheld his glory again, for it was upon him; and he heard a voice, saying: Blessed art thou, Moses, for I, the Almighty, have chosen thee, and thou shalt be made stronger than many waters; for they shall obey thy command as if thou wert God. And lo, I am with thee, even unto the end of thy days; for thou shalt deliver my people from bondage, even Israel my chosen" (Moses 1:24–26).

Then the Lord instructed Moses about the reality of the devil's life and mission. "I, the Lord God, spake unto Moses, saying: That Satan, whom thou hast commanded in the name of mine Only Begotten, is the same which was from the beginning, and he came before me, saying—Behold, here am I, send me, I will be thy son, and I will redeem all mankind, that one soul shall not be lost, and surely I will do it; wherefore give me thine honor. But, behold, my Beloved Son, which was my Beloved and Chosen from the beginning, said unto me—Father, thy will be done, and the glory be thine forever. Wherefore, because that Satan rebelled against me, and sought to destroy the agency of man, which I, the Lord God, had given him, and also, that I should give unto him mine own power; by the power of mine Only Begotten, I caused that he should be cast down; and he became Satan, yea, even the devil, the father of all lies, to deceive and to blind men, and to lead them captive at his will, even as many as would not hearken unto my voice" (Moses 4:1–4).

Lehi's Teachings

Lehi taught his sons about Satan, saying: "I, Lehi, according to the things which I have read, must needs suppose that an angel of God, according to that which is written, had fallen from heaven; wherefore, he became a devil, having sought that which was evil before God. And because he had fallen from heaven, and had become miserable forever, he sought also the misery of all mankind. . . . Wherefore, men are free according to the flesh; and all things are given them which are expedient unto man. And they are free to choose liberty and eternal life, through the great Mediator of all men, or to choose captivity and death, according to the captivity and power of the devil; for he seeketh that all men might be miserable like unto himself" (2 Nephi 2:17–18, 27).

Modern Application

In our day many find it hard to believe in the devil's reality, usually because of the scorn of others. But that is part of Satan's plan, for if he isn't believed in he can accomplish so much more in the manufacturing of misery. Thus Jacob cried: "O that cunning plan of the evil one! O the vainness, and the frailties, and the foolishness of men! When they are learned they think they are wise, and they hearken not unto the counsel of God, for they set it aside, supposing they know of themselves, wherefore, their wisdom is foolishness and it profiteth them not. And they shall perish" (2 Nephi 9:28).

However, in all wilderness experiences, those who seek the presence of God will, at some point, face the reality of Satan and his temptations. The youthful Joseph Smith was given this opportunity during his first visit to the hill Cumorah. Oliver Cowdery wrote that after Joseph had tried to take the plates and couldn't and then prayerfully repented, the angel Moroni "said, 'Look!' and as he thus spake [Joseph] beheld the prince of darkness, surrounded by his innumerable train of associates. All this passed before him, and the heavenly messenger said, 'All this is shown, the good and the evil, the holy and impure, the glory of God and the power of darkness, that you may know hereafter the two powers and never be influenced or overcome by that wicked one. Behold, whatever entices and leads to good and to

do good, is of God, and whatever does not is of that wicked one:
It is he that fills the hearts of men with evil, to walk in darkness
and blaspheme God; and you may learn from henceforth, that
his ways are to destruction, but the way of holiness is peace and
rest. . . . You have now beheld the power of God manifested and
the power of Satan: You see that there is nothing that is desirable
in the works of darkness; that they cannot bring happiness; that
those who are overcome therewith are miserable, while on the
other hand the righteous are blessed with a place in the
Kingdom of God where joy unspeakable surrounds them'" (*The
Papers of Joseph Smith*, edited by Dean C. Jessee [Salt Lake City:
Deseret Book Company, 1989], 1:87–88).

A Confrontation Will Occur

Wilderness wanderers may or may not see the devil; we
may or may not hear his voice or witness the manifestations of
his presence. Yet like Moses and Joseph, we will be required to
overcome our fear of him and confront him. Otherwise we will
surely experience at least somewhat the bitterness of hell, for
our fear is part of what gives Satan his power over us.

We must also reach the point where we can face him directly,
bear witness of our allegiance to Christ and His Father, spurn
completely his temptations, and finally, in the name of Christ,
command him to depart. And here again the powers we have
obtained through temple ordinances will serve us well. Brigham
Young stated: "The Spirit of the Lord and the keys of the priest-
hood . . . hold power over all animated beings" (in Hugh W.
Nibley, *Nibley on the Timely and the Timeless* [Provo, Utah: Brigham
Young University Religious Studies Center, 1978], p. 88). Joseph
Smith discussed this power over animated beings when he said:
"I preached in the grove on the keys of the kingdom, charity, etc.
The keys are certain signs and words by which false spirits and

personages may be detected from true, which cannot be revealed to the elders till the temple is completed. . . . There are signs in heaven, earth and hell; the elders must know them all, to be endowed with power, to finish their work and prevent imposition" (*Discourses of the Prophet Joseph Smith*, p. 116).

Elaborating on this theme, Joseph taught: "It is evident from the Apostles' writings, that many false spirits existed in their day, and had 'gone forth into the world,' and that it needed intelligence which God alone could impart to detect false spirits, and to prove what spirits were of God. The world in general have been grossly ignorant in regard to this one thing, and why should they be otherwise—for 'the things of God knoweth no man, but the Spirit of God.'

"There always did, in every age, seem to be a lack of intelligence pertaining to this subject. Spirits of all kinds have been manifested, in every age, and almost among all people . . . and all contend that their spirits are of God. Who shall solve the mystery? 'Try the spirits,' says John, but who is to do it? The learned, the eloquent, the philosopher, the sage, the divine—all are ignorant. . . .

" 'Try the spirits,' but what by? Are we to try them by the creeds of men? What preposterous folly—what sheer ignorance—what madness! Try the motions and actions of an eternal being (for I contend that all spirits are such) by a thing that was conceived in ignorance, and brought forth in folly—a cobweb of yesterday! Angels would hide their faces, and devils would be ashamed and insulted, and would say, 'Paul we know, and Jesus we know, but who are ye?' Let each man of society make a creed and try evil spirits by it, and the devil would shake his sides; it is all that he would ask—all that he would desire. Yet many of them do this, and hence 'many spirits are abroad in the world.'

"One great evil is, that men are ignorant of the nature of spirits; their power, laws, government, intelligence, etc., and imagine that when there is anything like power, revelation, or vision manifested, that it must be of God" (*Teachings*, pp. 202–3).

"As we have noticed before, the great difficulty lies in the ignorance of the nature of spirits, of the laws by which they are governed, and the signs by which they may be known; if it requires the Spirit of God to know the things of God; and the spirit of the devil can only be unmasked through that medium, then it follows as a natural consequence that unless some person or persons have a communication, or revelation from God, unfolding to them the operation of the spirit, they must eternally remain ignorant of these principles; for I contend that if one man cannot understand these things but by the Spirit of God, ten thousand men cannot; it is alike out of the reach of the wisdom of the learned, the tongue of the eloquent, the power of the mighty. And we shall at last have to come to this conclusion, whatever we may think of revelation, that without it we can neither know nor understand anything of God, or the devil; and however unwilling the world may be to acknowledge this principle, it is evident from the multifarious creeds and notions concerning this matter that they understand nothing of this principle, and it is equally as plain that without a divine communication they must remain in ignorance. The world always mistook false prophets for true ones, and those that were sent of God, they considered to be false prophets, and hence they killed, stoned, punished and imprisoned the true prophets, and these had to hide themselves 'in deserts and dens, and caves of the earth,' and though the most honorable men of the earth, they banished them from their society as vagabonds, whilst they cherished, honored and supported knaves, vagabonds, hypocrites, impostors, and the basest of men. . . .

212

"Every one of these professes to be competent to try his neighbor's spirit, but no one can try his own, and what is the reason? Because they have not a key to unlock, no rule wherewith to measure, and no criterion whereby they can test it. Could any one tell the length, breadth or height of a building without a rule? test the quality of metals without a criterion, or point out the movements of the planetary systems, without a knowledge of astronomy? Certainly not; and if such ignorance as this is manifested about a spirit of this kind, who can describe an angel of light? If Satan should appear as one in glory, who can tell his color, his signs, his appearance, his glory?—or what is the manner of his manifestation? Who can detect the spirit of the French prophets with their revelations and their visions, and power of manifestations? Or who can point out the spirit of the Irvingites, with their apostles and prophets, and visions and tongues, and interpretations, &c., &c. Or who can drag into daylight and develop the hidden mysteries of the false spirits that so frequently are made manifest among the Latter-day Saints? We answer that no man can do this without the Priesthood, and having a knowledge of the laws by which spirits are governed; for as 'no man knows the things of God, but by the Spirit of God,' so *no man knows the spirit of the devil, and his power and influence, but by possessing intelligence which is more than human, and having unfolded through the medium of the Priesthood the mysterious operations of his devices;* without knowing the angelic form, the sanctified look and gesture, and the zeal that is frequently manifested by him for the glory of God, together with the prophetic spirit, the gracious influence, the godly appearance, and the holy garb, which are so characteristic of his proceedings and his mysterious windings" (*History of the Church*, 4:573–74; emphasis mine).

Joseph Smith clearly knew a great deal about the nature

and powers of spirits, both those who followed Lucifer and we
who followed Christ. Much of this information he has left for
us to learn.

Satanic Assignments

Through the scriptural accounts mentioned above, we learn
that Satan has certain rights and powers, which he falsely calls
priesthoods. It was because of these rights to tempt and torment man that Jesus did not at first rebuke him. Concerning
these powers, Joseph Smith stated: "Without attempting to
describe . . . the design of God in relation to the human body
and spirit, I would just remark . . . that the spirits of good men
cannot interfere with the wicked beyond their prescribed
bounds, for Michael, the Archangel, dared not bring a railing
accusation against the devil, but said, 'The Lord rebuke thee,
Satan'" (*Teachings*, p. 208).

At another time the Prophet remarked: "It would seem
also, that wicked spirits have their bounds, limits, and laws by
which they are governed or controlled . . . and it is very evident
that they possess a power that none but those who have the
Priesthood can control" (ibid., p. 208).

Evil spirits or devils, who follow Lucifer in his task of
afflicting and tormenting and destroying mortals, do seem to
be assigned specific powers or missions. And interestingly, this
seems to be done in the manner of an organized assault, just as
Christ's missionary force is an organized assault against these
same powers of darkness. An example of such an assignment
is found in Alma, where we learn that Korihor was possessed
by a lying spirit, which may mean a spirit who had been given
the specific assignment by Satan of enticing mortals to become
liars (see Alma 30:42).

While in prison in Liberty, Missouri, Joseph Smith identi-

fied the evil spirit (or group of spirits with the same assignment) who was responsible for the woes of the Saints in
Missouri, and at the same time he taught some interesting
things about the character of that spirit, the spirit of confusion,
and thus of other spirits under Satan's dominion. He wrote: "It
is an imperative duty that we owe to God, to angels, with
whom we shall be brought to stand, and also to ourselves, to
our wives and children, who have been made to bow down
with grief, sorrow, and care, under the most damning hand of
murder, tyranny, and oppression, supported and urged on and
upheld by the influence of that *spirit* which hath so strongly riv-
eted the creeds of the fathers, who have inherited lies, upon the
hearts of the children, and [that spirit has] filled the world with
confusion, and has been growing stronger and stronger, and is now
the *very mainspring of all corruption,* and the whole earth groans
under the weight of its iniquity. It is an iron yoke, it is a strong
band; they are the very handcuffs, and chains, and shackles,
and fetters of hell" (D&C 123:7–8; emphasis mine).

As we have learned the names of the spirits of lying and
confusion from the Lord, so by asking we can learn the names,
or assignments, of all Satan's followers. When Christ was ready
to cast the unclean spirit from a man of the tombs possessed by
him (see Mark 5:1–13), He first asked the spirit's name. The spirits replied that their name was Legion, for they were many.
Christ acknowledged them, granted their bizarre request to be
allowed to possess a herd of swine, and then cast them out.
Perhaps we could do more good as we battle those same hosts
of devils if we also knew their names—not their personal names,
but the names of their powers or assignments.

Some of the Satanic names or assignments we read of in the
scriptures are:

Adultery and *whoremongering*—agitating a person's baser desires until control is lost and adultery is committed (see 1 Corinthians 6:9).

Divorce—influencing couples to feel more and more alienated until the family unit is finally destroyed (see Malachi 2:15–16).

Resistance—influencing a person to be unwilling to listen to or practice righteousness even when it is understood (see Zechariah 3:1).

Lying—influencing a person to abandon the truth more and more often until the truth is no longer even recognized (see Alma 30:42).

Infirmity—sometimes causing sickness and physical pain (see Luke 13:11).

Apostasy—influencing a person to become so emotionally disturbed over some point of doctrine, or over the perceived "unrighteous" actions of another, that the rest of the gospel is ignored and the entire Church is abandoned (see John 3:20; 2 Nephi 9:46).

Murder—influencing a person to thirst for another's life until at last it is taken (see 2 Nephi 9:9). These spirits go hand-in-glove with spirits of apostasy, for so often such murders occur following apostasy from the truth.

Confusion—influencing a person to lose understanding of a calling, a point of doctrine, or a divinely inspired purpose until failure in that righteous endeavor has occurred (see 1 Corinthians 14:3; D&C 123:7–8, 10). This spirit of confusion has such power that it is able to support, urge on, and uphold such lesser spirits as murder, tyranny, and oppression. Thus, once a spirit of confusion obtains power over someone, causing that person's testimony to falter and his or her righteous resolves to disintegrate against the wall of doubt and despair, then such other spirits as murder, tyranny, oppression, and most likely anger, affliction, and apostasy are invited to take up their abode within that same man or woman. It is not long, then, before the person is progressing through the three stages of apostasy, which were also identified by Joseph Smith as kicking against the pricks, persecuting the Saints, and ultimately fighting against God (see D&C 121:36–38).

Destruction—causing a person's physical body to deteriorate until physical death occurs (see 1 Corinthians 5:5).

Contention—influencing a person to argue, quarrel, fight, complain, and otherwise drive away the Spirit of God by his or her inability to get along with others (see 3 Nephi 11:29).

Anger—associated with the spirits of contention, the spirits of anger mentioned by Mormon (see Moroni 9:3) seem to have tremendous destructive powers. In fact, Mormon tells his son Moroni that Satan's implanted anger led Mormon's people to unbelievable acts of depravity and left them without order and mercy but strong in their perversions and brutality (see Moroni 9:4, 9, 18–19).

Devourer—causing a person to lose the ability to financially sustain and support his or her family (see Malachi 3:7–12; Revelation 13:1–9).

Fear—influencing a person to fear one thing or another until all ability to have faith in anything has been taken away (see 2 Timothy 1:7). From Moses' experience with this spirit, we can see the great danger inherent in allowing ourselves to be subject to fear. Only after Moses submitted to fear did he see the bitterness of hell (see Moses 1:20).

The Law Governing Satan and His Followers

The Lord says: "That wicked one cometh and taketh away light and truth, through disobedience, from the children of men" (D&C 93:39). Therefore, at least part of the heavenly eternal law under which Satan and his followers function is *that they are governed by each of us individually, according to how we choose to live.* Satan's power over us hinges upon our obedience or disobedience.

As we exercise agency, we either give Satan's followers power through our disobedience to God's laws, or we take power away from them by our righteous obedience. The more we choose to sin, the more we give them permission to afflict us. The less we choose to sin, the more free of them we will be. That is why Christ's gift of repentance is so dramatically important. If we want to get Satan and his hosts off our backs, all we need to do is repent, to receive and then retain a remission of our sins, which absolutely robs the old serpent of his power over us.

How Evil Spirits Act upon Mortals

Apparently the pattern of abuse of an evil spirit upon us mortals is to come at us from the outside, afflicting, tormenting with fears and temptations, wearing at us in our assignments or weaknesses. That continues until we finally get rid of the spirit through righteousness and rebuking or we succumb to it and partake of the sin. Once we have succumbed, the spirit may gain entry to our body, where it can exert even more power and influence than before. In this manner many diseases come, marriages are broken up, testimonies are lost, missions are abandoned, families are destroyed, callings are not fulfilled, and even peoples' lives are taken before their time.

As Joseph Smith taught: The greatness of [Satan's] punishment is that he shall not have a tabernacle. This is his punishment. So the devil, thinking to thwart the decree of God, by going up and down in the earth, seeking whom he may destroy—any person that he can find that will yield to him, he will bind him, and take possession of the body and reign there, glorying in it mightily, not caring that he had got merely a stolen body; and by-and-by some one having authority will come along and cast him out and restore the tabernacle to its rightful owner. The devil steals a tabernacle because he has not one of his own: but if he steals one, he is always liable to be turned out of doors" (*History of the Church*, 5:388).

Nephi says: "At that day shall he rage in the hearts of the children of men, and stir them up to anger against that which is good. And others will he pacify, and lull them away into carnal security, that they will say: All is well in Zion; yea, Zion prospereth, all is well—and thus the devil cheateth their souls, and leadeth them away carefully down to hell. And behold, others he flattereth away, and telleth them there is no hell; and thus he sayeth unto them: I am no devil, for there is none—and thus he whispereth in their ears, until he grasps them with his awful chains, from whence there is no deliverance" (2 Nephi 28:20–22).

Concerning this scripture, LDS scholar Dennis L. Largey writes: "A closer look at some of the keys words used in this passage is helpful to broaden our understanding of how Satan operates: First, he *pacifies*, which means he appeases or placates. Second, he *cheats*, swindles, misleads, fools, or practices fraud upon, which means he deceives by trickery. Third, he *flatters*, which means he compliments excessively and insincerely, especially to win favor, to feed vanity, or to persuade that what one wants to believe is the case. Fourth, he *leads* the way by going in advance, by conducting, escorting, or directing, by causing one to follow a certain course of action or line of thought. All of this—the pacifying, the cheating, the flattering, and the leading—is done carefully, which is synonymous with thoroughly, painstakingly, and conscientiously. Satan thus customizes his dishonesty according to the susceptibility of his target. His favorite approach is whatever works. In the pride of his heart, he does not drive from the rear but leads from the front. Knowing only a few would follow him if his true identity and design were manifested, he carefully draws people into the false conclusion of supposing they are winning when, in fact, they are slowly, but nevertheless effectively being destroyed" (Dennis L. Largey, "The Enemies of Christ: 2 Nephi 28," in *The Book of Mormon: Second Nephi, The Doctrinal Structure*, edited by Monte S. Nyman and Charles D. Tate, Jr. [Provo, Utah: Brigham Young University Religious Studies Center, 1989], pp. 297–98).

How to Detect Satan

Satan is always subject to the authority of Christ as manifested through Christ's righteous mortal servants. Occasionally, however, he will pretend to be an angel of light—a messenger from God. Joseph Smith taught: "When a messenger comes saying he has a message from God, offer him your hand and request him to shake hands with you. If he be an angel he will do so, and you will feel his hand. If he be the spirit of a just man made perfect he will come in his glory; for that is the only way he can appear—Ask him to shake hands with you, but he will not move, because it is contrary to the order of heaven for a just man to deceive; but he will still deliver his message. If it be the devil as an angel of light, when you ask him to shake hands he will offer you his hand, and you will not feel anything; you may therefore detect him" (D&C 129:4–8).

There may be times, as in the case of Moses, when Satan will refuse to depart. Concerning such occurrences, Joseph Smith taught: "The devil may appear as an angel of light. Ask God to reveal it; if it be of the devil, he will flee from you; if of

God, He will manifest Himself, or make it manifest" (*Teachings,* p. 162).

Mortals Have Power over Satan Because of Our Bodies

In addition to these things, Joseph Smith taught "that satan was generally blamed for the evils which we did, but if he was the cause of all our wickedness, men could not be condemned. The devil cannot compel mankind to evil; all was voluntary. Those who resisted the spirit of God, are liable to be led into temptation, and then the association of heaven is withdrawn from those who refuse to be made partakers of such great glory. God would not exert any compulsory means and the Devil could not; and such ideas as were entertained [on these subjects] by many were absurd" (*Times and Seasons,* 2:429). What beautiful harmony between the Prophet's doctrine and that of the Apostle James, who wrote: "Let no man say when he is tempted, I am tempted of God: for God cannot be tempted with evil, neither tempteth he any man: but every man is tempted, when he is drawn away of his own lust, and enticed. Then when lust hath conceived, it bringing forth sin: and sin, when it is finished, bringeth forth death" (James 1:13–15).

The Prophet also taught: "All beings who have bodies have power over those who have not. The devil has no power over us only as we permit him. The moment we revolt at anything which comes from God, the devil takes power" (*Teachings,* p. 181).

"We came to this earth that we might have a body and present it pure before God in the celestial kingdom. The great principle of happiness consists in having a body. The devil has no body, and herein is his punishment. He is pleased when he can obtain the tabernacle of man, and when cast out by the Savior he asked to go into the herd of swine, showing that he would prefer a swine's body to having none" (ibid.).

Satan's Intentions

One issue Joseph Smith addressed as being an intention of the devil is to separate what God has joined together (such as marriage and Church membership). He said: "The policy of the wicked spirit is to separate what God has joined together, and unite what He has separated, which the devil has succeeded in doing to admiration in the present society" (ibid., p. 103).

Another issue is being self-righteous. "All the religious world is boasting of righteousness; it is the doctrine of the devil to retard the human mind, and hinder our progress, by filling us with self-righteousness. The nearer we get to our heavenly Father, the more we are disposed to look with compassion on perishing souls; we feel that we want to take them upon our shoulders, and cast their sins behind our backs. My talk is intended for all this society; if you would have God have mercy on you, have mercy on one another" (ibid., p. 241).

The Prophet Lehi taught: "Because [the devil] had fallen from heaven, and had become miserable forever, he sought also the misery of all mankind. . . . Wherefore, men are free according to the flesh; and all things are given them which are expedient unto man. And they are free to choose liberty and eternal life, through the great Mediator of all men, or to choose captivity and death, according to the captivity and power of the devil; for he seeketh that all men might be miserable like unto himself" (2 Nephi 2:18, 27).

Our Safety

Finally, the Prophet gave us the key for avoiding the destruction the devil has planned for each of our souls: "He said he did not care how fast we run in the path of virtue; resist evil, and there is no danger; God, men, and angels will not condemn those that resist everything that is evil, and devils cannot; as well might the devil seek to dethrone Jehovah, as overthrow an innocent soul that resists everything which is evil" (*Teachings*, p. 226).

By learning to recognize Satan and then completely resisting evil, we who travel through the wilderness of the Lord will have overcome the devil in our lives, and he will be bound. And according to President Spencer W. Kimball: "When Satan is bound in a single home—when Satan is bound in a single life—the Millennium has already begun in that home, in that life" (*The Teachings of Spencer W. Kimball*, p. 172).

It seems worth the effort, doesn't it?

The Highest
Blessings
of the Gospel

23

All to Make Their Callings and Elections Sure

Once ancient wilderness travelers had been "called" as sons or daughters of Jesus Christ and had been "elected" as the elect of God, they were declared by the Spirit to be friends of Christ. Thereafter it remained for them to make their callings and elections sure and so become joint heirs with Christ. Thus Peter declared: "Give diligence to make your calling and election sure: for if ye do these things, ye shall never fall: for so an entrance shall be ministered unto you abundantly into the everlasting kingdom of our Lord and Saviour Jesus Christ" (2 Peter 1:10–11). "We have therefore a more sure knowledge of the word of prophecy, to which word of prophecy ye do well that ye take heed, as unto a light that shineth in a dark place, until the day dawn, and the day star arise in your hearts" (JST 2 Peter 1:19).

Joseph Smith says that when Peter "exhorts us to make our calling and election sure," it is the same thing as "the sealing power spoken of by Paul in other places" (*Teachings,* p. 149). As Elder Bruce R. McConkie puts it: "The illustrative quotation from Paul which the Prophet then quotes is: 'In whom ye also trusted, after that ye heard the word of truth, the gospel of your salvation: in whom also after that ye believed, ye were sealed with that holy Spirit of promise, Which is the earnest of our inheritance until the redemption of the purchased possession, unto the praise of his glory,' that we may be sealed up unto the day of redemption. (Eph. 1:13–14.) That is, the calling and election of Ephesian Saints had been made sure because they were sealed by the Holy Spirit of Promise" (*Doctrinal New Testament Commentary* [Salt Lake City: Bookcraft, 1973], 3:336).

The Meaning of the Phrase

Elder McConkie also explains: "All blessings promised in connection with the callings of God are conditional; they are offered to men provided they obey the laws upon which their receipt is predicated (D.&C. 130:20–21). 'For all who will have a blessing at my hands,' the Lord says, 'shall abide the law which was appointed for that blessing, and the conditions thereof, as were instituted from before the foundation of the world' (D.&C. 132:5).

"It follows, then, that when the law has been lived to the full, the promised blessing is guaranteed. 'I, the Lord, am bound when ye do what I say; but when ye do not what I say, ye have no promise' (D.&C. 82:10). Accordingly, when a man lives the law that qualifies him for eternal life, the Lord is bound by his own law to confer that greatest of all gifts upon him. And if by a long course of trial and obedience, while yet in this life, a man proves to the Lord that he has and will abide in the truth, the Lord accepts the exhibited devotion and issues his decree that the promised blessings shall be received. The

calling [and election], which up to that time [have been] provi-
sional, [are] then made sure. The receipt of the promised blessings are no longer conditional; they are guaranteed.
Announcement is made that every gospel blessing shall be
inherited. . . .

"To have one's calling and election made sure is to be
sealed up unto eternal life; it is to have the unconditional guarantee of exaltation in the highest heaven of the celestial world;
it is to receive the assurance of godhood; it is, in effect, to have
the day of judgment advanced, so that an inheritance of all the
glory and honor of the Father's kingdom is assured prior to the
day when the faithful actually enter into the divine presence to
sit with Christ in his throne, even as he is 'set down' with his
'Father in his throne' (Rev. 3:21)" (ibid., 3:329–31).

A Caution about Integrity

Before we can progress in this highly spiritual area, however, we must thoroughly understand the principle of integrity.
Brigham Young taught: "There is one principle that I wish the
people would understand and lay to heart. Just as fast as you
will prove before your God that you are worthy to receive the
mysteries, if you please to call them so, of the kingdom of
heaven—that you are full of confidence in God—that you will
never betray a thing that God tells you—that you will never
reveal to your neighbor that which ought not to be revealed, as
quick as you prepare to be entrusted with the things of God,
there is an eternity of them to bestow upon you. Instead of
pleading with the Lord to bestow more upon you, plead with
yourselves to have confidence in yourselves, to have integrity
in yourselves, and know when to speak and what to speak,
what to reveal, and how to carry yourselves and walk before
the Lord. And just as fast as you prove to Him that you will

preserve everything secret that ought to be—that you will deal out to your neighbors all which you ought, and no more, and learn how to dispense your knowledge to your families, friends, neighbors, and brethren, the Lord will bestow upon you, and give to you, and bestow upon you, until finally he will say to you, 'You shall never fall; your salvation is sealed unto you; you are sealed up unto eternal life and salvation, through your integrity'" (*Journal of Discourses*, 4:371–72).

The Voice of God out of the Heavens

Throughout history, even when for one reason or another the blessings of receiving the fulness of the priesthood have not been readily available, righteous Saints who have progressed spiritually to the fullest extent possible have obtained the voice of God out of the heavens declaring their callings and elections to be sure. Thus Moses taught: "[The fulness of the priesthood] was delivered unto men by the calling of his own voice, according to his own will, unto as many as believed on his name" (JST Genesis 14:29). In our day the Lord has declared: "Wo unto all those who come not unto this priesthood which ye have received, which I now confirm upon you who are present this day, by mine own voice out of the heavens" (D&C 84:42).

Joseph the Prophet declared: "There are three grand secrets . . . which no man can dig out, unless by the light of revelation. . . . I am going to take up this subject by virtue of the knowledge of God in me, which I have received from heaven" (*Teachings*, p. 304). These are the three secrets: "1st key: Knowledge is the power of salvation. 2nd key: Make your calling and election sure. 3rd key: It is one thing to be on the mount and hear the excellent voice . . . [as Peter did bearing witness of the Son], and another to hear the voice [of God] declare to you, You have a part and lot in that kingdom" (ibid., p. 306).

Some who obtained the voice of God out of the heavens declaring their exaltation were Adam (see Moses 6:51, 66–67), Abraham (see Abraham 1:16–19), Isaac (see Genesis 26:2–4, 24–25), Jacob (see Genesis 32:24–30), Moses (see Moses 1:1–5), the Brother of Jared (see Ether 3:13), Nephi (see 1 Nephi 11:6–7, 11), his brother Jacob (see 2 Nephi 2:2–4; 33:6), Moroni (see Ether 12:37–39), and our Savior, the Lord Jesus Christ (see D&C 93:11–22; *Teachings*, p. 308).

As an additional example of one who obtained the promise of exaltation in this manner, consider the experience of Nephi the son of Helaman. "As he was thus pondering—being much cast down because of the wickedness of the people of the Nephites, their secret works of darkness, and their murderings, and their plunderings, and all manner of iniquities—and it came to pass as he was thus pondering in his heart, behold, *a voice came unto him saying:* Blessed art thou, Nephi, for those things which thou hast done; for I have beheld how thou hast with unwearyingness declared the word, which I have given unto thee, unto this people. And thou hast not feared them, and hast not sought thine own life, but hast sought my will, and to keep my commandments. And now, because thou hast done this with such unwearyingness, *behold, I will bless thee forever; and I will make thee mighty in word and in deed, in faith and in works; yea, even that all things shall be done unto thee according to thy word, for thou shalt not ask that which is contrary to my will. Behold, thou art Nephi, and I am God. Behold, I declare it unto thee in the presence of mine angels*" (Helaman 10:3–6; emphasis mine).

For our day, the Prophet Joseph Smith is the classic example of one who was sealed up unto eternal life by obtaining the voice of God out of the heavens. Of him the scripture states: "I am the Lord thy God, and will be with thee even unto the end of the world, and through all eternity; for verily I seal upon you your exaltation, and prepare a throne for you in the kingdom of my Father, with Abraham your father" (D&C 132:49).

Mary Elizabeth Rollins Lightner related that, in a meeting in Kirtland in 1831 that she attended: "Joseph looked around very solemnly. It was the first time some of them had ever seen him. Said he, 'There are enough here to hold a little meeting.' They got a board and put it across two chairs to make seats. Martin Harris sat on a little box at Joseph's feet. They sang and prayed. Joseph got up and began to speak to us. As he began to speak very solemnly and very earnestly, all at once his countenance changed and he stood mute. Those who looked at him that day said there was a search light within him, over every part of his body. I never saw anything like it on the earth. I could not take my eyes off him; he got so white that anyone who saw him would have thought he was transparent. I remember I thought I could almost see the cheek bones through the flesh. I have been through many changes since but that is photographed on my brain. I shall remember it and see in my mind's eye as long as I remain upon the earth.

"He stood some moments. He looked over the congregation as if to pierce every heart. He said, 'Do you know who has been in your midst?' One of the Smiths said an angel of the Lord. Martin Harris said, 'It was our Lord and Savior, Jesus Christ.' Joseph put his hand down on Martin and said: 'God revealed that to you. Brethren and sisters, the Spirit of God has been here. The Savior has been in your midst this night and I want you to remember it. There is a veil over your eyes for you could not endure to look upon Him. You must be fed with milk, not with strong meat. I want you to remember this as if it were the last thing that escaped my lips. He has given all of you to me and has *sealed you up to everlasting life that where he is, you may be also.* And if you are tempted of Satan say, "Get behind me, Satan."'

"These words are figured upon my brain and I never took my eye off his countenance. Then he knelt down and prayed. I have never heard anything like it before or since. I felt that he was talking to the Lord and that power rested down upon the congregation. Every soul felt it. The spirit rested upon us in every fiber of our bodies" (Mary Elizabeth Lightner, "Address at Brigham Young University," April 14, 1905, typescript, BYU, p. 1; emphasis mine).

One other in this dispensation whose experience is worthy of note is Heber C. Kimball. In his published journal, under the date of April 6, 1839, he recorded: "I returned to Far West April 5th, and remained a few days. My family having been gone about two months (during which time I heard nothing from them), our brethren being in prison, and death and destruction following us wherever we went, I felt very sorrowful and lonely. While in this condition, the following words came to my mind, and the Spirit said unto me, 'Write.' I obeyed by taking a piece of paper and writing on my knee, as follows: ' . . . Verily, I say unto my servant Heber, thou art my son in whom I am well pleased; for thou art careful to hearken to my words, and not transgress my law nor rebel against my servant Joseph Smith; for thou hast a respect to the words of mine anointed, even from the least to the greatest of them; *therefore, thy name is written in heaven, no more to be blotted out forever,* because of these things; and this spirit and blessing shall rest down upon thy posterity forever and ever" (*President Heber C. Kimball's Journal,* Seventh Book of the Faith-Promoting Series [Salt Lake City, Juvenile Instructor Office, 1882], p. 70; emphasis mine).

Brigham Young felt so strongly about members of the Church obtaining this and similar experiences that he declared:

"Any person knowing and understanding the Scriptures as they are, and understanding the mind and will of God can understand at once that when he is shut out from the presence of the Lord, *when He does not hear His voice,* sees not His face, receives not the ministering of His angels or ministering spirits, and has no messenger from the heavens to visit him, he must surely be in hell" (*Journal of Discourses,* 2:137; emphasis mine).

And thus we see that, no matter the conditions of the world in which we may find ourselves, we should, and will be allowed to, progress spiritually as far as we wish to go.

Priesthood Power

But is this heavenly manifestation all there is? Not according to the Prophet Joseph, who said: "Abraham's was a more exalted power or priesthood (for he could talk and walk with God), and yet consider how great this man [Melchizedek] was when even this patriarch Abraham gave a tenth part of all his spoils and then received a blessing under the hands of Melchizedek, even the last law or a fulness of the law or priesthood, which constituted [Abraham] a king and a priest after the order of Melchizedek or an endless life" (*Words,* p. 246). "Melchizedek [had] power of an endless life, of which [the type] was our Lord Jesus Christ, which also Abraham obtained by the offering of his son Isaac. . . . [This was] not the power of a Prophet nor apostle nor patriarch only, but of King and Priest to God, to open the windows of heaven and pour out the peace and law of endless life to man. . . . No man can attain to this Joint heirship with Jesus Christ without being administered to by one having the same power and authority of Melchizedek" (ibid., p. 245; spelling and punctuation standardized).

"Now for the secret and grand key," Joseph declared. "Though they might hear the voice of God and know that Jesus was the Son of God, this would be no evidence that their election and calling was made sure, that they had part with Christ, and were joint heirs with Him. They then would want that more sure word of prophecy, that they were sealed in the heavens and had the promise of eternal life in the kingdom of God. Then, having this promise sealed unto them, it was an anchor to the soul, sure and steadfast" (*Teachings*, p. 298).

Thus the Lord declared: "All covenants, contracts, bonds, obligations, oaths, vows, performances, connections, associations, or expectations, that are not made and entered into and sealed by the Holy Spirit of promise, of him who is anointed, both as well for time and for all eternity, and that too most holy, by revelation and commandment through the medium of mine anointed, whom I have appointed on the earth to hold this power (and I have appointed unto my servant Joseph to hold this power in the last days, and there is never but one on the earth at a time on whom this power and the keys of this priesthood are conferred), are of no efficacy, virtue, or force in and after the resurrection from the dead; for all contracts that are not made unto this end have an end when men are dead" (D&C 132:7).

From the foregoing it is apparent that he whom the Lord calls His Anointed—the president of the Church—is responsible for the bestowal of all priesthood blessings throughout the Church. So it is with what the Lord calls "the fulness of the priesthood" (D&C 124:28), and which Bruce R. McConkie calls "the fulness of the sealing power" (*Mormon Doctrine*, p. 217). The president of the Church is responsible for its administration. Thus the Lord says: "The keys of the kingdom . . . belong always unto the Presidency of the High Priesthood" (D&C 81:2), and only one man on earth at a time, the president of the Church, can exercise them in their fulness (see D&C 132:7).

When he is instructed "by revelation and commandment" to exercise these priesthood keys of sealing power in their fulness in behalf of worthy Church members, the prophet's blessing or pronouncement can be called the more sure word of prophecy, for "whether by mine own voice or by the voice of my servants, it is the same" (D&C 1:38). The Lord declares: "The more sure word of prophecy means a man's knowing that he is sealed up unto eternal life, by revelation and the spirit of prophecy through the power of the Holy Priesthood" (D&C 131:5). Thus Joseph said: "I anointed [Judge James Adams] to the patriarchal power—to receive the keys of knowledge and power, by revelation to himself" (*Teachings*, p. 326).

Speaking of the power and authority of the prophet to do this work, President George Q. Cannon stated that "when he spoke by the power of God, it was the word of God to this people. When he sealed a man up to eternal life, he bestowed upon him the blessings pertaining to eternity, and to the Godhead, or when he delegated others to do it in his stead, God in the eternal world recorded the act; the blessings that were sealed upon that man or that woman, they were sealed to be binding in this life, and in that life which is to come; they became part of the records of eternity, and would be fulfilled to the very letter upon the heads of those upon whom they were pronounced. . . . There is no doubt about it" (*Journal of Discourses*, 24:274).

Though the Holy Ghost acting as the Holy Spirit of Promise must ratify all priesthood ordinances conditionally, in this one instance—receiving the fulness of the priesthood by the more sure word of prophecy—the ratification and seal are final. Elder Bruce R. McConkie explains: "When the Holy Spirit of Promise places his ratifying seal upon . . . someone whose calling and election is thereby made sure—because there are no more conditions to be met by the obedient person—this act of being sealed up unto eternal life is of such transcendent import that of itself it is called being sealed by the Holy Spirit of Promise, which means that in this crowning sense, being so sealed is the same as having one's calling and election made sure. Thus, to be sealed by the Holy Spirit of Promise is to be sealed up unto eternal life; and to be sealed up unto eternal life is to be sealed by the Holy Spirit of Promise" (*Doctrinal New Testament Commentary*, 3:335–36).

Thus the Lord declares: "If a man marry a wife by my word, which is my law, and by the new and everlasting covenant, and it is sealed unto them by the Holy Spirit of promise, by him who is anointed, unto whom I have appointed this power and the keys of this priesthood; and it shall be said unto them—Ye shall come forth in the first resurrection; and if it be after the first resurrection, in the next resurrection; and shall inherit thrones, kingdoms, principalities and powers, dominions, all heights and depths—then shall it be written in the Lamb's Book of Life, that he shall commit no murder whereby to shed innocent blood, and if ye abide in my covenant, and commit no murder whereby to shed innocent blood, it shall be done unto them in all things whatsoever my servant hath put upon them, in time, and through all eternity; and shall be of full force when they are out of the world; and they shall pass by the angels, and the gods, which are set there, to their exaltation and glory in all things, as hath been sealed upon their heads, which glory shall be a fulness and a continuation of the seeds forever and ever" (D&C 132:19).

The Keys of Elijah

These sealing powers we have been speaking of are the keys restored by Elijah to Joseph and Oliver Cowdery in the

Kirtland Temple (see D&C 110:13–16). Joseph Smith taught: "The spirit, power, and calling of Elijah is, that ye have power to hold the key of the revelations, ordinances, oracles, powers and endowments of the fulness of the Melchizedek Priesthood and of the kingdom of God on the earth; and to receive, obtain, and perform all the ordinances belonging to the kingdom of God" (*Teachings*, p. 337).

Therefore: "the power of Elijah is sufficient to make our calling and Election sure" (*Words*, p. 330). To be sealed by the Holy Spirit of Promise is to be sealed by the spirit and power of Elijah (ibid., p. 335). "God . . . shall send Elijah . . . [to] reveal the covenants, to seal the hearts of the fathers to the children and the children to the fathers—anointing and sealing—called, elected, and made sure—without father, etc., [which is] a priesthood which holds [power] by right from the eternal Gods—and not by descent from father and mother" (ibid., p. 244; spelling and punctuation standardized).

And: "A measure of this sealing is to confirm upon their head in common with Elijah the doctrine of election or the covenant with Abraham . . . where it says . . . they shall seal the servants of God in their foreheads, etc. It means to seal the blessing on their heads, meaning the everlasting covenant, thereby making their calling and election sure . . . which when a father and mother of a family have entered into, their children . . . are secured by the seal wherewith the parents have been sealed [and such children] cannot be lost. . . . And this is the oath of God unto our Father Abraham, and this doctrine shall stand forever" (ibid., pp. 241–42; spelling and punctuation standardized).

And finally: "The doctrine or sealing power of Elijah is . . . that degree of power which holds the sealing power of the Kingdom. . . . Make your calling and election sure. Go from

grace to grace until you obtain a promise from God for yourselves that you shall have eternal life. This is eternal life, to
know God and his son Jesus Christ—it is to be sealed up unto
eternal life and obtain a promise for our posterity. Whatever
you shall bind on earth shall be bound in heaven. This is the
power of Elijah" (ibid., pp. 331, 334; punctuation standardized).

It is interesting to note that, according to Joseph Smith, this
sealing power may also be used to seal certain individuals to
the buffetings of Satan in order that they might ultimately
obtain eternal lives. As he declared: "This spirit of Elijah was
manifested in the days of the Apostles in delivering certain
ones to the buffetings of Satan that they may be saved in the
day of the Lord Jesus. They were sealed by the spirit of Elijah
unto the damnation of Hell. . . . [However], the power of Elijah
cannot seal against [the unpardonable] sin, for this is a reserve
made in the seals and power of the priesthood" (ibid., p. 330;
spelling and punctuation standardized).

The Spirit of Elijah

In the chapter dealing with the ministering of angels the
Prophet Joseph was quoted concerning Elias, Elijah, and
Messiah. The full quotation is: "The spirit of Elias is first, Elijah
second, and Messiah last. Elias is a forerunner to prepare the
way, and the spirit and power of Elijah is to come after, holding
the keys of power, building the Temple to the capstone, placing
the seals of the Melchizedek Priesthood upon the house of
Israel, and making all things ready; then Messiah comes to His
Temple, which is last of all. Messiah is above the spirit and
power of Elijah, for He made the world, and was that spiritual
rock unto Moses in the wilderness. Elijah was to come and prepare the way and build up the kingdom before the coming of

the great day of the Lord, although the spirit of Elias might begin it" (*Teachings*, p. 340).

It should now be more evident why Joseph hinted that the expected visitation of these three personages was broader than their appearance in the Kirtland Temple. All angelic ministrants are acting in the role of Elias as they labor with those who have been born again, serving as forerunners in preparing their charges for the higher sealing blessings of Elijah. And when people are sealed up unto eternal life by having their calling and election made sure through the more sure word of prophecy, then in that sense they received the ministration and sealing powers of Elijah.

Long after the Kirtland Temple experience, Elder Orson Pratt taught: "We need never look for the coming of the Son of God—for the day when he shall suddenly come to his temple and sit like a refiner of silver, and as with fuller's soap to purify and purge the sons of Levi, &c., until Elijah the Prophet is sent. . . . He will be sent with power and authority, like other angels sent from heaven, to bestow the same authority that is upon himself on some individuals on the earth, that they may go forth holding that same authority that Elijah himself held, having the same keys, receiving the same instructions, in regard to the Latter-day dispensation,—a mission, in other words, sent from heaven by Elijah as a ministering angel to seek out the chosen vessels, and ordain them, and send them to administer to the inhabitants of the earth (*Journal of Discourses*, 7:78).

The Significance of the Temple

Since Elijah could not restore his keys of sealing the fulness of the priesthood upon worthy individuals to Joseph until a proper temple had been erected (see D&C 124:28), it follows that the temple must also be significant in their administration. Thus the Prophet Joseph said: "If a man gets a fullness of the priesthood of God he has to get it in the same way that Jesus Christ obtained it, and that was by keeping all the commandments and obeying all the ordinances of the house of the Lord. . . . All men who become heirs of God and joint-heirs with Jesus Christ will have to receive the fulness of the ordinances of his kingdom; and those who will not receive all the ordinances will come short of the fulness of that glory, if they do not lose the whole" (*Teachings*, pp. 308–9).

Priests and Kings

One of the honors given to those who have made their callings and elections sure is that they are made priests and kings to God. It was not enough that Joseph be a king and a priest to the Most High, but he also insisted that his people be a society of priests "as in Paul's day, as in Enoch's day," through the full ordinances of the temple (see *Words*, pp. 54–55). As he put it: "What was the power of Melchizedek? 'Twas not the Priesthood of Aaron which administers in outward ordinances, and the offering of sacrifices. Those holding the fulness of the Melchizedek Priesthood are kings and priests of the Most High God, holding the keys of power and blessings" (*Teachings*, p. 322).

Elder Bruce R. McConkie elaborates: "Holders of the Melchizedek Priesthood have power to press forward in righteousness, living by every word that proceedeth forth from the mouth of God, magnifying their callings, going from grace to grace, until through the fulness of the ordinances of the temple they receive the fulness of the priesthood and are ordained *kings and priests*. Those so attaining shall have exaltation and be kings, priests, rulers, and lords in their respective spheres in the eternal kingdoms of the great King who is God our Father (Rev. 1:6; 5:10)" (*Mormon Doctrine*, p. 425).

It was ever Joseph's intention that these priests and kings act in their office in communing with God. Speaking to the Twelve on February 23, 1844, Joseph Smith said: "I want every man that goes [west to explore for a new home for the Saints] to be a king and a priest. When he gets on the mountains [the Lord's temple] he may want to talk with his God" (*History of the Church*, 6:224).

Finally, lest the foregoing imply that such blessings are for men only, consider the following from Elder James E. Talmage: "In the restored Church of Jesus Christ . . . in accordance with Divine requirement . . . it is not given to woman to exercise the authority of the Priesthood independently; nevertheless, in the sacred endowments associated with the ordinances pertaining to the House of the Lord, woman shares with man the blessings of the Priesthood. When the frailties and imperfections of mortality are left behind, in the glorified state of the blessed hereafter, husband and wife will administer in their respective stations, seeing and understanding alike, and co-operating to the full in the government of their family kingdom. Then shall woman be recompensed in rich measure for all the injustice that womanhood has endured in mortality. Then shall woman reign by Divine right, a queen [and priestess] in the resplendent realm of her glorified state, even as exalted man shall stand, priest and king unto the Most High God. Mortal eye cannot see nor mind comprehend the beauty, glory, and majesty of a righteous woman made perfect in the celestial kingdom of God" ("The Eternity of Sex," *Young Woman's Journal*, October 1914, pp. 602–3).

The Order of the Son of God

Those whose callings and elections have been made sure are brought into what is called the order of the Son of God. President Ezra Taft Benson has said: "To enter into the order of the Son of God is the equivalent today of entering into the fulness of the Melchizedek Priesthood, which is only received in the house of the Lord" ("What I Hope You Will Teach Your Children About the Temple," *Ensign,* August 1985, p. 8).

Alma wrote: "Now, as I said concerning the holy order, or this high priesthood, there were many who were ordained and became high priests of God; and it was on account of their exceeding faith and repentance, and their righteousness before God, they choosing to repent and work righteousness rather than to perish; *therefore they were called after this holy order,* and were sanctified, and their garments were washed white through the blood of the Lamb. Now they, after being sanctified by the Holy Ghost, having their garments made white, being pure and spotless before God, could not look upon sin save it were with abhorrence; and there were many, exceedingly great many, who were made pure and entered into the rest of the Lord their God" (Alma 13:10–12; emphasis mine).

Among a host of others, Alma was a member of this order (see Alma 4:20), as was Jacob the son of Lehi (see 2 Nephi 6:2), Melchizedek, and Enoch. Of these latter two prophets Moses wrote: "Melchizedek lifted up his voice and blessed Abram. Now Melchizedek was a man of faith, who wrought righteousness; and when a child he feared God, and stopped the mouths of lions, and quenched the violence of fire. And thus, having been approved of God, he was ordained an high priest after the order of the covenant which God made with Enoch, *it being after the order of the Son of God;* which order came, not by man, nor the will of man; neither by father nor mother; neither by begin-

243

ning of days nor end of years; but of God; and it was delivered unto men by the calling of his own voice, according to his own will, unto as many as believed on his name" (JST Genesis 14:25–29; emphasis mine).

President Benson says: "Because Adam and Eve complied with these requirements, God said to them, 'Thou art after the order of him who was without beginning of days or end of years, from all eternity to all eternity' (Moses 6:67). Three years before Adam's death, a great event occurred. He took his son Seth, his grandson Enos, and other high priests who were direct-line descendants, with others of his righteous posterity, into a valley called Adam-ondi-Ahman. There Adam gave to these righteous descendants his last blessing. The Lord then appeared to them. The vast congregation rose up and blessed Adam and called him Michael, the prince and archangel. The Lord himself declared Adam to be a prince forever over his own posterity. Then Adam, in his aged condition, rose up and, being filled with the spirit of prophecy, 'predicted whatsoever should befall his posterity unto the latest generation' (D&C 107:56; see also vv. 53–65).

"The Prophet Joseph Smith said that 'Adam blessed his posterity' because 'he wanted to bring them into the presence of God' (*Teachings*, p. 159). Here is an illuminating passage from section 107 of the Doctrine and Covenants that tells us how Adam was able to bring himself and his righteous posterity into God's presence: 'The order of this priesthood was confirmed to be handed down from father to son, and rightly belongs to the literal descendants of the chosen seed, to whom the promises were made. This order was instituted in the days of Adam, and came down by lineage [in order] . . . that his posterity should be the *chosen of the Lord*, and that *they should be preserved unto the end of the earth*' (D&C 107:40–42; italics added).

"How did Adam bring his descendants into the presence of

the Lord? . . . [By entering] into the priesthood order of God [and then bringing them in after him]. Today we would say they went to the House of the Lord and received their blessings.

"The order of priesthood spoken of in the scriptures is sometimes referred to as the patriarchal order because it came down from father to son. But this order is otherwise described in modern revelation as an order of family government where a man and a woman enter into a covenant with God—just as did Adam and Eve—to be sealed for eternity, to have posterity, and to do the will and work of God throughout their mortality. . . .

"Adam followed this order and brought his posterity into the presence of God. He is the great example for us to follow. Enoch followed this pattern and brought the Saints of his day into the presence of God. Noah and his son Shem likewise followed the same pattern after the flood.

"Abraham, a righteous servant of God, desiring, as he said, 'to be a greater follower of righteousness,' sought for these same blessings. Speaking of the order of the priesthood, he said, 'It was conferred upon me from the fathers; it came down from the fathers, from the beginning of time, . . . even the right of the firstborn, or the first man, who is Adam, or first father, through the fathers unto me.' So Abraham declared, 'I sought for mine appointment unto the Priesthood according to the appointment of God unto the fathers' (Abraham 1:2–4)" (Ezra Taft Benson, "What I Hope You Will Teach Your Children About the Temple," *Ensign*, August 1985, pp. 8–9).

Moses also attempted to bring his people into the same holy order of the Son of God, but they hardened their hearts against such an opportunity, and so the Lord would not allow them into His rest, "which rest is the fulness of his glory" (see D&C 84:23–25). An interesting detail of the Lord's action against the children of Israel was made known to Joseph Smith, who wrote: "I

245

will take away the priesthood out of their midst; *therefore my holy order, and the ordinances thereof*" (JST Exodus 34:1; emphasis mine).

We know of one significant group yet to appear who will be ordained to this sacred order. The Prophet Joseph wrote in response to a question: "What are we to understand by sealing the one hundred and forty-four thousand, out of all the tribes of Israel—twelve thousand out of every tribe? We are to understand that those who are sealed are high priests, *ordained unto the holy order of God,* to administer the everlasting gospel; for they are they who are ordained out of every nation, kindred, tongue, and people, by the angels to whom is given power over the nations of the earth, to bring as many as will come to the church of the Firstborn" (D&C 77:11; emphasis mine).

Power in the Priesthood

The righteous who are anointed unto this holy order are given powers commensurate with the spiritual position they have obtained before the Lord. As Moses proclaimed: "God having sworn unto Enoch and unto his seed with an oath by himself; that every one being ordained after this order and calling should have power, by faith, to break mountains, to divide the seas, to dry up waters, to turn them out of their course; to put at defiance the armies of nations, to divide the earth, to break every band, to stand in the presence of God; to do all things according to his will, according to his command, subdue principalities and powers; and this by the will of the Son of God which was from before the foundation of the world. And men having this faith, coming up unto this order of God, were translated and taken up into heaven. . . .

"And now, Melchizedek was a priest of this order; therefore he obtained peace in Salem, and was called the Prince of peace. And his people wrought righteousness, and obtained heaven,

246

and sought for the city of Enoch which God had before taken, separating it from the earth, having reserved it unto the latter days, or the end of the world" (JST Genesis 14:30–34).

Enoch used this power according to the holy order of the Son of God with great effectiveness. In the writings of Moses as revealed to Joseph Smith we read: "So great was the faith of Enoch, that he led the people of God, and their enemies came to battle against them; and he spake the word of the Lord, and the earth trembled, and the mountains fled, even according to his command; and the rivers of water were turned out of their course; and the roar of the lions was heard out of the wilderness; and all nations feared greatly, so powerful was the word of Enoch, and so great was the power of the language which God had given him" (Moses 7:13).

The scriptures contain other accounts of the remarkable powers that accompany the granting of the fulness of this patriarchal order of the priesthood. For instance, we know that the Lord said to Nephi, the son of Helaman: "Behold, thou art Nephi, and I am God. Behold, I declare it unto thee in the presence of mine angels, that ye shall have power over this people, and shall smite the earth with famine, and with pestilence, and destruction, according to the wickedness of this people. Behold, I give unto you power, that whatsoever ye shall seal on earth shall be sealed in heaven; and whatsoever ye shall loose on earth shall be loosed in heaven; and thus shall ye have power among this people. And thus, if ye shall say unto this temple it shall be rent in twain, it shall be done. And if ye shall say unto this mountain, Be thou cast down and become smooth, it shall be done. And behold, if ye shall say that God shall smite this people, it shall come to pass" (Helaman 10:6–10).

A final example of this power would be the Brother of Jared, whose faith brought him to the veil, where he saw the finger of the Lord. As Moroni wrote: "There were many whose faith was so exceedingly strong, even before Christ came, who could not be kept from within the veil, but truly saw with their eyes the things which they had beheld with an eye of faith, and they were glad. And behold, we have seen in this record that one of these was the brother of Jared; for so great was his faith in God, that when God put forth his finger he could not hide it from the sight of the brother of Jared, because of his word which he had spoken unto him, which word he had obtained by faith. And after the brother of Jared had beheld the finger of the Lord, because of the promise which the brother of Jared had obtained by faith, the Lord could not withhold anything from his sight; wherefore he showed him all things, for he could no longer be kept without the veil" (Ether 12:19–21).

Thereafter the Brother of Jared ordered the mountain Zerin to remove and it was removed (see Ether 12:30). But he was given another power that is even more remarkable and that was almost the envy of the great Moroni, who wrote in prayer: "Behold, thou hast not made us mighty in writing like unto the brother of Jared, for thou madest him that the things which he wrote were mighty even as thou art, unto the overpowering of man to read them" (Ether 12:24).

Modern Application

Joseph Smith taught: "After a person hath faith in Christ . . . then let him continue to humble himself before God, hungering and thirsting after righteousness and living by every word of God and the Lord will soon say unto him, 'Son thou shalt be exalted,' etc. When the Lord has thoroughly proved him and finds that the man is determined to serve him at all hazards, then the man will find his calling and election made sure" (*Words*, p. 5; spelling and punctuation standardized).

Those wilderness wanderers who have accomplished this have become patriarchs over their own families in the full and complete sense of the word. Having the fulness of the priesthood and reigning as kings and priests unto God, they have received the sealing power, or keys, of Elijah, which is called the Patriarchal Priesthood, and can therefore speak with absolute authority, as did Nephi the son of Helaman, within their own callings and stewardships. They have fulfilled the declaration of Joseph Smith, who said: "The Bible says 'I will send you Elijah . . . that he shall turn the hearts of the fathers to the children & the hearts of the children to their fathers. . . . ' Now the word 'turn' here should be translated bind or seal. But what is the object of this important mission or how is it to be fulfilled? The keys are to be delivered, the Spirit of Elijah is to come, the gospel to be established, the Saints of God gathered, Zion built up, and the Saints to come up as Saviors on Mount Zion. But how are they to become Saviors on Mount Zion? By building their temples, erecting their baptismal fonts, and going forth and receiving all the ordinances, baptisms, confirmations, washings, anointings, ordinations *and sealing powers* upon [their] heads" (*Words*, p. 318; emphasis mine; spelling and punctuation standardized).

Finally, it is vital that we keep in mind that, though mortal death may come upon us before we receive a fulness of these blessings, yet "even so in Christ shall [we] all be made alive" (1 Corinthians 15:22) and be made "partakers of the inheritance of the saints" (Colossians 1:12) or "the heavenly gift" (4 Nephi 1:3) of the fulness of the priesthood. Our challenge, therefore, is to become fully worthy of the fulness of the priesthood and to endure to the end in that state or condition.

And that, of course, is preparatory to receiving the Messiah as the Second Comforter, the ultimate blessing available to mortals.

CHAPTER

24

The Second Comforter

As the majestic finale of the wilderness experience, wanderers must progress steadily forward in the Spirit, clinging steadfastly to every word that proceeds out of the mouth of God. That diligent seeking permits them to "have the privilege of receiving the mysteries of the kingdom of heaven, to have the heavens opened unto them, to commune with the general assembly and church of the Firstborn, *and to enjoy the communion and presence of God the Father, and Jesus the mediator of the new covenant*" (D&C 107:19; emphasis mine). "This greater priesthood administereth the gospel and holdeth the key of the mysteries of the kingdom, even the key of the knowledge of God" (D&C 84:19).

As a further explanation of this, Joseph Smith wrote that "the Keys of this priesthood consisted in [Noah's] obtaining the voice of Jehovah that [Jehovah] talked with him in a familiar and friendly manner, that he continued to him the Keys, the Covenants, the power and the glory with which

[Jehovah] blessed Adam at the beginning. . . . Elijah was the last prophet that held the Keys of this priesthood, and who will, before the last dispensation, restore the authority and deliver the keys of this priesthood in order that all the ordinances may be attended to in righteousness" (*Words*, pp. 42–43).

According to Joseph Smith, these keys of access to God, held in fulness by the president of the Church, enable the least member in the church to have power in his priesthood to also bring himself into the presence of God (see *Teachings*, p. 149). Scripturally this is called beholding the face of Christ, who has said: "It shall come to pass that every soul who forsaketh his sins and cometh unto me, and calleth on my name, and obeyeth my voice, and keepeth my commandments, shall see my face and know that I am" (D&C 93:1). This experience, of course, is true worship, and according to Moses, it occurs when we call upon God through the name of His Only Begotten in mighty prayer (see Moses 1:17), which is accomplished with greatest effectiveness through temple worship.

The crowning blessing of the wilderness experience, then, is to see and know personally our Savior. As Elder Bruce R. McConkie says: "The purpose of the endowment in the house of the Lord is to prepare and sanctify his saints so they will be able to see his face, here and now, as well as to bear the glory of his presence in the eternal worlds" (*The Promised Messiah* [Salt Lake City: Deseret Book Company, 1978], p. 583).

Ultimately, therefore, if we are to successfully conclude the Lord's wilderness school, we must see Christ face to face as one person sees another, speak with Him in like manner, and feel the wounds in His hands and feet. That is called receiving the Second Comforter.

All Are to Know the Lord

"I am going on in my progress for eternal life," Joseph said of himself; and then in fervent pleading to all the Saints, he exclaimed: "Oh! I beseech you to go forward, go forward and make your calling and your election sure" (*Teachings,* p. 366), "for the day must come when no man need say to his neighbor, Know ye the Lord; for all shall know Him (who remain) from the least to the greatest. How is this to be done? It is to be done by this sealing power, and the other Comforter spoken of, which will be manifest by revelation" (*Teachings,* p. 149).

The Prophet continues: "The other Comforter spoken of is a subject of great interest, and perhaps understood by few of this generation. After a person has faith in Christ, repents of his sins, and is baptized for the remission of his sins and receives the Holy Ghost, (by the laying on of hands), which is the first Comforter, then let him continue to humble himself before God, hungering and thirsting after righteousness, and living by every word of God, and the Lord will soon say unto him, Son, thou shalt be exalted. When the Lord has thoroughly proved him, and finds that the man is determined to serve Him at all hazards, then the man will find his calling and his election made sure, then it will be his privilege to receive the other Comforter, which the Lord hath promised the Saints, as is recorded in the testimony of St. John, in the 14th chapter, from the 12th to the 27th verses" (*Teachings,* pp. 149–50).

In a revelation to a group of Latter-day Saints in December 1832, the Lord said that the alms of their prayers were "recorded in the book of the names of the sanctified, even them of the celestial world" (D&C 88:2). That meant they had "overcome by faith" and were "sealed by the Holy Spirit of promise, which the Father sheds forth upon all those who are just and true" (D&C 76:53). "Wherefore," the Lord said to them, "I now send upon you another Comforter, even upon you my friends, that it may abide in your hearts, even the Holy Spirit of promise; which other Comforter is the same that I promised unto my disciples, as is recorded in the testimony of John. This Comforter is the promise which I give unto you of eternal life, even the glory of the celestial kingdom; which glory is that of the church of the Firstborn, even of God, the holiest of all, through Jesus Christ his Son" (D&C 88:3–5).

Seeing and Knowing God

In this volume we have discussed many individuals who have experienced the Second Comforter and have seen and known God. While I do not wish to be repetitious, perhaps it would be worthwhile to reconsider them.

Abraham records his relief upon finally obtaining this grand blessing by declaring: "After the Lord had withdrawn from speaking to me, and withdrawn his face from me, I said in my heart: Thy servant hast sought thee earnestly; now I have found thee" (Abraham 2:12). So will we all feel that great relief.

Mahonri Moriancumer, the Brother of Jared, was also able to attain to this remarkable spiritual experience while dwelling in the wilderness. His account is interesting because of the amount of knowledge the Lord was willing to impart once the veil had been opened. Moroni, in recording the event, states that "the veil was taken from off the eyes of the brother of Jared, and he saw the finger of the Lord; and it was as the finger of a man, like unto flesh and blood; and the brother of Jared fell down before the Lord, for he was struck with fear. And the Lord saw that the brother of Jared had fallen to the earth; and the Lord said unto him: Arise, why hast thou fallen? And he saith unto the Lord: I saw the finger of the Lord, and I feared lest he should smite me; for I knew not that the Lord had flesh and blood.

"And the Lord said unto him: Because of thy faith thou hast seen that I shall take upon me flesh and blood; and never has man come before me with such exceeding faith as thou hast; for were it not so ye could not have seen my finger. Sawest thou more than this? And he answered: Nay; Lord, show thyself unto me. And the Lord said unto him: Believest thou the words which I shall speak? And he answered: Yea, Lord, I know that thou speakest the truth, for thou art a God of truth, and canst not lie.

"And when he had said these words, behold, the Lord showed himself unto him, and said: Because thou knowest these things ye are redeemed from the fall; therefore ye are brought back into my presence; therefore I show myself unto you. Behold, I am he who was prepared from the foundation of the world to redeem my people. Behold, I am Jesus Christ. I am the Father and the Son. In me shall all mankind have life, and that eternally, even they who shall believe on my name; and they shall become my sons and my daughters. And never have I showed myself unto man whom I have created, for never has man believed in me as thou hast. Seest thou that ye are created after mine own image? Yea, even all men were created in the beginning after mine own image. Behold, this body, which ye now behold, is the body of my spirit; and man have I created after the body of my spirit; and even as I appear unto thee to be in the spirit will I appear unto my people in the flesh."

"Therefore," Moroni concludes, "it sufficeth me to say that Jesus showed himself unto this man in the spirit, even after the manner and in the likeness of the same body even as he showed himself unto the Nephites. And he ministered unto him even as he ministered unto the Nephites; and all this, that this man might know that he was God, because of the many great works which the Lord had showed unto him. And because of the knowledge of this man he could not be kept from beholding within the veil; and he saw the finger of Jesus, which, when he saw, he fell with fear; for he knew that it was the finger of the Lord; and he had faith no longer, for he knew, nothing doubting. Wherefore, having this perfect knowledge of God, he could not be kept from within the veil; therefore he saw Jesus; and he did minister unto him" (Ether 3:6–20).

Moses, Nadab, Abihu, and seventy of the elders of Israel were successful in obtaining the Second Comforter (see Exodus 24:9–10), but most of the Israelites were not—because they *chose* not to be. That angered the Lord, and because of their rebelliousness the entire generation was never allowed to see the face of God and enter into the Lord's rest" (see D&C 84:23–24). Therefore "the children of Israel walked forty years in the wilderness, till all the people that were men of war, which came out of Egypt, were consumed, because they obeyed not the voice of the Lord: unto whom the Lord sware that he would not shew them the land, which the Lord sware unto their fathers that he would give us, a land that floweth with milk and honey" (Joshua 5:6).

On the other hand, Nephi records that both he and his younger brother, Jacob, were successful in being brought into the presence of the Lord. To our benefit, he also tells us that this marvelous blessing was accomplished not because of age or ecclesiastical experience but through intense desire, great diligence, and lowliness of heart.

"I, Nephi, being exceedingly young, nevertheless being large in stature, and also having great desires to know of the mysteries of God, wherefore, I did cry unto the Lord; and behold *he did visit me,* and did soften my heart that I did believe all the words which had been spoken by my father; wherefore, I did not rebel against him like unto my brothers. And I spake unto Sam, making known unto him the things which the Lord had manifested unto me by his Holy Spirit. And it came to pass that he believed in my words. But, behold, Laman and Lemuel would not hearken unto my words; and being grieved because of the hardness of their hearts I cried unto the Lord for them. And it came to pass that the Lord spake unto me, saying: Blessed art thou, Nephi, because of thy faith, for thou hast sought me diligently, with lowliness of heart" (1 Nephi 2:16–19; emphasis mine). And "I spake unto him as a man speaketh; for I beheld that he was in the form of a man; yet nevertheless, I knew that it was *the Spirit of the Lord;* and he spake unto me as a man speaketh with another" (1 Nephi 11:11; emphasis mine).

Nephi also wrote: "I will send [Isaiah's words] forth unto all my children, for he verily saw my Redeemer, even as I have seen him. And my brother, Jacob, also has seen him" (2 Nephi 11:2–3).

Lehi said to his son Jacob: "Thy soul shall be blessed, and thou shalt dwell safely with thy brother, Nephi; and thy days shall be spent in the service of thy God. Wherefore, I know that thou art redeemed, because of the righteousness of thy Redeemer; for thou hast beheld that in the fulness of time he cometh to bring salvation unto men. And *thou hast beheld in thy youth his glory;* wherefore, thou art blessed even as they unto whom he shall minister in the flesh; for the Spirit is the same, yesterday, today, and forever. And the way is prepared from the fall of man, and salvation is free" (2 Nephi 2:3–4; emphasis mine).

Jesus among the Nephites

One of the most supernal witnesses of Christ's personal mingling in the lives of mortals occurred in the Land Bountiful almost a year after the Savior's crucifixion and resurrection in Jerusalem (see 3 Nephi 8:5; 10:18). There at the temple, once the people had exercised sufficient faith (see Ether 12:7), the resurrected Lord made himself physically manifest to more than twenty-five hundred of them (see 3 Nephi 17:25).

The record states that they twice heard a voice out of heaven but did not understand it. "And again the third time they did hear the voice, and did open their ears to hear it; and their eyes were towards the sound thereof; and they did look steadfastly towards heaven, from whence the sound came. And behold, the third time they did understand the voice which they heard; and it said unto them: Behold my Beloved Son, in whom I am well pleased, in whom I have glorified my name— hear ye him. And it came to pass, as they understood they cast their eyes up again towards heaven; and behold, they saw a Man descending out of heaven; and he was clothed in a white robe; and he came down and stood in the midst of them; and the eyes of the whole multitude were turned upon him, and they durst not open their mouths, even one to another, and wist not what it meant, for they thought it was an angel that had appeared unto them.

"And it came to pass that he stretched forth his hand and spake unto the people, saying: Behold, I am Jesus Christ, whom the prophets testified shall come into the world. . . .

"And it came to pass that when Jesus had spoken these words the whole multitude fell to the earth; for they remembered that it had been prophesied among them that Christ should show himself unto them after his ascension into heaven" (3 Nephi 11:5–10, 12).

In the days, months, and years that followed, the number of Nephite people who saw the resurrected Lord swelled to unknown thousands as He "did show himself unto them oft" (3

Nephi 26:13). Jesus continued to manifest himself unto the righteous among them until the last prophet, Moroni, was visited by Him more than four hundred years later (see Ether 12:39).

The Fulness of His Glory

It should be remembered that for most wilderness travelers, receiving the Second Comforter will be a series of relatively small but increasingly significant events, such as the Brother of Jared experienced when he first heard the voice of the Lord (see Ether 1:40–43; 2:14), saw the Lord's finger (see Ether 3:6), and finally was admitted fully into the presence of the Lord (see Ether 3:13). Nevertheless, the ultimate goal is to obtain the fulness of this divine manifestation. Thus, Moroni, who had obtained this fulness, could declare: "I, Moroni, bid farewell unto the Gentiles, yea, and also unto my brethren whom I love, until we shall meet before the judgment-seat of Christ, where all men shall know that my garments are not spotted with your blood. And then shall ye know that I have seen Jesus, and that he hath talked with me face to face, and that he told me in plain humility, even as a man telleth another in mine own language, concerning these things" (Ether 12:38–39).

Remembering the sequence of visitations Joseph Smith taught—Elias, Elijah, and then Messiah—brings us, therefore, to the nature of the mission of Messiah, or the Lord Jesus Christ, as he fully manifests himself to an individual through the true veil. As Joseph Smith taught: "The Spirit of Messiah is all power in Heaven and in Earth—Enthroned in the Heavens as King of Kings and Lord of Lords" (*Words*, p. 336). In a personal visitation in which the Messiah "comes to his Temple which is last of all" (*Words*, p. 332), the Messiah's mission is to confirm power upon the righteous, temple-oriented people that is equal to his own. They then become joint heirs with Christ to rule and reign with him forever.

When we are preparing for graduation from the Lord's wilderness school and have had such an experience, it is said that we have received the fulness of His glory, meaning that we have beheld Him in His glory (see D&C 76:20; 84:24; *Journal of Discourses*, 13:241). Joseph Smith taught: "All those who keep [the Father's] commandments shall grow up from grace to grace, and become heirs of the heavenly kingdom, and joint-heirs with Jesus Christ; possessing the same mind, being transformed into the same image or likeness, even the express image of him who fills all in all; *being filled with the fullness of his glory,* and become one in him, even as the Father, Son and Holy Spirit are one.

"As the Son partakes of the fullness of the Father through the Spirit, so the saints are, by the same Spirit, to be partakers of the same fullness, to enjoy the same glory; for as the Father and the Son are one, so, in like manner, the saints are to be one in them. Through the love of the Father, the mediation of Jesus Christ, and the gift of the Holy Spirit, they are to be heirs of God, and joint heirs with Jesus Christ" (*Lectures on Faith*, pp. 50–52; emphasis mine; see also 3 Nephi 28:10–11).

By way of further explanation, President Joseph Fielding Smith taught: "As sons and daughters then, we are heirs of his kingdom and shall receive by right the fulness of the glory and be entitled to the great blessings and privileges which the Lord in his mercy has revealed to us in the dispensation of the fulness of times. 'For as many as are led by the Spirit of God,' Paul has written, 'they are the sons of God. . . . The Spirit itself beareth witness with our spirit, that we are the children of God: And if children, then *heirs; heirs of God,* and *joint-heirs with Christ;* if so be that we suffer with him, that we may be also glorified together'" (*Doctrines of Salvation*, 2:38–39). And: "*The Lord has made it possible for us to become members of the Church of the Firstborn, by receiving the blessings of the house of the Lord and over-coming all things.* Thus we become *heirs, 'priests* and *kings,* who have received of his fulness, and of his glory,' who shall 'dwell in the presence of God and his Christ forever and ever,' with full exaltation. Are such blessings worth having?" (ibid., 2:42).

It is this promise of sharing in the same glory with Christ that is intended by the words of the revelation that states in part: "I, John, bear record that I beheld his glory, as the glory of the Only Begotten of the Father, full of grace and truth, even the Spirit of truth, which came and dwelt in the flesh, and dwelt among us. And I, John, saw that *he received not of the fulness at the first,* but received grace for grace; and he received not of the fulness at first, but continued from grace to grace, until he received a fulness; And thus he was called the Son of God, because he received not of the fulness at the first.

"And I, John, bear record, and lo, the heavens were opened, and the Holy Ghost descended upon him in the form of a dove, and sat upon him, and there came a voice out of heaven saying: This is my beloved Son. And I, John, bear record that *he received a fulness of the glory of the Father; And he received all power, both in heaven and on earth,* and the glory of the Father was with him, for he dwelt in him. . . .

"I give unto you these sayings that you may understand and know how to worship, and know what you worship, that you may come unto the Father in my name, and *in due time receive of his fulness. For if you keep my commandments you shall receive of his fulness, and be glorified in me as I am in the Father;* therefore, I say unto you, you shall receive grace for grace" (D&C 93:11–17, 19–20; emphasis mine).

A Joint Heir with Christ

Many of the references quoted above pertaining to receiving the fulness of the Lord's glory also make reference to becoming joint heirs with Christ of all that the Father has. That is because obtaining a fulness of His glory would include obtaining everything else Christ is heir to. As Bruce R. McConkie puts it: "Christ is the *Heir of God* (Matt. 21:33–41; Mark 12:1–12; Luke 20:9–18; Rom. 4:13–14; Heb. 1:1–4). . . . As the literal Son of God—the Firstborn in the spirit, the Only Begotten in the flesh—Christ is the natural *heir* of his Father. . . . It thus became his right to inherit, receive, and possess all that his Father had (John 16:15). . . . And his Father is possessor of all things: the universe; all power, wisdom, and goodness; the fulness of truth and knowledge; and an infinity of all good attributes. By heirship and by obedience, going from grace to grace, the Son attained these same things. . . . He gained every endowment, quality, attribute, perfection, power, and possession so that 'in him dwelleth all the fulness of the Godhead bodily' (Col. 2:9). He has received the 'fulness of the glory of the Father' (D.&C. 93:4–20; Col. 1:19).

"A joint-heir is one who inherits equally with all other heirs including the Chief Heir who is the Son. Each joint-heir has an equal and an undivided portion of the whole of everything. If one knows all things, so do all others. If one has all power, so do all those who inherit jointly with him. If the universe belongs to one, so it does equally to the total of all upon whom the joint inheritances are bestowed" (*Mormon Doctrine*, pp. 349, 394–95).

Once we know that we have obtained this joint heirship, according to the Prophet Joseph, this knowledge of our heirship becomes "an anchor to the soul, sure and steadfast. Though the thunders might roll and lightnings flash, and earthquakes bellow, and war gather thick around, yet this hope and knowledge would support the soul in every hour of trial, trouble and tribulation. Then knowledge through our Lord and Savior Jesus Christ is the grand key that unlocks the glories and mysteries of the kingdom of heaven" (*Teachings*, p. 298).

The Rest of the Lord

In the revelation on priesthood, the Lord told the Prophet Joseph that the Lord's rest was the fulness of his glory (see D&C 84:24). The Lord's rest, therefore, is to enter into the fulness of the Lord's glory, which wilderness travelers have all been striving for. As Alma declared: "I would that ye should humble yourselves before God, and bring forth fruit meet for repentance, that ye may also enter into that rest" (Alma 13:13).

Feeling the Savior's Wounds

When the Savior appeared to his disciples in the upper room shortly after his resurrection, one of his first actions was to invite them to step forward and feel for themselves the wounds in his hands and feet. Luke records: "Jesus himself stood in the midst of them, and saith unto them, Peace be unto you. But they were terrified and affrighted, and supposed that they had seen a spirit. And he said unto them, Why are ye troubled? and why do thoughts arise in your hearts? Behold my hands and my feet, that it is I myself: handle me, and see; for a spirit hath not flesh and bones, as ye see me have. And when he had thus spoken, he showed them his hands and his feet" (Luke 24:36–40).

To the Nephites at the temple in Bountiful, the message was the same: "Arise and come forth unto me," the resurrected Lord declared, "that ye may thrust your hands into my side, and also that ye may feel the prints of the nails in my hands and in my feet, that ye may know that I am the God of Israel, and the God of the whole earth, and have been slain for the sins of the world. And it came to pass that the multitude went forth, and thrust their hands into his side, and did feel the prints of the nails in his hands and in his feet; and this they did do, going forth one by one until they had all gone forth, and did see with their eyes and did feel with their hands, and did know of a surety and did bear record, that it was he, of whom it was written by the prophets, that should come" (3 Nephi 11:14–15).

It was with this in mind—the necessity of feeling for ourselves the Savior's wounds as He brings us through the true veil—that Joseph Smith declared on Sunday, May 1, 1842: "No one can truly say he knows God until he has handled something, and this can only be in the holiest of holies" (*History of the Church*, 4:608; see also John 17:3; 1 John 1:1–3; D&C 45:51–53; 50:45; 67:10; 84:98; 132:22–24).

It is in connection with this transcendent experience that individuals are given what Joseph Smith called the grand key word of the priesthood. As the Prophet explained: "The g[rand] key word was the first word Adam spoke and is a word of supplication. He found the word by the Urim and Thummim—it is that key word to which the heavens [are] opened" (William Clayton, "Journal," 15 June 1844, Private Custody).

The Vision of All

Joseph Smith taught that "when any man obtains this last Comforter he will have the personage of Jesus Christ to attend him or appear unto him from time to time. And even he will manifest the Father unto him and they will take up their abode with him, and *the visions of the heavens will be opened unto him* and the Lord will teach him face to face and *he may have a perfect knowledge of the mysteries of the Kingdom of God,* and this is the state and place the Ancient Saints arrived at when they had such glorious visions Isaiah, Ezekiel, John upon the Isle of Patmos, St. Paul in the third heavens, and all the Saints who held communion with the general assembly and Church of the First Born." (*Words,* p. 5; emphasis mine; spelling and punctuation standardized).

"While the Prophet stated there were things they received that were unlawful to utter (2 Corinthians 12:4[1–4]; 3 Nephi 17:17; 19:34[32–34]; 28:12–14; D&C 76:115), yet there was a general theme revealed to all. That theme pertained to the future destiny of man before and during the earth's millennial state" (*Words,* p. 311, footnote 4).

Thus Moses beheld every particle of the earth, "and he beheld also the inhabitants thereof, and there was not a soul which he beheld not; and he discerned them by the Spirit of God; and their numbers were great, even numberless as the sand upon the sea shore. And he beheld many lands; and each land was called earth, and there were inhabitants on the face thereof" (Moses 1:28–29).

Nephi was shown what was most likely the same vision, and he recorded by commandment that portion of it pertaining to the doings of mankind up until the last days (see 1 Nephi 11–14). From that point forward the vision was to be recorded by John, known as the Revelator (see 1 Nephi 14:25). His record is today called the book of Revelation in the Bible.

The Brother of Jared was also shown this magnificent vision. The scripture relates: "[The Lord] showed unto the brother of Jared all the inhabitants of the earth which had been, and also all that would be; and he withheld them not from his sight, even unto the ends of the earth. For he had said unto him in times before, that if he would believe in him that he could show unto him all things—it should be shown unto him; therefore the Lord could not withhold anything from him, for he knew that the

Lord could show him all things. And the Lord said unto him: Write these things and seal them up; and I will show them in mine own due time unto the children of men" (Ether 3:25–27).

Following the Lord's visit to the Nephites, this vision recorded by the Brother of Jared was made available to the people (see Ether 4:2). However, once they had dwindled again in unbelief, the Lord commanded Moroni that he should hide up the vision in the earth. Moroni then says: "I have written upon these plates the very things which the brother of Jared saw; and there never were greater things made manifest than those which were made manifest unto the brother of Jared. Wherefore the Lord hath commanded me to write them; and I have written them. And he commanded me that I should seal them up [at least part of the sealed portion of the gold plates]; and he also hath commanded that I should seal up the interpretation thereof; wherefore I have sealed up the interpreters, according to the commandment of the Lord" (Ether 4:4–5).

However, this glorious vision is not always to remain sealed. Moroni continues: "The Lord said unto me: They shall not go forth unto the Gentiles until the day that they shall repent of their iniquity, and become clean before the Lord. And in that day that they shall exercise faith in me, saith the Lord, even as the brother of Jared did, that they may become sanctified in me, then will I manifest unto them the things which the brother of Jared saw, even to the unfolding unto them all my revelations, saith Jesus Christ, the Son of God, the Father of the heavens and of the earth, and all things that in them are.

"And he that will contend against the word of the Lord, let him be accursed; and he that shall deny these things, let him be accursed; for unto them will I show no greater things, saith Jesus Christ; for I am he who speaketh. . . . But he that believeth these things which I have spoken, him will I visit with the manifestations of my Spirit, and he shall know and bear record" (Ether 4:6–8, 11).

These are some of the blessings we as wilderness travelers should anticipate as we obtain the fulness of the Second Comforter. Once we have obtained them, we are fully worthy of being ushered into the Promised Land of the Lord and of helping to build up and strengthen the Lord's Zion.

Epilogue

We have now come full circle in this volume, from a discussion about Joseph Smith and the Kirtland Saints obtaining the blessings of celestial glory while in this world to a fairly comprehensive review of the fact that, if it is our true desire, we may do the same. Moreover, we have determined that if we really want to live without fear during the prophesied calamities occurring all about us, we must progress spiritually until, whether in this life or the next, we have obtained a fulness of the blessings most of the Kirtland Saints obtained. We would then be part of the group Joseph Smith was referring to when he said that "many of us have gone at the command of the Lord in defiance of everything evil, and obtained blessings unspeakable, in consequence of which our names are sealed in the Lamb's book of life, for the Lord has spoken it" (*Teachings*, p. 9).

Unfortunately, based upon my own limited experience in discussing the issue of spiritual progression with others, I am forced to conclude that not many will so press forward—not because we can't, mind you, but solely because we won't. Why? Primarily, I believe, because we fear. We know something of our own carnal natures—the natural man we all inherited at birth— and we fear that we cannot put it behind us. And even when we actually overcome the natural man by being born again, we continue to fear, like Laman and Lemuel, that the Lord will make no such glorious things known to us as He has promised (see 1 Nephi 15:8–10).

I have pondered long on this, and I believe that such spiritually paralyzing fear, while satanically inspired, stems almost wholly from not understanding our eternal natures and identities. I also believe that many of the difficulties we experience in mortality could be avoided or at least made lighter if we could only come to such an eternal understanding more quickly. As President John Taylor taught: "This is the reason why we are here, and kicked and cuffed round, and hated and despised, by the world. The reason why we do not live in peace is because we are not prepared for it. We are tempted and tried, driven, mobbed, and robbed; apostates are in our midst, which cause trouble and vexation of spirit, and it is all to keep down our pride and learn us to honor the God of Jacob in all things *and to make us appear [who] we really are*" (*Times and Seasons*, 6:1,100–101; emphasis mine).

Our Eternal Identities

Who we really are, as well as the course of spiritual progression we will have ultimately pursued if we stick to it, was shown in vision to Joseph Smith. He wrote under the Spirit of revelation: "They are they who received the testimony of Jesus, and believed on his name and were baptized after the manner of his burial, being buried in the water in his name, and this according to the commandment which he has given—that by keeping the commandments they might be washed and cleansed from all their sins, and receive the Holy Spirit by the laying on of the hands of him who is ordained and sealed unto this power; and who overcome by faith, and are sealed by the Holy Spirit of promise, which the Father sheds forth upon all those who are just and true. They are they who are the church of the Firstborn. They are they into whose hands the Father has given all things—they are they who are priests and kings, who have received of his fulness, and of his glory; and are priests of the Most High, after the order of Melchizedek, which was after the order of Enoch, which was after the order of the Only Begotten Son. Wherefore, as it is written, they are gods, even the sons of God—wherefore, all things are theirs, whether life or death, or things present, or things to come, all are theirs and they are Christ's, and Christ is God's. . . . These shall dwell in the presence of God and his Christ forever and ever. These are they whom he shall bring with him, when he shall come in the clouds of heaven to reign on the earth over his people. These are they who shall have part in the first resurrection. These are they who shall come forth in the resurrection of the just. . . . These are they who are just men made perfect through Jesus the mediator of the new covenant, who wrought out this perfect atonement through the shedding of his own blood. These are they whose bodies are celestial, whose glory is that of the sun, even the glory of God, the highest of all, whose glory the sun of the firmament is written of as being typical" (D&C 76:51–59, 62–65, 69–70).

An Intriguing View

But even knowing all that, many of us continue to say: "But that isn't me God is talking about. It can't be! I know myself too well, and I'll never make it that far—at least not in this life."

If you find yourself entertaining such thoughts, which are more typical than you might imagine, then please consider the following, which I have found helpful. On Christmas day in 1844, W. W. Phelps wrote a letter that was published in *The Times and Seasons* 5:758, wherein he spoke of the meaning of *eternity.* Brother Phelps wrote: "That eternity [the one during which Christ's doings have been known], agreeable to the records found in the catacombs of Egypt, has been going on in this system . . . almost two thousand five hundred and fifty-five millions of years."

Elder Bruce R. McConkie, who quotes a small portion of this letter, adds: "That is to say, the papyrus from which the Prophet Joseph translated the Book of Abraham, to whom the Lord gave a knowledge of his infinite creations, also contained this expression relative to what apparently is the universe in which we live, which universe has been created by the Father through the instrumentality of the Son" (*The Mortal Messiah, Book I,* [Salt Lake City: Deseret Book Company, 1979], pp. 32–33, footnotes).

Thus, Jehovah began His eternal reign some two thousand five hundred fifty five million years ago, or, said another way, two and a half billion years. That was when. But how, where, and why did Christ's eternal reign begin?

In answer, Joseph Smith spoke of "the head of the Gods" calling "a council of the Gods" to arrange for the creation and peopling of the earth (see D&C 121:30–32; *Teachings,* pp. 348–49), as well as of "the Grand Council of heaven" in which those destined "to minister to the inhabitants of the world" were "ordained" to their respective callings (see *Teachings,* p. 365). It was at one of these councils, held only a little less than 2,555,000,000 years ago, that Jehovah offered himself as the one to go down to earth and bring to pass the Father's plan of salvation through His own life and death and resurrection (see Abraham 3:27; Moses 4:1–2; Isaiah 14:13–14; see also Bruce R. McConkie, *The Promised Messiah,* p. 48).

What astounds me is that each of us was also in attendance at at least one of those councils on that long-ago date, offering a sustaining vote in our Savior's behalf, rejecting Lucifer's counterfeit plan, and being absolutely certain of our own individual identities as we did so. And once Jehovah had been sustained as God and Christ, we who had thus kept our first estates were foreordained to our own future mortal assignments, and set about learning how to accomplish them. Elder McConkie writes: "Since men are foreordained to gain exaltation, and since no man can be exalted without the priesthood, it is almost self-evident that worthy brethren were foreordained to receive the priesthood. And so we find Alma teaching that those who hold the Melchizedek Priesthood in this life were 'called and prepared from the foundation of the world according to the foreknowledge of God' (Alma 13:1–12)" (*Doctrinal New Testament Commentary*, 3:328). Remember—the foundation of the world was 2.5 billion years ago. "And Joseph Smith said, 'Every man who has a calling to minister to the inhabitants of the world,' and this includes all who hold the Melchizedek Priesthood, 'was ordained to that very purpose in the Grand Council of heaven before this world was. I suppose that I was ordained to this very office in that Grand Council' (*Teachings*, p. 365)" (*Doctrinal New Testament Commentary*, 3:329).

Therefore I conclude that, despite the fairly negative pictures most of us have of ourselves as struggling and usually failing weak mortals (which picture is based on satanically inspired doubts as well as an incredibly brief span of time here on earth that we are allowed to remember), we are all, in reality, ancient beings filled with glory, light, and knowledge. And we acquired those godly traits by exercising "exceeding faith and good works" (Alma 13:3) over *at least* two and a half billion years of time.

With that mind-boggling fact before us, consider these questions. (1) Since I know that I had an eternal premortal identity separate from who I am today, what do I suppose my name was during that lengthy life we call the first estate? (2) Is not that glorious and ancient identity more properly the "true" me than the one I now know, which is at best no more than a few decades old? (3) Is two and a half billion years sufficient time for me to have become acquainted not only with Christ and our Father but also with all the holy angels such as Gabriel, Raphael, and Michael? (4) Is it not possible that I not only knew such great beings but also mingled among them as an eternal equal, even with similar assignments? And (5) Since I successfully kept my first estate for at least two and a half billion years, isn't it foolish and shortsighted for me to doubt my ability to keep my second estate for a mere seventy or eighty years?

It is no wonder that the devil, who has an intimate knowledge of our true identities, tries so hard to convince us that we are without spiritual merit. If he can't, then he knows he has lost, and we will never be miserable like him.

As I conclude this volume, which for me has been a tremendous exercise in understanding and pressing forward with my own spiritual quest, I bear solemn witness of two things. First, virtually any one of us, no matter our station in mortality, has the capacity to achieve the spiritual goals outlined in this book. And second, Jesus Christ lives and stands waiting with outstretched arms to "take up his abode with us," and He will do so as quickly as we are willing to put aside the world and give our hearts and lives wholly to Him.

"Behold," He says with words that fairly ring through the eternities, "that which you hear is as the voice of one crying in the wilderness—in the wilderness, because you cannot see him—my voice, because my voice is Spirit; my Spirit is truth; truth abideth and hath no end; and if it be in you it shall abound. And if your eye be single to my glory, your whole bodies shall be filled with light, and there shall be no darkness in you; and that body which is filled with light comprehendeth all things. Therefore, sanctify yourselves that your minds become single to God, and the days will come that you shall see him; for he will unveil his face unto you, and it shall be in his own time, and in his own way, and according to his own will" (D&C 88:66–68).

That such should be so, I humbly testify in His holy name. Amen.

Index

Index

34

Kirtland Temple, 38–39; enemy to, 53; stranger to, 54; fellow-citizen in kingdom of, 54; servant or handmaiden of, 54; son or daughter of, 55, 104–8, 113–15; elect of, 55–56, 107; joint heir with, 56–57, 107, 234, 258–60; how to return to, 60–61; seeking, through compliance to laws, 83–84; taking on name of, through baptism, 87–88; witness of, by the Father, 90–91; promises to, through the sacrament, 91–92; our responsibility for the suffering of, 93; being made clean through, 93–94; as our owner, 94–95; brings about a change of heart, 97–98; justification through, 99–102; in the wilderness, 121–22, 137, 150, 204–6; hearing voice of, in the wilderness, 126–28; delivers from danger in the wilderness, 127–28; directs wilderness travelers, 138–43; blesses those in the wilderness, 145–47; sacrifice of joint heirs with, 148–50; will show us our weaknesses, 157–58; angels as messengers for, 166–70; presides over heavenly church, 168; basic teachings of, 173–74; personal revelation from, 180; being brought into presence of, 194–96; commanding Satan in the name of, 210; friends of, 55–56, 227; second coming of, 240; as Second Comforter, 251–53; receiving fulness of glory of, 259–62; as heir of the Father, 261; feeling wounds of, 262–63
John the Baptist, 122
Just men made perfect, 168–69, 269
Justification, 99–102

Joint heirs with Christ, 56–57, 107, 149–50, 234, 258–59, 261–62

Keys: of conversing with God, 20–21; of knowledge of God, 26; to be revealed in temple, 32; of Restoration, 38–39, 196–97, 201–3, 237–39
Kimball, Heber C., sealed to exaltation, 233
Kirtland Temple, 32–33, 36–40, 42, 196–97, 232–33
Knight, Newell, vision of, 22
Knowledge: greater, given in Nauvoo, 40; of spiritual progression, 112; available to wilderness travelers, 140–41; godly, must be sought, 199; unlocks mysteries, 262. *See also* Mysteries of Godliness

Land speculation, 42, 44–45
Language of God, 20, 31
Law of the true last moment, 162
Lehi in the wilderness: afflictions of, 121, 144; left worldly possessions behind, 122; was delivered into the wilderness, 127; sought separation from worldly people, 133–35; left Jerusalem in secret, 136; traveled as the Lord directed, 138; had difficulties and blessings, 147; had needs provided for, 160; received reprieve, 163; received the Liahona, 176; had scriptures, 178; sought the Lord, 193–94
Liahona, 176–77
Limitations, personal, 58–62
Lying, 216

Marbles, example of, 68–69
Melchizedek, 241, 243, 246–47
Melchizedek Priesthood: powers of,

of, 215–17; methodology of,
219–20; discerning, from a
messenger from God, 220; cannot
compel to do evil, 221; plan of,
222; overcoming, 222–23
School of the Prophets, 26–27, 29–31
School of the Wilderness, 121. *See also*
Wilderness
Scriptures, 112–13, 177–78
Scorners, 10–11
Sealed with Holy Seal of Promise,
228–29, 237
Sealing powers of Elijah, 237–39
Second Comforter, 251–53
Secrets, three grand, 230
Self-righteousness, 222
Servant of God, 54–55, 59–60
Service, 59
Seventy, members of, 34–35
Sins: favorite, 68–70; as bonds of
iniquity, 74–77; having, revealed,
80–82; abhorrence of, after change
of heart, 97–98, 102–3, 110;
tendency to commit, 155–56
Smith, Hyrum, vision of, 35
Smith, Joseph: early spiritual
experiences of, 21–22; saw visions,
25, 28, 34–35; organized School of
the Prophets, 26–27; held back
revelations, 50; encountered Satan,
209–10; had exaltation sealed,
231–32; received Second
Comforter, 258–59
Sons and daughters of Jesus Christ,
55, 104–7, 112
Sorrow, godly, 82–84, 92, 100–101, 110
Spirit beings. *See* Angels
Spirit, contrite, 82–84, 87, 89–90, 110,
112
Spirit of Truth. *See* Holy Ghost
Spirits: false, 211–13; evil, 214–17
Spiritual levels, 53–57
Spiritual manifestations: to early

Saints, 33–38; declined during
apostasy, 47; available today,
48–50, 54–55. *See also* Angels
Stakes, setting up, 58–62
Stranger to God, 54
Suicide, 7–8

Temple: attendance, 8, 203;
endowment, 32, 200; worship,
73–74, 191; mountains as, 193–94;
ordinances of, 200–201, 210–11;
and restoration of keys, 240
Temporal needs, 159–62
Temptation, 221
Teton Dam disaster, 15
Three Witnesses, 22, 42–43
Tithing, 8
Translated beings, 168–170
Tribes of Israel, 246

United States, 5, 13–14
Urim and Thummim, 176

Visions: as communication with God,
9; seen by early Saints, 25, 28–30,
33–35; opened to those who have
the Second Comforter, 263–64. *See
also* Angels

Water, baptism of, 85–88
Whitlock, Harvey, vision of, 25
Whitmer, David, vision of, 37
Wickedness, 13
Wight, Lyman, vision of, 25
Wilderness: School of, 121, 126, 141;
deliverance from danger in,
127–28; repentance before
experience of, 129–30; forsaking of
family and friends in, 131–35;
teaching by those who have
traveled in, 136–37; isolation of
travelers in, 135–36; difficulties in,
144–52; sacrifices and fasting in,

Books authored or coauthored by Blaine M. Yorgason

Spiritual Progression in the Last Days

Joseph Smith: Tarred and Feathered

The Life of Arch L. Madsen
(private printing)

To Soar with the Eagle

Secrets

Prayers on the Wind

Namina: Biography of Georganna
Bushman Spurlock *(private printing)*

The Life Story of Roger and Sybil
Ferguson *(private printing)*

Obtaining the Blessings of Heaven

To Mothers and Fathers from the Book of
Mormon

Receiving Answers to Prayers

Spiritual Survival in the Last Days

Into the Rainbow

The Warm Spirit

Here Stands a Man

Decision Point

KING—The Biography of Jerome Palmer
King *(private printing)*

Pardners: Three Stories of Friendship

In Search of Steenie Bergman *(Soderberg
Series #5)*

The Greatest Quest

Seven Days for Ruby *(Soderberg Series #4)*

Joseph Smith's Eleven Dollar Surgery

Becoming

The Shadow Taker

Tales from the Book of Mormon (The
Loftier Way)

Brother Brigham's Gold *(Soderberg Series #3)*

Ride the Laughing Wind

The Miracle

The Thanksgiving Promise

Chester, I Love You *(Soderberg Series #2)*

Double Exposure

Seeker of the Gentle Heart

The Krystal Promise

A Town Called Charity, and Other Stories
About Decisions

The Bishop's Horse Race *(Soderberg Series #1)*

And Should She Die (The Courage
Covenant)

Windwalker *(movie version—out of print)*

Windwalker

Others

Charlie's Monument

Tall Timber *(out of print)*

Miracles and the Latter-day Teenager
(out of print)